HEAVILY MEDITATED

| ALSO BY DAVE ASPREY |

Super Human

Fast This Way

Game Changers

Head Strong

Bulletproof: The Cookbook

Smarter Not Harder

HEAVILY MEDITATED

THE FAST PATH TO REMOVE YOUR TRIGGERS, DISSOLVE STRESS, AND ACTIVATE INNER PEACE

DAVE ASPREY

HARPER

An Imprint of HarperCollins*Publishers*

HarperCollins books may be purchased for educational, business, or sales promotional use. For information, please email the Special Markets Department at SPsales@harpercollins.com.

FIRST EDITION

Library of Congress Cataloging-in-Publication Data has been applied for.

ISBN 978-0-06-320476-8

25 26 27 28 29 LBC 5 4 3 2 1

To the seekers who know there must
be more than you can see.

| CONTENTS |

UNLOCKING YOUR ZEN

Ever feel like your brain is stuck in traffic while everyone else is on the express lane? Do you feel anxious and stressed-out? Is your energy in the gutter, and you can't find the motivation to be productive? Are your cravings for external pleasures out of control? Maybe minor setbacks feel monumental, or you feel challenged by your daily responsibilities. You're not alone.

For most of my life, I was more anxious than I realized. More accurately, I was a ticking time bomb just waiting to explode. Every injustice felt personal; every slight left a deep wound. It was exhausting. By the time I was in my twenties, I weighed more than 300 pounds and was constantly battling debilitating brain fog and chronic fatigue. Determined to upgrade my MeatOS ("meat operating system," aka my body), fix my brain, and hack my biology to live past 180, I embarked on a lifelong quest to push the boundaries of human potential.

This book is the ultimate guide to upgrading your brain, unlocking altered states of consciousness, removing the triggers holding you hostage, and tapping into unlimited energy, happiness, and inner peace.

Over the past decade, I've built a $100-million-a-year company and created the biohacking movement, now a $63 billion industry helping millions lose weight and switch their brains back on. This journey required more self-mastery than I ever imagined, but it equipped me with the knowledge and tools necessary to accomplish my mission, which I'm excited to share with you in this book.

I've studied and faced my share of challenges: family members trying to steal from me, trusted colleagues embezzling funds, internal company disputes fueled by lies, and investors kicking me off the board of a company I founded. I've even survived a public cancellation attempt by one of our time's most prominent media figures, driven by financial motives and devoid of truth. It's a lot to handle and enough to drive anyone mad. But this isn't a pity party. I've also experienced unimaginable success alongside these betrayals and losses. I've experienced the peaceful end of a long-term marriage, figured out how to extend human life, and discovered how to enhance brain function. I've fasted in caves, learned to eat so I'm never hungry, and gotten into the best shape of my life. And I've helped millions improve their health, which is the biggest reward. But the hardest lesson I've learned through this process is how to let go of the things that hurt me, so they don't control my emotions, my actions, and my life.

You don't always have to be hungry, tired, anxious, or worried. Even under enormous stress, learning to find inner peace is possible, no matter what's happening on the outside. And here's the good news: we have the technology to help us find that inner peace faster and more effectively than ever.

| PAVING THE WAY TO PEACE |

Our ancestors knew the path to inner peace thousands of years ago. They've hidden these secrets in caves, monasteries, shrines, ashrams, and temples; ancient libraries filled with wisdom, locked vaults of the Vatican, and traditional practices handed down over fires by wise elders. The world has changed, though. We don't have time to do it the old way when everything about our lives now is fast-paced and overstimulating. But we can use these ancient teachings combined with modern technology to upgrade our reality and ground us in the present to experience more fulfillment and inner peace.

Because let's face it: few of us can lock ourselves in a monastery or embark on a vision quest, sleeping alone in a cave for days without food. But I've had the great honor and privilege of learning from many masters, people of different lineages and practices, and am now able to bring their teachings back to earth to help you understand what's happening in your mind, body, and soul. Why do we suffer, and how can we fix it? This book stems from overcoming enormous challenges and spending six months with electrodes on my head. I tried every piece of technology and every kind of mind-altering experience or substance that seemed safe to figure out what was going on in my brain. Then I took the time to make enough sense of all that knowledge to share it with you here so you could learn how to manage yours, too.

There is a reason you experience what you're experiencing, and the reason is not what you think. I wrote this book to give you more effective tools than to just "try harder." Tools that can help calm your mind and upgrade your life without having to spend forty years meditating or seeking serenity in ancient places of worship, although both do sound peaceful.

By combining ancient wisdom with modern science, I discovered that you can achieve profound changes in your mental and physical states. Whether through biohacking techniques, neurofeedback, or simply understanding how your body responds to stress and stimuli, there are ways to take control of your brain and body's performance. But you need enough energy for your efforts to be effective.

If you're one of the tens of millions who've listened to my podcast, *The Human Upgrade*, or read my previous books, you know that I use something called the "F-word framework" to understand our unconscious behaviors. But if you're new here and this sounds strange, welcome! And don't worry. I'll guide you through these foundational F-words as we explore the tools and techniques to transform your life. This framework is integral to your human upgrade journey.

| THE FOUNDATIONAL FIVE |

Your mitochondria, tiny organelles inside your cells, are the front-line decision-makers in your body. They are the sensors of reality, programmed with bacteria-level decision-making methods. Although their role in your body is enormous, these little guys aren't very smart. But they decide where you allocate your energy. Their primary directive begins with the first F: fear. If something is scary, your mitochondria will make you run away, kill, or hide. This is the first instinct of all life on earth, and it's happening, constantly, in your subconscious.

Once you address fear, the second F: food, is mitochondria's next priority when spending energy. If you can eat it, eat everything, because famine can kill you (says fear). Then comes the third F: fertility. "Mate and save the species!" Pleasure aside, the real driver is ensuring humankind lives on. Then there's the fourth F: friends, your connection to humanity.

If you have enough energy left after dealing with fear, food, and fertility, you can focus on friendships and becoming a valuable member of society. This is when you feel inspired to, and capable of, giving back, helping little old ladies across the street, buying a stranger a cup of coffee, and generally doing your best to be a good person. But you won't have time for friends if your energy is deficient or your stress levels are through the roof. If you're a busy entrepreneur or parent, you know what I'm talking about.

When you can control where and how you allocate your energy, you can take action toward your goals and create the life you want. If you're putting all of your energy into fear or food, you won't evolve. Being stuck in fear, especially, is uncomfortable and an acute dream killer. But there is a way to hack this.

This brings me to the newest addition to the framework. I'm excited to introduce you to the fifth F: forgiveness. Forgiveness is a game changer. It's not about condoning poor behavior or letting toxic people back into your life. It's about letting go of pain, so it doesn't control how you treat yourself or others. This is the true essence of biohacking. Just like you don't have to suffer to lose weight, you don't have to lose your mind to find peace.

| HACK YOUR ZEN |

About fifteen years ago, before my kids were in the world, I read Dharma Singh Khalsa's book *Meditation as Medicine*. Despite a lifetime of being a committed night owl, I wanted to see if I could rewire myself to become a morning person. My natural bedtime since I was about ten years old was approximately 2:02 a.m.—at least, that's what my sleep trackers said. No matter what I did, this was natural for me. Then, no surprise, I'd end up sleeping in, only to be shamed by myself and by society for being so-called "lazy." But I was curious: Could I change my natural inclination for the witching hour and become a morning lark?

You've probably heard people say they're a night owl or a morning lark (early bird). They're referring to their chronotype, the body's natural preference for sleep timing. The assumption is that a person's chronotype is fixed, like a life sentence to either late-night Netflix binges or sunrise yoga sessions. But, like any dedicated biohacker, I decided to challenge the theory. For eighteen months, my mornings began at 5 a.m. I figured my body would adapt.

New findings from Baylor University's Sleep Neuroscience and Cognition Laboratory reveal that our chronotypes are more adaptable than we thought. The study, published in *Chronobiology International*, shows that while genetics can and does influence your body's natural preference for day or night, your habits and choices can shift your sleep patterns.[1] So, being a night owl isn't just about biology; it's also about your behavior and lifestyle. Your biological clock, schedule demands, and personal habits influence your sleep health, alertness, and performance.

My experiment certainly yielded results, but not the ones I was hoping for. After eighteen months of trying to become a morning person, I was less functional, less happy, and less creative, so I stopped. However, these days I do wake up earlier, around sunrise; I have a cup of Danger Coffee, maybe do a cold plunge, and stay outside for twenty minutes. While a rigid wake-up time didn't work for me, I was able to change my sleep habits because I changed my environment and stopped punishing myself for being a night person.

Would I recommend becoming an early bird if you're not one? No. Would I recommend controlling light and sun exposure so that you can become at least a regular morning bird? Yes. It has improved my brain function and productivity significantly. But if you plan to stay up staring at bright screens and having a late-night dinner, successfully changing your sleep patterns won't work. That weird connection between all the different things your nervous system and your body's operating system consider determines your success. When did it get dark? When did the temperature change? When did the food stop? If those line up, waking up early for morning meditation might be incredible for you. And if it's not? Don't force it.

| BIOHACKING YOUR BRAIN SYMPHONY |

As you explore the pathways to inner peace and meditation, it's crucial to understand the science behind your brain states. We'll explore these more deeply throughout the book, but I want to start off with some of the basics.

Imagine your brain as a complex orchestra, producing different types of brainwaves. They operate at different frequencies, measured in hertz (Hz). Delta (1–4 Hz), theta (4–8 Hz), alpha (8–12 Hz), beta (13–37 Hz), and gamma (38–100 Hz) each play a unique role in your mental and emotional well-being. These brain waves are the electrical symphony that conduct everything from your moments of stress to your most profound states of relaxation.

Starting with delta waves, these slow and steady giants are your ticket to deep, restorative sleep, where your body heals and regenerates. Think of delta waves as the janitors of your brain, cleaning up the messes of the day while you're off in dreamland. Next, theta waves dominate during light sleep and deep meditation, fueling creativity and intuition. Then, alpha waves move in. They're about relaxation (when you're awake but calm), bridging the conscious and subconscious. Consider this your brain's "chill" mode.

Then we hit the beta waves, which take over when you're focused, problem-solving, or actively thinking. Like all good things, moderation is crucial. Overthinking can too easily lead to stress. Finally, gamma waves, the brain's high-frequency overachievers, kick in during peak mental activity, enhancing problem-solving, learning, and memory. Think of gamma waves as your brain's secret weapon, turning you into a mental warrior. Together these brain waves create a perfect mental harmony for every state you need to conquer your day, from Zen master to productivity powerhouse.

The technologies we use at 40 Years of Zen to influence these brain states are extraordinary. EEG (electroencephalography) Q-EEG (quantitative electroencephalography), and neurofeedback act like high-tech conductors, helping us precisely quantify and guide your brain's performance. These tools allow our team to monitor and adjust brain activity, making achieving desired states of calm or focus easier. By leveraging these technologies, you tap into the brain's natural ability to rewire itself, a phenomenon known as neuroplasticity.

We've mastered using these technologies to help people achieve profound mental states. The tools and techniques I share in this book induce similar transformative states. Our most powerful tool, the Reset Process, is your guide. This process has helped countless individuals achieve significant breakthroughs, and it's outlined for you here in this book.

Brain training takes this a step further. Just as you train your body for peak physical performance, you can train your brain to reach profound mental states. Neurofeedback, for example, provides real-time feedback on your brain activity, helping you adjust and improve over time. Combining this with the Reset Process is incredibly powerful and can enhance cognitive function, reduce stress, and help you achieve a state of inner peace that feels almost effortless.

The path to inner peace is both a science and an art. It's about understanding your body's natural rhythms and leveraging tools that align with your biology. Get ready to learn how to control your light exposure, embrace meditation, dive into breathwork, harness sexual energy, safely and consciously induce pain, explore psychedelics, geek out with EEG and neurofeedback, and simply allow yourself to let go and forgive.

The journey to self-mastery is within your reach. This book serves as a reminder that no one is in charge of you but you. Let it guide you through its practical strategies and profound insights to help you navigate life's challenges with grace and resilience and become the person you were born to be.

PART I

HOW TO HACK REALITY

HURRY, MEDITATE FASTER

Do you know that feeling where you're trying to remember a word or focus on something, and it just doesn't work no matter what you do? If you're like most people, this happens every day, and it happens more than once. We're facing an epidemic of brains that don't work as well as they used to. You may find your car keys in the refrigerator or walk into a room and forget why you went in there. And worse, you're more likely to be reactive on those days. Maybe you yell at your kids or get angry at something trivial. Well, you're in good company. I had this problem in spades. For years, my brain was a mess.

It started in my twenties, right before I landed an impressive job in Silicon Valley. My train of thought would vanish midsentence, and just like that, poof, words would disappear. It was embarrassing. My brain felt like it had its own navigational agenda, and I was just along for the ride. Leaving meetings without remembering the conversation, followed by a feeling of helplessness I couldn't shake, was terrifying. It felt like I was getting dumber by the minute with no possible fix in sight.

There I was, in the land of tech giants, feeling like my brain was betraying me. Imagine trying to keep up with the industry's sharpest minds while your brain plays hide-and-seek with basic information. It was like being in a mental fog that I couldn't clear, no matter how hard I tried. I had to do something or else risk losing my job, confidence, and sense of self.

Those days are long gone. But back then, this kind of brain fog was just business as usual. These days, if I forget even one word in a day, it's a red flag. When I think about it, I can always trace it back to something I did—a food-based toxin, chemical exposure, or a poor night of sleep. There's always a reason. It's important to be aware of your state so you can "track it back." The good news is, this is a skill you can learn and master.

It's normal to feel anxiety when your brain betrays you by not working the way you want it to. The problem is, we've been programmed to hide that anxiety because it's embarrassing and because no one wants to acknowledge that they feel stupid, even when their brain isn't working right. But here's the thing: It's not about feeling stupid. It's about understanding your body and mind well enough to recognize when something's off. When you start paying attention, you can catch those little signs and adjust before things worsen. Tracking what you eat, how you sleep, and even your stress levels will present patterns that your body's been hiding from you. You'll start to see connections between your actions and your brain's performance, putting the power back in your hands to change what's not working. Imagine pinpointing exactly why you're having an off day and knowing how to fix it. It's not magic; it's biohacking. For me, learning to decode these signals changed everything.

During that time, my brain had some really bad days. On other days, it was average. And on a very rare day, it was amazing. I started looking for a tool to track how well it worked on any given day, leading me to a game called FreeCell. It's like an old-school version of solitaire, and strongly tests your working memory. The game flows if you play a couple of rounds and your brain is firing on all cylinders. When your brain is off, solving even the simplest moves takes forever. So, I started using this as a personal brain performance barometer. It was the quickest way to determine if my brain was having a good or bad day, because sometimes it's hard to tell. Some days, you might just feel groggy and spacey. But other days, you might feel slower than usual by 15–20 percent without knowing why or having a way to measure it. FreeCell became a real-time measuring tool for brain capacity and performance.

Today there are lots of brain games that directly measure how your brain is doing. The reality is that your brain is not the same every day, but you're unlikely to know what's going on unless it's at the extremes. The tools in this book can help you solve that problem and a whole bunch of other invisible issues that suck your energy and make you show up in the world in a way that you didn't choose, because you're not in charge when this foggy state is your default.

By tracking your brain's performance, you can build a habit of noticing patterns and triggers. Maybe you find that a particular food or lack of sleep throws you off your game. Or perhaps stress from work or family issues sends you spiraling. Once you identify these triggers, you can take steps to avoid them, or at least mitigate their impact. It's all about becoming the detective of your own mind.

Imagine waking up and knowing exactly what to do to have a great brain day. No more guessing, no more frustration. Just clarity, focus, and control. It's like upgrading your brain's operating system to the latest version with all the bugs fixed. And the best part? Anyone can do it. You don't need a PhD in neuroscience to understand what's happening in your head. You just need the right tools and a bit of curiosity.

In hindsight, I can recognize that I was doing a lot of things that caused my brain to betray me. I was eating the wrong food and living in a house with toxic mold. Eventually I was diagnosed with brain damage caused by that mold. I also dealt with blood sugar issues, work stress, and hormones that were out of whack. Imagine being in your twenties but feeling like an old man with no mojo left. And none of the so-called "solutions" seemed to make a dent, which only piled on more stress.

Emotional reactivity became my norm. It felt like, on the days my brain decided to clock out, my emotions followed suit. Maybe this sounds familiar; maybe it doesn't. But when the brain lacks the support it needs to transform into the kind of brain that provides power, support, and calmness no matter what life throws at you, chaos usually follows. However, if you get good at tracking your symptoms and know how to support your brain in shifting your state when you want to, you'll save time and energy.

For my part, I realized my brain needed more than just the basics to function well. It needed the right fuel, a clean environment, and a solid foundation of good habits. This meant making significant changes in my life, but the payoff was worth it. I learned to prioritize high-quality, nutrient-dense foods that supported brain health. I also had to clean up my environment. Getting rid of mold, clutter, and other toxins made a huge difference. And then there was the stress. Managing stress is a critical part of living a peaceful life. Meditation, biofeedback, and other relaxation techniques became the go-to helpers to keep my brain calm and allow my body to follow its lead.

| YOUR BRAIN ON NEUROFEEDBACK |

But all the self-driven changes in the world couldn't quite get me to where I wanted to be with my brain health. It was the late 1990s, and I'd had enough. It was time to act and head to the only spot in the Bay Area that dabbled in brain training. I was already using smart drugs (you may know them as nootropics or "cognitive enhancers," things like Qualia Mind, aniracetam, modafinil, nicotine, bacopa, gingko, or now, Brain 101 from Suppgrade Labs). But despite all that, something still felt off. The constant yo-yo between laser focus and mental haze, what we now call brain fog, was driving me nuts. So, like a typical engineer, the next step was clear: gather data.

I went to a local chiropractor's office with its glaring artificial lights and murky fish tank, hoping he could shed some light on what was happening in my head. Stepping through the door, a tornado of a kid ran up to me, screaming and running in circles. His frenetic energy made me want to bolt out of there, but getting answers was more important, which meant enduring the chaos in the waiting room and preparing for my first training session.

On the next visit, about six weeks later, the same kid was in the lobby again. Anticipating another chaotic encounter, all I could think was, *Uh-oh, time to make a beeline for the car.* But that's not what happened.

Instead of the usual chaos, the kid calmly walked up to me, extended his hand, and introduced himself like a pint-sized gentleman: "Hi, my name's Bobby." It was shocking. Is this even the same kid? It turns out Bobby was on the spectrum and was benefiting greatly from the therapy he was receiving, showing noticeable improvements in focus. One of the reasons for being at the chiropractor's office was that I was also on the spectrum, a realization that came in my midtwenties after reading an enlightening article in *Wired* magazine about Asperger's syndrome (now referred to as ASD, autism spectrum disorders) in adults. It was like someone flipped on a switch. I took a diagnostic test, scoring in the 40s out of 50, and even more of what I felt about my brain made sense. Not surprisingly, my PhD grandmother and grandfather, as well as six out of seven of my aunts and uncles on one side of the family, also took the test and scored high. These are engineering masterminds of the family, and suddenly, it all clicked. Plus, having witnessed Bobby's transformation, it became apparent that whatever brain therapy the chiropractor did with him was working. Maybe "broken" brains could be fixed after all.

Seeing this kid come back, seemingly more focused and relaxed than before, only six weeks later gave me an understanding of what might be possible. So, like any curious engineer, I bought an EEG machine for at-home neurofeedback sessions to accelerate my progress. How hard could it be? Looking back, this is like seeing someone do brain surgery and then purchasing some scalpels to do it yourself. But that's the Silicon Valley mindset for you—tackle the challenge head-on and figure it out as you go.

The first few sessions were a mess. Wires were everywhere, and figuring out how to properly interpret the data was challenging. But I was determined. I spent hours tweaking my setup, reading research papers, and experimenting with different protocols. The more I learned about neurofeedback, the more I realized its potential. It wasn't just a tool for people like Bobby and me; it could help anyone looking to improve their brain function. The idea that you could train your brain to perform better was revolutionary. It was like discovering a hidden user manual for the most powerful organ in your body.

It didn't take long before realizing that this DIY approach might not be the brightest idea. I had zero training to do this kind of work, and as you can imagine, there was a lot to learn. Home-use EEG machines can be unreliable at best. Sure, they might help you chill out a bit, but when tackling the big issues, they're like bringing a water pistol to a forest fire. As a longtime fan of danger and the creator of a coffee brand literally called Danger Coffee (with its tagline of *Who knows what you might do?*), I genuinely believe that you can't do anything meaningful in your life without the ability to take risks or a willingness to face danger. But in this case, I'll be the first to say: don't do what I did. When you're dealing with an already damaged brain, the risk isn't worth it.

| WEIRD BRAINS |

I learned to read at eighteen months old—an achievement that might sound impressive, like I was some sort of baby genius (spoiler alert: I wasn't). There are books about teaching babies to read at that age, so it wasn't exactly unheard-of. What we didn't know was the potential harm this could cause a baby's developing nervous system back then. So, while other kids were out there feeling their way through the world, I was often buried deep in books, disappearing constantly into my own version of it.

Looking back, spending more time nurturing a healthy nervous system would have likely made a difference. Maybe not. Growing up in an environment with toxic mold and other factors contributing to neuroinflammation and autoimmune issues was a recipe for future challenges in the brain and body anyway.

People with ASD often face challenges in social interactions and decoding nonverbal cues. These quirks usually begin in childhood and develop into adulthood. But recognizing the signs can be like finding a needle in a haystack if you don't know what to look for. You might just think you're different from others, and that's because you are (and it's awesome).

The signs were there growing up, but for years nobody talked about weird brains like we do today. People with unconventional neurological wiring were just considered "different" and left to fend for themselves in a world that refused to learn about, support, or understand them. This made life more complicated and confusing because of the lack of genuine connection with others, a universal need for human survival.

But like everything, there's another side of the coin to consider. Sure, navigating life with a brain that's wired differently comes with its fair share of challenges. But these differences shape resilient, adaptable, and incredibly creative individuals. I'm talking about those who don't just think outside the box; they obliterate it. They're the ones who go on to do extraordinary things for themselves and often for humanity as a whole.

As I grew older, the gap between my brain's capabilities and everyday performance became more apparent. I excelled in subjects that interested me but struggled with social interactions and the unpredictability of life outside structured learning. My brain was a powerful engine but often felt like a runaway train. Picture this: An awkward eighth-grade kid, the principal's office, and my parents sitting there with concerned looks. And then, the bomb drops. The principal throws down a massive folder filled with disciplinary reports and declares, "Houston, we have a problem." Or, more accurately, "Dave's parents, we have a problem."

Looking at the folder, all I could think of was that my grades were solid, so what was the big deal? But then, like a floodgate opening, all those internal voices that come with having a weird brain decided to chime in. Suddenly, I had an overwhelming sense of, *What's wrong with me? I need to hide who I am. Why is the world so confusing? Why are people treating me differently? Why does everyone love loud places when they make me feel crazy?* It's like being stuck in a whirlwind of thoughts, each adding another layer to feeling totally out of sync with the world around you. The cacophony of thoughts only makes that sense of disconnection even more intense. You know you're different but can't quite understand why. It's like being stuck in a puzzle with missing pieces; no matter how hard you try, you don't fit in.

Ever wonder why navigating social situations feels like trying to solve a Rubik's Cube blindfolded? It's because the parts of your nervous system responsible for making connections run on low battery during those crucial developmental stages. So, while other kids were busy picking up on social cues and mastering the art of small talk, your brain was like, "Hold up, I'm still trying to figure out how gravity works." It doesn't make you bad or wrong; you just have a unique perspective that others don't. While everyone else is busy deciphering social nuances, your brain is out here tackling the big questions of the universe. Sounds like a superpower, right? Because it is.

You know that feeling when your surroundings feel like they're at an 11, and you're just trying to keep your head above water?

That's the reality for many people with weird brains. Maybe you don't even realize you're overwhelmed because overwhelm is your default setting. You're swimming in a sea of chaos without realizing it's chaotic because it's all you've ever known. You're acutely aware that the feelings of disconnection and loneliness suck, but it's harder to pinpoint the reasons they're there in the first place. It's incredibly challenging when you're a kid trying to fit in and make sense of a world that just doesn't get you. This creates confusion, irritation, shame, and loneliness; they become constant companions.

You might feel like you're operating on a different wavelength from everyone else. You might think, "Why can't they see what's obvious to me?" But it's not about being superior or having secret insight. It's just that your brain works a little differently—a remarkable distinction, even if it doesn't always feel that way. For some, these challenges lead to problems in school. Admittedly, I got into dozens of fights, which explains that lovely family meeting in the principal's office. Though I never initiated the fights, my words usually provoked the first punch.

People like us are searching for connection in a world that feels like it's speaking a foreign language and refusing to teach it to us. Social interactions can feel like traversing a minefield blindfolded, which makes forming meaningful relationships challenging. Subtle nuances in language, like irony and sarcasm, might as well be written in hieroglyphics for all the sense they make to us. Nonverbal cues like hand gestures and facial expressions can be unclear, rendering social situations overstimulating or confusing. But because the state of overwhelm is your baseline, you may not think much of it.

Sensory sensitivities add another layer of complexity that makes every day feel like a roller-coaster ride. Bright lights, loud noises, and certain textures can be kryptonite, triggering discomfort or anxiety. Additionally, disrupted routines and unexpected plan changes can spiral you into panic mode. You might ask yourself, *Why does this feel like such a big deal to me and not to anyone else?* Just remember, there's nothing wrong with you. You're simply processing your environment with a more discerning lens. It's a gift, not a flaw.

Initially, you imagine everyone else must feel the same way you do because you think everyone else is just like you—until you understand what's happening in your brain.

So, as you can see, it's already challenging to navigate the world with a "weird brain." But it's likely you're also dealing with an onslaught of energy-sapping environmental toxins like I was. Talk about trial by fire. When you hit the sweet spot where your energy levels are off the charts, and your efficiency is through the roof, you reach a state where you feel like an unstoppable superhero.

| UNIQUE GENIUS |

Everyone perceives the world through their own unique lens, but neurodivergent people have an array of exceptionally distinct perspectives. While our understanding of reality may differ from others in some ways, that difference also makes our "weird brains" invaluable.

The existence of ASD in adults, particularly in Silicon Valley— a hub teeming with "weird brains"—sparked a wave of curiosity as to its prevalence. One theory suggested environmental toxins as a potential culprit. But it's more about laws of attraction and the environment itself. Think about it: Silicon Valley, with its heavy focus on engineering and computer sciences, is like a magnet for people with neurodivergent traits. In this fast-paced world, being able to hyperfocus is like having a golden ticket, but it's a double-edged sword. Sure, there are plenty of moments of brilliance, but there's also a susceptibility to distraction, showcasing the dual nature of having a weird brain.

With nearly two million engineers crammed into a few dozen square miles of Northern California, rubbing elbows and making babies, it's no surprise that the likelihood of passing on those neurodivergent traits skyrockets. However, as we know from the study of epigenetics, it usually takes some sort of lifestyle trigger to create genetic susceptibility. It could be many factors—EMFs, gluten, toxic mold, or all of the above. However, the common thread in these environmental hazards is their contribution to mitochondrial weakness, a primary factor in inflammatory conditions such as ASD and autoimmunity. Autoimmunity is when your body's defense system gets confused and starts attacking your own cells, thinking they're the enemy. It's like friendly fire in your immune system, leading to various health issues.

But this isn't a book solely about ASD. It's about understanding that the pattern-matching abilities of our "weird brains" result from our unique brains evolving in their own way.

Having a "weird" brain allows you to recognize things differently than a neurotypical brain would or could. The cognitive process mirrors artificial intelligence with the ability to sift through tons of information and pull out patterns that "normal" brains miss.

Some say I'm an "event correlation machine" because sometimes, just looking at something sparks an intuitive understanding that's not obvious to others. Whether you have a weird brain or not, you've likely experienced this before in some capacity. For example, look at the amazing people with the innate ability to comprehend math in unconventional ways that blow other people's minds. It's wild. And so cool.

Consider Temple Grandin, an animal behaviorist and well-known advocate for autism awareness.[1] When she was two, she was diagnosed with brain damage. Then, when she was four, having never spoken a word and refusing any sort of physical touch, the doctors told her mother she would likely never talk and that a lack of bonding with her mother caused her autism. But Temple defied the odds and graduated from college as a diagnosed autistic savant. Despite being different, the potential for weird brains to flourish is remarkable.

Temple is famously known for her unique ability to shift animal behavior based on a "knowing" she gets when entering their environment. For instance, she can walk into a cattle facility and tell you why the cows are afraid and what you need to do to calm them down. She knows this, not because she's fluent in cow language, but because her brain notices patterns and matches them to solutions others can't. It's incredible and very useful. Her "weird" brain has saved people tons of time and money (energy), and the livestock get to live their best lives. Happier cows mean happier humans simply because we take on the energy of whatever we consume.

Having a weird, highly effective lens—a unique worldview—allows me to sit down with people for interviews on *The Human Upgrade* podcast, rapidly understand biology, life, and consciousness, and come out on the other side with an understanding of why it all makes sense. Those lightning-fast insights prove to be accurate and pave the way for new avenues of inquiry and business ventures to help upgrade society.

This ability is the driving force behind many of my ventures. Long before validating its benefits, I championed MCT oil for cognitive enhancement. MCT stands for medium-chain triglycerides. These are fats that are easier for your body to use as fuel, helping you power through your day with more energy and focus. The studies on MCT oil came out five years after I published its efficacy. So how did I know? It was obvious to me, but only to others once they tried it. It's a superpower and a vulnerability, traits we all have varying degrees of.

When I finally understood my autism diagnosis, it was like a weight had lifted. I realized my brain was different, not broken. Things that didn't make sense for decades were no longer confusing. There was more clarity on how people with weird brains experience life, which isn't good or bad. It's just undeniably distinct. This realization was empowering. It helped me embrace my strengths and work on my weaknesses. With the question of "why" behind me, a sense of peace and excitement took its place. Weird brains are not a liability but an asset that needs fine-tuning.

Whether you're dealing with brain fog or stress, or just trying to make sense of your unique wiring, know that there's a way forward. Embrace your quirks, leverage your strengths, and remember that you can unlock incredible potential with the right tools and mindset. The path to high performance is not just for the so-called "broken" or "weird" brains; it's for anyone who wants to operate at their best.

With all this knowledge and inspired by Bobby's transformative results at the chiropractor's office, the dots finally connected. If Bobby could do it, couldn't anyone? It was time to train my brain, learn how to hack it, and then spread that information to the masses. And so began the journey down the rabbit hole of biohacking the brain. I soaked up every last bit of information about rewiring and training the brain for high performance. It was a journey in preparation, laying the groundwork for opening the doors to 40 Years of Zen decades later.

| THE MISSING LINK TO INNER PEACE |

In my books *Fast This Way* and *Smarter Not Harder*, we explored the concept of the four F's: fear, food, fertility, and friends. The purpose of the book you're reading now is partly to introduce the fifth F: forgiveness. Forgiveness is an essential component and the missing link to a life of peace. It's the only way we can evolve to higher states. Just ask any spiritual master on the planet what the secret is to achieving Zen, and invariably, the answer will land on forgiveness. Fortunately, forgiveness isn't some rare commodity reserved for the chosen few. It's accessible to every one of us—anywhere, anytime. You unlock a whole new world of possibilities by tapping into your conscious awareness and opening your heart to the power of forgiveness.

Scott Barry Kaufman[2] is a friend, psychologist, professor at Columbia University, and the author of ten published books. He is known as a "modern-day Abraham Maslow." You've probably heard of Maslow if you've ever taken a psychology class. He is most famous for his groundbreaking theory on the Hierarchy of Needs, which includes physiological, safety, love and belonging, self-esteem, and self-actualization. When Scott discovered Abraham Maslow's unpublished journals, lectures, and essays, revealing an unfinished theory of transcendence, he felt a deep connection to his own work. Driven by curiosity and a desire to explore deeper, Kaufman dedicated himself to completing Maslow's theory and updating it with seven decades of new scientific discoveries. The result is Scott's book *Transcend: The New Science of Self-Actualization.*

With the addition of self-transcendence to Maslow's originally published hierarchy, Scott stresses the importance of transcending the self and connecting with something greater, whether it be other people, nature, or a purpose. He focuses on gratitude, compassion, and the profound sense of interconnectedness we share with others and the world around us. While he doesn't explicitly mention forgiveness as a part of his updated hierarchy, compassion, resilience, and empathy are central to his work.

Forgiveness is not about ignoring lousy behavior or letting those who have wronged you off the hook. It's about rising above your ego and making space for compassion and understanding to flourish, both within and outside yourself. Extending these positive states to others is like planting seeds of peace, understanding, and empathy that grow into happier, healthier humans.

Being exposed to Scott's work helped expand my knowledge from systems of biology and mitochondria to studies of consciousness and the impact of forgiveness on our inner peace. In 2004, after three months of spiritual exploration through Buddhist monasteries, traversing the awe-inspiring landscapes from Kathmandu to Lhasa to Mount Kailash, and even my religious studies during undergrad, it became apparent that having a forgiveness practice is part of mastering peace. For years this concept seemed foreign and bewildering. So many people are operating from a reactive place, holding grudges instead of letting go of the stuff causing anxiety, often unknowingly. Wouldn't it be great if you could simply tell yourself not to be pissed-off about something, and it worked? But it doesn't. Because anger, frustration, and even forgiveness are feelings, not thoughts.

For years, the belief persisted that there was no logical reason for feeling anxious or afraid. But really, there were just no words to articulate the feelings inside. Looking at all the research, it's clear that forgiveness is the antidote to negative emotions—the ego. Yet in the West, shaped by parental teachings such as "Tell your sister you're sorry," we equate apologizing with forgiveness. But words are empty if you don't believe them. So, your hollow apology given at the request of your parents (or society) is a lie. Without true forgiveness, you'll still feel anger, regardless of any apology delivered or received. Holding resentments based on fake forgiveness takes up precious space in your brain and body, making you sick and sad.

Years ago, my sister attempted to steal one of my companies in a deliberate act that we later discovered in court. The Reset Process that we do at 40 Years of Zen helped me to forgive her. But that doesn't mean she gets to be in my life. The very definition of forgiveness is that you let go of resentment and thoughts of revenge. It doesn't mean that you will allow someone who hurt you back into your life. You can forgive someone who hurt you significantly, physically, or emotionally, but you don't have to invite them to dinner.

Western cultural norms confuse forgiveness as being about the other person when it has nothing to do with anyone else. Forgiveness is about your body, nervous system, cells, and heart. Your mind is barely even a part of it because these parts of you *feel*, and then they relay the feeling to your mind. We think forgiveness is a thought when it's actually a *feeling*. It's like feeling love, sadness, compassion, or anger. And it turns out that forgiveness—which means being nonreactive to stuff that doesn't matter—is tied to what Scott Barry Kaufman says about humans desiring transcendence. Humans seek transcendence because we strive to evolve. We evolve by truly forgiving, and we forgive by feeling gratitude.

At a recent Zen experience, we incorporated ketamine into the training, which we will discuss in Part II, Chapter 8, on psychedelics. We discovered that ketamine allows you to experience profound gratitude and forgiveness. Our studies also helped our team distinguish between gratitude and grace.

You hear a lot about gratitude, but grace, often thrown around in conversation, is a higher state of tranquility. It's not a word I tend to think of unless we're talking about a gymnast or religion. But grace is so much more than either of these things. It is the state that the masters, monks, and deeply spiritual people have trained themselves to access at any time, no matter their circumstances or surroundings. The way we do that as humans is to turn on gratitude as a muscle and practice gratitude until we're gratitude athletes. We know how to do that with neurofeedback, medicine, and meditation. We know how to do it with various thought processes, spiritual teachings, and psychological practices and then layering those things as the switch that allows you to go into gratitude more easily. But what's the state when things no longer trigger you, and you feel profound gratitude without negativity? If you said "grace," you'd be right. And grace happens when you practice forgiveness and gratitude together. This occurs in the Reset Process; it allows you to create "grace on demand" by fusing these feelings into one life-altering state whenever you want.

So, before you stop at gratitude, challenge yourself to go further. Learn to become a "grace guru" and experience life as monks do, making forgiveness a part of your peace practice. If you don't know how to do that yet, don't worry. That's what the Reset Process in Chapter 11 is for.

| THE FOUR LESSONS |

Not everyone is willing to spend thousands (or millions) of dollars to rewire and train their brains. And that's okay. It's part of the reason I wrote this book for you. The good news is that you don't need a bottomless wallet to kick-start your transformation journey. All you need is an open mind and a willingness to dive into the centuries of wisdom and decades of personal experience outlined in these pages.

The lessons and principles in this book will allow you to upgrade your brain and life without spending decades meditating or millions on the latest, strangest, and sometimes inherently dangerous gadgets. Chances are, you don't have an EEG machine collecting dust at home. And you don't need one. My journey went far beyond the norm. I went to extremes to heal and expand my brain, but you don't have to do everything named here to see results. I'll show you what's worth your time to get the best results in the least amount of time.

There are shortcuts you can take right now to make up for lost time and rewire your brain for high performance. And you don't have to spend six months with your brain hooked up to machines or hibernate alone in a cave while on a four-day vision quest in the wilderness like I did. Life-changing results are within your reach, and you don't need to be guided by a shaman named Delilah to achieve them.

Lesson #1: All Anxiety Is Hackable

One of the things I learned on my four-day fasting journey in a cave outside Sedona, Arizona, which I wrote about in *Fast This Way*, was that you can reset almost any kind of anxiety. I didn't know it when I entered the cave, but it became apparent as I sat by myself in the dark without food that I had a fear of being alone and an extreme fear of being hungry.

Ultimately, I had taken things around friends, food, and fertility and moved them all into the fear category. By fasting all by myself in a cave where there were no people or food around, I consciously chose to wrestle with my demons using exposure therapy. Exposure therapy is a method where you gradually and repeatedly face whatever triggers your fear and anxiety, but in a controlled, safe way. Over time, your brain gets used to it and stops reacting so intensely.

My journey into understanding and managing my brain's behavior didn't start in that cave, but it was a pivotal moment. The exposure therapy I underwent there mirrored the kind of intense self-exploration and biohacking I had been doing for years. This included identifying the impact of my environment, like toxic mold, on my mental and physical health.

Living with intense anxiety wasn't new. If you've ever lived in a house with toxic mold, walking into a room with even the slightest mold smell may cause your body to contract. Poisoned for years by toxic mold—with chunks of my brain showing no metabolic activity—the smell of it brings me back to that traumatizing experience. Dr. Daniel Amen calls this "toxic mold-induced brain damage." Intense anxiety takes over the whole body, and it's debilitating. This is a cell danger response, and it starts in the mitochondria.

The cells get inflamed, stop making energy, and begin causing inflammation to protect the body. That inflammation settles in your brain and nervous system, and you think, *Something's attacking me;*

I don't know what it is, but it feels like I'm under threat, and I don't know why. You get dizzy, your mouth feels dry, and your heart starts racing. This happens to people often, and many learn to live with the symptoms, thinking they're just "anxious." However, this chronic inflammation causes debilitating long-term health effects on your brain and body if you don't address it.

In the post-COVID era, this cell danger response is happening to more people than before, especially if you experience long COVID. That's because around 30 percent of people exposed to the spike protein, one way or another, have these symptoms now because their cell danger response is chronically activated. This response then turns into feeling more physical anxiety (fear). But what I've learned through 40 Years of Zen is that you can reset almost any kind of anxiety. Whether it's from toxic mold exposure, a virus, or a past abusive relationship, having a functioning mind and body aimed toward peace is still possible.

Lesson #2: Not All Anxiety Is the Same

There are three distinct types of anxiety—physical, reactive, and emotional. **Physical anxiety** is from being sick or depleted. Physical anxiety happens before you can think because your body gets a signal that it's in danger before your rational brain has a chance to interpret it.

If you expose yourself to something or someone that causes your body to feel stress, your brain will look for a story to match and validate that feeling. This is typically from past experiences that felt similar, even if they are totally different—your body doesn't know the difference between stored and new emotions. This is why the cause of the stress you're experiencing *feels* like it's from your spouse or partner when it might have nothing to do with them.

On a trip with a past partner, we were in a jungle exploring the ruins, and she ate a piece of beef jerky with monosodium glutamate (MSG). Within five minutes, she screamed at me for walking too fast even though we had a guide, and I wasn't the one directing our path. Her outburst came out of nowhere, but then a lightbulb went off. *Oh my gosh, her sudden mood change, like Jekyll and Hyde, was biochemical.* But in her mind, it felt like I was to blame simply because I was the one with her when the anxiety hit. Her brain swelled and panicked because there was too much excitatory glutamate from MSG in the spaces between her nerve cells.

I've had a dozen or so top neuroscientists and physicians on *The Human Upgrade* podcast talk about MSG. It's used in rats to induce diabetes.[3] The big packaged-food industry wants you to believe that concerns about MSG are just "fake news" and somehow rooted in racism, but that's total nonsense. The reality is, these companies are pumping way more MSG into their products than you'd ever find in traditional Asian cooking, and it's making people sick.

Biochemical reactions are also why so many people, including me, quit coffee and feel better. I didn't drink coffee for five years because an hour after having a cup, I'd get major anxiety. It felt like a surge of electricity shooting through my body paired with an overactive mind. Scanning traffic for the driver who cut me off or getting angry at the smallest things was normal. But it wasn't me reacting; it was my body's reaction to the crappy cup of coffee laden with mold toxins and who knows what else. This is why I created Danger Coffee.

The difference with Danger Coffee, and why people can drink it without any issues, is that it's mold-toxin-free. It's also remineralized, providing your body with the trace minerals it needs to carry out the thousands of processes that keep you running at full power. You can have a cup of Danger Coffee and feel energized, knowing you're supporting your biochemistry instead of poisoning yourself with anxiety-inducing mold toxins. Imagine enjoying your morning coffee without the jitters and subsequent energy crash. Yeah, it's possible. Remove the junk, add in the magic, and voila!

Other times, something unsuspected in your environment, like bright LED lights (what I call "junk light"), is what's causing you to feel stressed. This is because your mitochondria are overly stressed, and your physical reaction is a projection of the biochemical reaction happening inside your body. And then you act like a jerk while making up a story about why the other person you're with is actually the jerk (because it couldn't *possibly* be you). This is why creating awareness of your current state and stored traumas is so important. Not to be used as an excuse but to better understand your programming and learn to shift your state from that place.

Next, you've got **reactive anxiety** from trauma or old patterns. Like physical anxiety, reactive anxiety also happens pre-thought.

In 2014, when I was building Bulletproof and running a few other flourishing companies, a guy suggested I go on the Joe Rogan podcast. Despite us both being podcasters, I had never heard of him at the time because content creation was our business focus, not listening to other shows. Joe was well-known then but not as famous as he is now.

When I walked into his office in Los Angeles, a life-sized werewolf was in the lobby (obviously not real). I couldn't resist getting a picture with it before proceeding with the interview, where we talked about grass-fed nutrition, eating meat, and drinking coffee to help with his attention-deficit/hyperactivity disorder (ADHD). Afterward, Joe was enthusiastic in his praise on dozens and dozens of podcasts. It felt great knowing that the information I shared was helpful.

Soon after our interview aired, a group of devout Joe Rogan fans, self-identified as the "Death Squad," welcomed me to the family and made a profile for me within their community. This group consisted of adult men who, having endured childhood bullying, perpetuated similar behaviors in adulthood. They would decide when someone needed a "lesson" and rally together to engage in online harassment—a familiar pattern of human bullying, deeply entrenched in tribalism. It was an "us versus them" mentality, which is not my thing. But whatever, right? It didn't matter much at that point.

Soon after, the guy who got me on Rogan's show proposed a partnership to launch a Bulletproof Coffee truck. And I said yes. It sounded exciting. Then a bunch of unexplained delays kept happening. Despite the setbacks, I returned to Rogan's show and got the same effusive praise as the first time. Just as before, I was grateful and happy to help.

During the second recording, Rogan expressed his newfound enthusiasm for kale smoothies, a trend also embraced by his audience. Taking the chance to offer valuable insight, I shared my perspective on the downsides of kale consumption and suggested some better alternatives. He appeared genuinely receptive and appreciative, fueling the desire to keep providing input. Then afterward, his friend, who originally got me on the show, backed out of our coffee truck collaboration, revealing his ulterior motives to launch a competing coffee brand. This left me stunned and disheartened. "Well, at least tell me it's tested for mold," because that was a critical aspect of our previous discussions. He admitted to neglecting this step, opting to "leave it to the community" to figure it out. He knew mold was toxic, and when you're creating something like coffee, which many people drink daily, knowingly injecting this into their system could wreck their brains, guts, and bodies. So, having mold-free coffee matters a lot. This threw me for a loop.

The next day, there were discussions in online forums falsely sharing my support of this guy's new coffee brand. Consumer well-being matters, so I spoke up to set the record straight: "That coffee likely has mold in it; it's not tested. I don't know what's in there, so I don't recommend it." What began as a well-intentioned agreement to join forces and expand the positive impact quickly spiraled into unwanted competition. This guy's company was trying to copy my marketing without doing lab testing, while Joe's company, Onnit, decided to launch their own MCT oil and coffee brand; his previous praise was obviously driven by financial interests. Despite my honesty and integrity, my reputation came under attack. Joe launched a smear campaign against me, labeling me a liar and a cheat, while the Death Squad flooded my social media with personal insults.

I was immediately in crisis mode. This ungrounded me for a couple of months. I had been sitting in this state of gratitude for being able to help others and was completely caught off guard by this entire experience. I hired a PR firm because I had no idea what to do. Despite stable sales, I became increasingly reactive. I was unaware of how profoundly this whole thing was impacting my leadership until one of the guys on my team, a former convoy commander who served in Iraq, confronted me about my behavior. This intervention brought me back to reality, and I decided six months of wallowing was long enough. It was time to figure out why this bothered me so much. What people said was false, so why did it trigger such an intense, visceral reaction?

I worked with EMDR (eye movement desensitization and reprocessing) therapy, but mainly within the 40 Years of Zen Reset Process framework. I asked myself when I first felt this uneasy feeling of doom. And for some reason, a memory from first grade popped into my head that I had forgotten entirely about. This memory meant nothing to me as an adult, and it's pretty funny looking at it now. But it had resurfaced during an altered state, prompting further examination.

In that examination, I thought back to a moment in first grade when I went to the boys' bathroom and saw a kid peeing on the wall. And, by the way, if you're not a boy or a parent of a boy, first-grade boys pee everywhere. So I immediately walked out of the bathroom and told a teacher in the hallway that little Johnny peed on the wall. Just as we were talking, little Johnny walked out. The teacher asked him, "Did you pee on the wall?" He replied, "No, that was Dave." I was sent to the principal's office, furious because I had done the right thing and was getting punished for it. It formed a core memory that had been hiding out for years, which was eye-opening. The sense of injustice I felt being accused of doing something wrong when I hadn't was unbearable, just like it was in the situation with Joe.

Both experiences come down to one common trauma: injustice. Recognizing that familiar emotional sensation from an experience that had occurred decades earlier, I ran the Reset Process to tackle that childhood trauma head-on. Within minutes, the chaos surrounding the situation with Joe seemed to shrink and lose its power. It was as if the clouds had parted, and the sun could shine again.

The other reality is something that Tim Ferriss brought to my attention when I interviewed him for the first time on my podcast about how to deal with critics. It's okay if someone doesn't agree with you; let's be curious about it, right? But attacking someone's character without cause is unacceptable. It's an equation; blocking negative energy costs me half a second, but hurling insults takes far more time and energy. Over time, I learned that all the fear, anxiety, and reactivity weren't necessary. The core of my emotions stemmed from a pivotal moment of injustice in first grade; it wasn't about Joe at all. It's astonishing how something seemingly insignificant from childhood can have such a profound impact in adulthood.

The Joe Rogan situation no longer bothers me because I've done the work to resolve the underlying trauma that made me vulnerable to his behavior. While he may have profited from it, I won't shy away from saying he's a bully. And despite the past, I have no ill feelings toward the man. I've seen his live comedy show; I wore my Bulletproof Coffee T-shirt, although I don't think he saw me. I also think he was a hero during the pandemic.

I want everyone who reads this to understand that trauma comes in many forms, big or small. Even with a loving upbringing, certain events can leave lasting scars. Recognizing your triggers is so important because when you do, you can track it back to where it all began and do the work to get to the other side. With the Reset Process, you erase your triggers and regain control.

The third and final type of anxiety is **emotional anxiety** from thought patterns; this happens *post-thought*. You feel before you think, and then you might feel some more.

This is when you learn something about the world and believe it to be true when it's not. So, you create a story from a belief or situation *in your past* that causes feelings of stress and danger in the present. For instance, if you believe that everyone's looking at you and judging you, you will be among most people in the U.S. who say public speaking is the scariest thing. These people believe everyone's judging them because it *feels* that way based on the memory-based feelings they hold in their bodies. In reality, no one's thinking about you more than they're thinking about themselves. Very often, if you're onstage, the audience is likely rooting for you to be successful; they want to see you win.

Your belief about being judged or not being good enough causes stress, not the people in front of you. But unless you have an awareness of the stories you're still holding on to in your cells, you will continue to project your fears onto others and into the world.

The bad news is that everything feels like emotional anxiety, even when it's not.

Lesson #3: Clinical-Grade Neurofeedback Can Rewire Your Brain for Peak Performance

You can rewire your brain to stop being reactive and perform way better than you think it ever could. The easiest way to improve brain function is to *stop being reactive* because you stop wasting energy on reactivity. When you stop wasting energy on reactivity, you have more energy for peace and performance.

After diving into exposure therapy and facing my unconscious fears—hunger and being alone—that had been brought to the surface when I spent time in a cave, clinical-grade neurofeedback was the answer to go deeper. After asking different experts around the country about their experiences with neurofeedback and seeing so many highly intelligent, successful people getting in their own way or simply feeling stuck or unfocused, I started doing executive coaching.

Working with executives around the country and using clinical-grade neurofeedback in licensed clinics, I discovered a noticeable gap in the industry. At that time, nearly all neurofeedback was focused on "fixing" broken brains. But something was missing. *I have a Wharton MBA and work in Silicon Valley. I'm a successful guy; is my brain really broken?* I thought.

Was "fixing" brains the answer? Or did our brains just need to be rewired and trained away from anxiety toward peace?

Lesson #4: What People Really Want Is Energetic Peace

After working with thousands of clients, it's exceptionally clear between executive coaching and those who've gone through 40 Years of Zen: People want energy and focus, yes. But more than anything, they want peace. Specifically, energetic peace.

The billionaires I was coaching claimed they wanted to be smarter. But it didn't take long to discover they actually wanted to be peaceful. And I don't mean wearing a flower crown while twirling around in the middle of a field, smoking herbs, and singing "Kumbaya" kind of peace. People want internal peace and to hold that state no matter what happens in their lives. It's no surprise it is the ultimate goal of many spiritual practices. Peace feels good in the mind and body. And it's possible to get it through many different pathways.

One of my clients ran a large hedge fund, and part of the coaching program was to use a rudimentary feedback device so he could see his stress levels. Like a true hedge fund manager, he only used it when he got bored on an airplane and had nothing better to do. A few days later, my phone rang. "You know what, Dave? I finally did what you suggested, and it felt really good, so I'm going to use it."

After we got off the phone, he put the device back on his ear and returned to work. The second the market bell rang, he noticed his device turned red, signaling he was in fight-or-flight mode—without knowing it! A hedge fund manager, responsible for *billions* of dollars of other people's money, didn't know when his body was in fight-or-flight mode. It sounds crazy, but this happens all the time. You're probably now, or have been in the past, just like him. Many people, especially in today's chaotic society, have adopted this unconscious state as their usual way of being. But it's not normal when your brain functions as it should. And it certainly won't set you up for a life of peace. In fact, it's quite the opposite.

This guy was at the top of his game. He was super happy and loved his life, but there was an invisible stress brewing within, causing him to be triggered by the alarm bells he heard every day at work. He'd gotten so used to this heightened state that it became his baseline. Without the data to know this was happening, he would have continued operating this way, likely creating more stress and health issues down the road. For the next six weeks, my client used the feedback device for the recommended twenty minutes daily and realized he could always be at peace or at least return to this state quickly with some training. He said that once he figured out how to calm his nervous system and bring himself back to peace, he started to come home at the end of the day with energy for the first time in twenty years. He could finally be present with his kids. It changed his life.

Don't get the wrong idea here. Striving for and achieving peace doesn't necessarily mean you'll always *be* at peace. But once you know what it feels like to be at peace, training your mind to return to that state when you fall out, even if really big things happen, becomes much easier. This raises your capacity to show up for anyone, anywhere you're called to show up. And it may just be for your family, your close friends, maybe for your career, or perhaps something much greater. But if you're at war with yourself or others, you're wasting energy and moving away from that peace, which is counterproductive.

You're wasting energy if you're easily triggered like my client was, going into fight-or-flight mode when an alarm goes off. But if you're at peace, and your energy production works well, you can see the world with a different, more reality-based lens than most people. You're harder to deceive. You're harder to program, and people can't push you around. And it's not that they can't push you around because they're afraid of you. *They can't push you around because you're at peace and unbothered by things outside your control.*

There are two kinds of peace. There's the kind of peace where you're so tired, so downtrodden, so exhausted and overwhelmed that you're peaceful simply because you *don't have the energy* to do anything about it. That's the peace of the defeated.

Then there's energetic peace, which I am talking about here. This is when you have trained your brain to consciously choose peace no matter what's happening in the world. Consider this your Zen state. Truly dangerous people are the ones who choose to be peaceful no matter what. In this case, being dangerous isn't about having physical weapons used to harm but a mental weapon (your brain) used for good. Energetic peace means having enough energy to handle whatever comes your way and maintain a Zen state. Or, as my good friend Vishen Lakhiani likes to say, it means you're "unfuckwithable."

| CURIOSITY CANCELS FEAR |

What would happen if you had the resilience to thrive, kick ass, and enjoy life in any situation, no matter what life throws at you? The problem is that this usually takes decades of meditation to achieve this consistently optimistic default state. But what if there was a way to get these life-changing benefits in days instead of years? What if you could be better now, not later? That's what this book is all about.

I've designed this process, as explained in this book, to teach you how to rewire your brain and supercharge your life. All I need from you is your willingness to dive in and try some potentially weird things. I promise I won't ask you to do anything I haven't done (I suppose that's not exactly saying much). I also promise you that the information in this book works. I'm proof, as are the thousands of others who have traversed through the teachings I'm about to share.

So, let's get into it.

| 2 |

WHY YOUR BODY
WILL PUNCH ITSELF
IN THE FACE

Like a finely tuned machine, your body constantly strives for efficiency, determined to keep you alive at all costs. This is built into your "meat operating system," or MeatOS. Just like a computer's operating system, your MeatOS is constantly running in the background with the sole intention of keeping you safe. This is what keeps your eyes blinking, your lungs breathing, and your heart beating without you even having to think about it. And just like you can hack a computer, you can also hack your MeatOS for high performance. The key is efficiency.

Did you know that you can actually measure your brain speed? This is where the magic happens. In neuroscience, it's called P300D. This is the gap between snapping your fingers and your brain processing the sound—roughly a third of a second. During this snapshot in time, which is superfast, your MeatOS takes the reins, calling the shots faster than you can blink. You can't see the gap, but it is measurable, and we monitor it at 40 Years of Zen and our Upgrade Labs centers.[1]

Seeing what's happening inside our brains without our conscious awareness is creepy. It's like having a stalker watching you from outside your window at night; only your MeatOS is there to keep you safe, not terrorize you. This lag time increases with age, so you may notice that the older you get, the longer it takes to process information. With all the brain-hacking stuff that I've done, I still have an eighteen-year-old's response time. It shows that age has nothing on us when it comes to hacking our biology.

But your MeatOS isn't just about keeping you alive; it's also why you might find yourself tempted by pizza and a lazy night on the couch instead of hitting the gym after a long day. It's like your MeatOS gives you a nudge toward comfort and relaxation. You know, the energy-saving route. If you've ever wondered why you'd rather sit around and veg instead of work out, it's all thanks to your primitive MeatOS working behind the scenes so you can perform at your highest level just in case you're suddenly chased by a tiger.

You can stop feeling guilty about your lazy impulses. They are natural, even healthy, and designed to help you make decisions that save energy. This is the laziness principle, which I discussed in detail in my book *Smarter Not Harder*. It's a fresh new perspective in neuroscience that's shaking things up.

Believe it or not, laziness has fueled all human progress. We got tired of walking and figured out we could ride horses. We got tired of feeding the horses, so we built cars. Progress happens when we find ways to make our lives easier. When done intentionally, laziness creates more efficiency, which is what we want at the end of the day.

We want more energy to do the things that matter, like fostering relationships with our loved ones, building meaningful businesses, and caring for our minds and bodies so we can give back to society. It's noble to only do things that matter. Wasted effort is precisely that: a waste.

It's okay to be lazy—we all are—and it doesn't have to be a bad thing. Let your innate laziness motivate you, even if you've been taught since childhood that anyone who's even slightly lazy is a bad person. Those were just scare tactics designed by parents to get you to do your homework and take out the trash. Brilliant, I might add.

It's time to ditch the outdated programming and flip the script. Say to yourself, "Hey, I'm gonna be picky about where I put my energy. It's okay to focus on the things that matter and let the rest go." If the word *lazy* doesn't feel good, fine. Pick a different word—the meaning is still the same. The point is to understand that even your noble intentions and efforts may come with some pushback from your operating system. It's only because your body is trying to do its job to use the least amount of energy possible. When this pushback happens, don't fight it. Feed it what it wants: a little dose of laziness. Think of it as giving yourself permission to recharge so you can go crush it in the areas of life that matter.

Think about it this way. Have you ever snagged a discount on a purchase and felt like a champ? You probably wouldn't rush home to your spouse to tell them how much you spent, but you'd instead tell them how much money you saved. Why do we focus so much on savings? Well, blame it on your lazy operating system—it loves conserving energy, whether it's time or money.

Marketers have figured out that a discount feels ten times bigger than it is, and they use it to their advantage. Ever notice how a discount feels like winning the jackpot? They're hacking us with their flash sales and "limited time" offers. And we are eating it up, making their lives easier.

Let's get real for a minute. If you could get the same results from a quick ten-minute workout without breaking a sweat or changing clothes compared to an hour-long sweat session followed by a shower and wardrobe change, which would you pick? Forget what you think sounds like the "right" answer—what genuinely feels better? Yeah, that's what I thought.

Instead of telling yourself you'll do something hard, tell yourself you'll save a bunch of energy, and your body will make it look attractive to choose the lazy option. Harness your desire for laziness to get yourself moving, whether it's hitting the gym, tackling brain-training exercises, or indulging in whatever excites you. Just shift your focus from how much you're doing to how much you're saving and watch your energy soar.

You've heard me say it before, but your body is both lightning-fast *and* dumb. It'll listen to whatever you feed it, so why not serve it a dish of energy-saving goodness? This fast-acting system inside you is running the show, *not you*. And while it can be annoying at times, it's natural. Your laziness does not make you wrong; it makes you human. Once you wrap your head around this idea and embrace it, you've got the upper hand. Use it to your advantage, noticing what your MeatOS is doing so it can't trick you anymore.

| NOISE: OFF; ENERGY: ON |

Your body lies to you constantly. It tells you what other people think about you when you don't actually know what they think of you—unless you're telepathic, in which case I'm pretty sure it's not the same as the nagging voice in your head spewing nonsense. Learning to recognize what's real and what's coming from a misinterpretation of reality caused by your MeatOS is life-altering.

Your MeatOS is like your body's survival coach, constantly whispering mean things to you to keep you on your toes. Your body is not thrilled about you meddling in its affairs, trying to complicate things. It wants to call the shots and hates that your conscious mind has a say in the matter. You want your body to be in charge of things like pumping blood, breathing, or running when you see a tiger. But you don't want it going into panic mode every time you encounter your mother-in-law (who is not a tiger). Those run-ins require two very different responses. Or maybe not. I don't know your mother-in-law. It's a constant tug-of-war between who's in charge—you or your body.

This constant push-pull is why turning off notifications on your devices is so important. The nonstop beeps, dings, and alarms make you jump or trigger your nervous system into fight-or-flight mode when there's no tiger in sight. You're wasting energy on outside stimuli, letting them hijack your body and throw you into panic mode instead of focusing on the present moment and responding from peace.

Fluorescent and LED lights are another example of how we unconsciously waste energy. These lights might seem harmless, but your MeatOS picks up on things you can't see. They are flickering at an invisible rate to the naked eye, but your body feels the strain. It's a silent stressor on your mitochondria, causing eye strain, sleepiness, sugar cravings, or headaches. It takes a lot of background energy to deal with the flickering lights, just like those annoying phone notifications. And yet we've adopted these background noises as a part of our lives, not considering the long-term negative impact.

As previously mentioned, one way to combat these harmful lights is to wear a specific type of lens, like the ones in TrueDark glasses,[2] to improve sleep and brain stress. These lenses filter out the wavelengths of junk light that mess with your biology.

A study[3] by the Theoretical and Applied Cognitive Neuroscience Laboratory at the University of Victoria found that just fifteen minutes of wearing TrueDark glasses puts your brain in the same state as meditation. We used our "Sunset lenses" to filter light in the study. Typically these are for nighttime use, but they're beneficial for all hours of the day or night. You put them on and feel your brain sigh in relief—and in the study, the brain waves proved this. Having the right lenses to look through during the workday can dramatically increase your brain's capacity to focus and think so you are more productive and feel better. You only need to wear them for 10–15 minutes to notice the benefits. I wear mine for about an hour before bed and sleep much better than I do without them.

Clinical-grade neurofeedback is another great way to upgrade your focus and performance—it's like hitting the gym for your brain. Upgrade Labs' Human Upgrade Centers are opening nation-wide, but you don't have to visit one of my facilities to experience it. Just know that this kind of support is now available without buying an at-home EEG machine and praying you don't wreck your brain trying to figure out how it all works.

Training your brain to do something that matters is much better than letting it operate on autopilot and do things that aren't useful, like wasting energy thinking about or doing hard things. And anything you don't care about will inevitably feel more challenging than the things that matter to you.

BECOME A WORLD-CLASS ATHLETE AT ALLOCATING ENERGY

The body has a deep-seated fear of running on empty. It's constantly asking itself, "What is the least amount of energy I can expend to make a decision?" Of course, the lowest-energy decision is to say "no," but that's not always an option, or the decision that feels best. Becoming a world-class energy allocator is a skill set you can master. With a bit of practice and even more intention, you will be an energy-allocating athlete in no time (even if you're horribly uncoordinated or failed miserably at sports). Energy is more than output; it's also about how well you utilize your inputs.

Do you ever wake up feeling like you got hit by a truck instead of refreshed and ready to tackle the day? Or maybe you're cruising along just fine, and then BAM! That midafternoon slump hits, and suddenly you're reaching for a cookie. How about after a long day of work? Do you still have enough juice left to hang out with loved ones, or are you ready to hibernate for the next twelve hours?

What if I told you that, with the proper training, you could have more energy than you know what to do with? It's true. By understanding what's happening inside your brain and body, and training it to operate more efficiently, energy will no longer be something you wish for. It will be your new state of being.

A classic example of poor energy allocation is attention-deficit/hyperactivity disorder (ADHD), which is, at times, a Band-Aid diagnosis to another underlying issue. So what is it, exactly?

Attention is the ability to consciously focus on what's in front of you. Most people can filter out distractions and concentrate on the task at hand. But people with ADHD have extra holes in their filter, letting in distractions and preventing them from using energy efficiently. Instead of being locked into the present moment, their MeatOS lets in all sorts of irritating sounds, noises, smells, and other things, distracting them from what matters. Think of it like a window screen with holes in it. It kind of works, but it's not as effective.

This is because your nervous system is compromised if you have ADHD, probably triggered by toxins[4] or inflammation[5] from auto-immunity,[6] diet,[7] or lifestyle.[8] And let's not forget about the sneaky culprit lurking in the shadows: stored trauma. We will dive deep into that in Part II.

So, what would happen if you fixed energy allocation, fixed trauma, and then retrained your brain? You could do what I did and finally experience life with more clarity and focus. And most importantly, more peace.

I was diagnosed with ADHD and ASD ages ago, and life was a bit of a blur until diving headfirst into brain training. Clinical-grade neurofeedback changed everything for me, which is what we do at 40 Years of Zen, along with other brain-boosting techniques. By consciously shifting blood flow to the front of the brain, you can train your brain to pay attention in unimaginable ways. And the best part? This level of cognitive training is possible for all brains; you are not doomed to live a life of foggy thinking unless you want to.

By excavating the remnants of stagnant energy inside you, upgrading your brain, and rewiring the patterns of trauma stored deep inside, you will finally see reality for what it is: an epic movie of your creation. If left unattended, however, you will view reality through a very different lens. It will be clouded by all the stories, limiting beliefs, and past experiences ultimately holding your mind hostage. This conscious shift and effort toward more efficiency will allow you to use your energy for meaningful things. No more wasting time and brainpower on energy suckers like anxiety, fear, blame, and shame.

Think about doing something scary, like giving a TED Talk to a packed audience, knowing it will be broadcast to the whole world afterward. Suddenly, right before you're about to step onstage, you notice an itchy tag on the back of your shirt that's pissing you off. It takes everything in your power to ignore the itch and give a talk that will leave a lasting impression when what you want to do is jump off the stage, rip the tag from your shirt, and vigorously scratch your skin raw.

Chances are, something like this has happened to you. It's annoying, right? Your body often does stuff like this to keep you from doing something that's even more computationally expensive. Your body says, "Don't use your energy to do that big, scary thing. SAVE, SAVE, SAVE. If I can distract you with something trivial (like an itchy tag), then you won't use your energy to evolve (i.e., change), and we will remain safe." This is how your body sabotages your attempts to improve your mind. And ultimately, your life. Staying exactly where you are is predictable and, therefore, safe. Evolving is a giant, scary leap into the unknown, and unfortunately, fear uses the most energy. This is why so many competent people stay stuck. They're paralyzed by fear, without enough energy to act toward their vision.

Speaking of changing your brain, I used to say that I have ASD, but not anymore. A lot of times after hearing this, people get upset because they claim you can't get rid of ASD. However, there's a growing body of evidence to show that, while there is no known cure or method to reverse ASD completely, there are therapies like neurofeedback,[9, 10, 11] to improve brain quality and outcomes for people with ASD. It's promising. I've done a lot of work on my brain to change the way it operates, and I have a completely different brain than I used to. The symptoms that used to plague me—brain fog, forgetfulness, anxiety, rage—no longer exist. Yet, although there are various interventions and support strategies to reduce these symptoms, the incidence of autism is on the rise. There are a variety of reasons for this.

At its core, there are two main drivers. One is chronic neuro-inflammation, usually autoimmune-related, and the other has to do specifically with your mitochondria—the powerhouses of your cells. Both factors can be upgraded and healed.

Imagine trying to watch your favorite show on Netflix or dive into a good book, but there's this annoying static buzzing in the background, making it nearly impossible to focus. You catch bits and pieces, but the signal you're receiving is jumbled. Having ASD is like dealing with constant static. This irritating noise on the line makes it hard for your brain to understand what you just heard or read. Your brain is distracted and using massive amounts of energy to sift through all the buzz happening at once.

The other thing that happens with ASD is that your body doesn't make enough energy because your mitochondria—the parts of your cells that produce energy to fuel your brain and body—are compromised. Trying to focus without enough energy is like trying to run a marathon with one arm tied behind your back. I don't want to say it's impossible, but it takes a lot of extra energy.

So now you don't have enough energy to focus, and focusing takes way more work than it does for a typical brain. And while other people are picking up on facial expressions and body language, you may miss social cues because you're so focused on understanding what people are saying and making sense of it all. Then throw in a mix of toxins and environmental factors, infections, injections, and who knows what else, and you've got a recipe for sensory overload and frustration. While there might not be a single cause, one thing's for sure: toxic mold is a major culprit for many people. It was for me. And sometimes it's all of the above. However, understanding the problem is the first step in finding a solution.

Understanding this and digging into the research available from some of the top experts in their industry, I successfully rewired and retrained my brain to reverse all the symptoms that created these feelings of helplessness, frustration, and embarrassment. While I may not identify as having ASD anymore, it's not about denying the past—it's about embracing the potential for growth and change. There's a whole world of healing and transformation available, waiting for you to take a leap of faith and see what happens.

| IT'S A MARATHON, NOT A SPRINT |

Fixing your brain without understanding all the components responsible for its sludge is hard. This book exists today to help you navigate the sea of information and train your brain for high performance, genuine happiness, and inner peace.

I'd love to tell you this is a quick process; your brain will be "fixed" overnight. But that would be a lie, and we're here to be truthful, right? So, understand this: where you are now did not happen without time or effort, whether consciously or not. Understandably, changing the course of your life will take some time and effort, too. The time it will take to get you to a sustainable and enjoyable place will likely happen much faster because now you have a road map to follow (this book) to achieve positive results. Focus on what you want instead of all the reasons it won't work, can't work, shouldn't work, hasn't worked; likely the same excuses that have kept you stuck in the first place. This is not a judgment, but an observation after working with thousands of highly successful and intelligent people just like you.

This book is a guide to help you through the process of—and this is big—*changing your entire life*. It starts in your brain, moves into your body, and, brick by brick, becomes your reality. Be patient with yourself and the process. The specifics shared here may differ from your individualized approach; do whatever works best for you. Neither is wrong. Honor the place you're in now and get excited about where you still have left to go. Just remember: fear consumes the most energy. Let go of anything that's creating that feeling and feel your energy rise!

After realizing everything that's been in the way and embarking on a journey of life-changing, lasting results, the path to fixing my brain was abundantly clear. First, get out of the toxic environment. Then fix the mitochondria and restore the immune system. You have to free the lines of static to power the system back up for efficiency.

All of that sounds great, right? And it is. But what happens when you handle these crucial components without addressing the brain? Now you have a system that doesn't know how to interpret all the new data it's in contact with daily. This means you may have to relearn how to hear, see, speak, and move your body. It means relearning how to interact with people using the full spectrum of human capabilities. Changing your way of being takes a lot of energy, but once you shift toward what you want to experience, it's nearly impossible to go back. This is the sweet spot. This is where your focused effort becomes your vibrant new reality.

Clinical-grade neurofeedback and meditation are like a dynamic duo when it comes to tackling the anxiety swirling around in your mind—whether you're dealing with ASD, other spectrum disorders, or past trauma, or are just navigating life in this crazy world.

You're anxious because you don't have enough energy to interpret the world within or around you. It's constantly noisy, causing stress and an overall feeling of unease. But it's all you know. A life without anxiety is foreign until you reset your system and train your brain to chill out and experience more peaceful states. When you finally break free from the anxious cycle, you'll ask yourself, *Why didn't I do this sooner?* If you're nodding along now, welcome to the club. We're all in this together.

Here's the thing: whether you're on the spectrum or not, feeling different from your peers is a challenge that doesn't discriminate by age or diagnosis. You don't need a label like ASD to feel the implications. And although it might help bring some clarity, it doesn't define who you are. Remember, we're all trying our best to navigate this strange universe. Be you, no matter what. That's what we need more of: authentic people showing up to improve the world.

All this talk about ASD brings me back to pattern-matching and the ability to see things others can't, like Temple Grandin's example from Chapter 1. The body allocates energy where it's needed to see these patterns clearly. When you become a world-class athlete at allocating energy, plus you have a "weird brain," you will see these patterns with more efficiency, leaving more energy for things (and people) that keep your energy high and your heart full.

Even if you're not on the spectrum, the magnetic pull of your MeatOS toward efficiency is universal. You may not have extraordinary pattern-matching abilities but rather something else unique to you. Ultimately, that's what you want: more energy, used more efficiently, so you can do what you want, with and for the people you love. This could be your family, community, clients, colleagues, or friends. Having the resources available to thrive so you don't spend your days like a starved zombie searching for food (or, in this case, energy) only to hit your pillow at night, absolutely exhausted, is the real reward.

| MENTAL CONSTIPATION |

The body wants you to use less energy. This is where confirmation bias swoops in. Once you've decided on something, your brain goes into overdrive, hunting down evidence to support it and boosting your confidence in the process—all to affirm that you just made the right decision (even if you didn't).

People joke about kids having selective hearing. Well, confirmation bias is like that. It's like having selective hearing on steroids, only for your brain. This happens due to multiple cognitive mechanisms, including memory recall, selective attention, and your understanding of information. When you decide, your brain tends to latch on to information that backs up your current beliefs while ignoring anything that doesn't fit the narrative. Essentially, you can talk yourself into or out of anything you want. Pretty sneaky, isn't it?

Think about how you make decisions. There are many ways to do so, but you probably have a preferred method.

The first method, something we train on at 40 Years of Zen, is intuition. Once you get fear and ego (negative emotions) out of the way, you can train your body to listen to your inner voice. This is one of the best decision-making methods and requires the least energy allocation once you know how to do it properly. You can align your heart and head when you quiet the surrounding noise and tune into yourself. The real magic happens when your wisdom speaks, and you're brave enough to listen, regardless of society's programming, the "should have, could have, would have" thoughts, and the old stories that tell us, "This is how things have always been and should continue to be." You know yourself better than anyone. It's a matter of honoring your wise inner guide when your innate truth whispers (or screams).

The next decision-making technique is: asking others for advice before checking in with yourself. Being inundated with multiple opinions and left to filter through all the information to form a decision makes this a much higher energy-allocating option. Everyone has a viewpoint, but you'll have to choose what you do with all the information presented. Don't forget to check in with yourself, particularly when considering a decision that impacts you.

Or there's the more spiritual approach of needing time and space to reflect and decide. Maybe you take a whole day off work to visit your favorite coffee shop, write in your journal, sit under a tree, or make a spreadsheet. This is the "overview" decision method, where you look at it from all angles and then make a well-thought-out decision. For some this creates analysis paralysis, which of course takes a lot of energy.

Herein lies the problem. If your body will affirm whatever decision you make (and it will), why not choose the most efficient route to make a decision and save yourself some energy? If you're like most people, you're probably overcomplicating things and unknowingly draining your energy in the process. But don't worry. Your decision-making preference can also be rewired and trained with the proper support.

The information in this book will help you to stop wasting so much energy and become much more efficient at allocating energy to the point that the body says, "You know what? I have so much energy; deciding doesn't feel that hard anymore. I think I'll use my resources to make a better decision." You'll use your energy to drop the ego and rely on your intuition (the most efficient path), or you'll still drop the ego but choose to think about it before deciding. The amazing news is that even if you prefer the overview decision-making method, you will have the energy to ponder. So you will make much better decisions regardless since you have more energy.

One of the most straightforward caveman-level ways of thinking is *if something is good, more is better; if something is bad, less is better.* But it turns out there's a Goldilocks zone where too much of a good thing is bad—for example, water. Water is essential for life, but too much or too little water will kill you. If you drink too much water without enough sodium in your system, you can die from a condition called hyponatremia. It happens every year during marathons when people overhydrate. On the other hand, you can die of thirst if you don't have enough water. So maybe there's a better way, like adding quality salt to your water, which hugely upgrades your hydration and energy.

One of the most toxic things you can do is to say *more is better.* Much like water, there are plenty of examples where more is not necessarily better. Meditation is one of them. In fact, with some of the more powerful techniques available, there are warnings like "Don't do this for more than twenty minutes a day, or you'll probably lose your job and get lost in la-la land." Obviously, that's verbatim (or something like that).

In advanced Buddhist teachings, it's very common to hear about people going crazy from something called "fast-path Buddhism." It's like taking the express lane to enlightenment using hacks and tools designed for people who want results without spending years in a monastery.

Years ago, I embarked on a ten-day silent meditation experience at a Buddhist monastery with a beautiful temple in Nepal. The monastery's library had a locked room that you were only allowed to enter once you reached a certain level of enlightenment. This was for the participants' safety because even with meditation, *more* can quickly become *too much.*

There's a Goldilocks zone for diet, too. Some people attempt a plant-based diet; I used to be vegan, so I understand this. But now it's proven that eating only plants is terrible for you,[12] yet people do it anyway. Conversely, a diet with no plants is probably not good, either. However, if given the choice, I would tilt more in the direction with a focus on meat. Somewhere in there is your "just-right" zone, and only you know what that is.

Just as there is a Goldilocks zone for water, food, or meditation, there's a Goldilocks zone for how many decisions you can make in one day. If you make too few decisions, you're probably not in control of your life. If you make too many decisions during your day, you'll run into "decision fatigue." If you reach this threshold, you'll start making poor decisions because your brain has run out of energy. Even if you're using your intuition, there's a limit.

In one study,[13] researchers examined judges' parole decisions throughout the day. There was a significant interrelationship between the timing of the decisions and the judges' energy levels. As the judges grew fatigued, particularly right before meal breaks, their probability of granting parole decreased dramatically. The judges' mental fatigue influenced their decision-making. Sucks for the people with parole meetings right before lunch, right? Moral of the story: don't make too many decisions, and definitely don't make them when you're "hangry." But really, don't make decisions when you know you don't have the energy to make sound ones.

| BUILD A BRAIN LIKE BRUCE LEE |

When you see martial artist and actor Bruce Lee using nunchucks or playing Ping-Pong and whacking balls like it's the easiest thing in the world, he has clearly trained his brain for exceptional response times. Now, I'm not Bruce Lee, not by a long shot. But it illustrates that no matter how old you are, you can train your brain and enhance its function for peak performance. This is because of neuroplasticity—the brain's ability to change and adapt throughout your lifetime—and having more energy in the brain to be able to master whatever you choose.

Bruce Lee, who died in 1973 at just thirty-two years old, said that by subtracting the things (and people) from your life that are "nonessential" or take away from your life in any way, you can multiply what's possible in your experience. I've seen this proven repeatedly.

If you want to go within, neurofeedback provides an intricate path to self-awareness; "Know thyself" is the perfect phrase. It will help you realize which nonessentials you can remove from your life. Neurofeedback also increases neuroplasticity[14] so you can play Ping-Pong like Bruce Lee. Or your neurofeedback journey can be a path to better movement in your body or improved self-regulation. It's really up to you. But if awareness work is your aim, just know it's a spiritual practice with many layers. It's beautiful work that can be hard at times. However, allowing yourself to dive in and learn what you need to know will help you get where you want to go.

Neurofeedback can help you go within and do the inner work, but it can also help you go without. At 40 Years of Zen, we're not in the business of fixing broken brains. Instead, we use neurofeedback to superpower a capable brain with strengths and weaknesses. It's a totally spiritual experience. There are no words for the scope of this powerful work; understanding its magnitude is a felt experience.

| BIGGER IS NOT ALWAYS BETTER |

This book exists to help you make sound decisions that feel easy, so you free up your energy to spend on the last two F's: friends and forgiveness. Even some of the AI tools we're using at Upgrade Labs focus on using data to remove the difficulty (and save you energy). It doesn't necessarily take a lot of work to *do* something; it takes a lot of work (energy) to *think* about doing something. The thinking is where the body is going to fight you. If you think about doing something through the lens of a crappy algorithm, and it tells you that you made a good decision when you didn't, you're just wasting energy. Your goal is to be efficient.

An example of this is Albert Einstein's brain. While some regions of his brain showed unique characteristics and differences compared to other brains researched, it wasn't bigger. *It was more efficient.* Studies on Einstein's brain showed that certain regions, like the parietal lobe, connected to mathematical and spatial reasoning, were highly developed. He also had more glial cells than the average brain, which support and nourish neurons. This combination of unique qualities contributed to enhanced neural connectivity and efficiency in his brain but did not increase its size.

So, which is better? A computer chip that requires a nuclear reactor to run and is lightning-fast, or a million small ones that run off the sun's power and do the same computing? It turns out efficiency is where the game is. Efficiency always wins. Life is efficient once you remove the barriers. It's humans and our thinking minds that over-complicate it.

Part of life's efficiency is understanding how efficient your brain is. From there, how much reality can you handle? If your brain is low-efficiency, it can't handle as much reality (remember, this is where anxiety pops up). But if your brain is more efficient, it can handle more reality, which means more peace.

There are infinite things around you that you will never know about, and they're happening all the time. Ignorance, in this case, is bliss because it helps you be more efficient. For instance, what is the amount of air pressure that's on your little finger? Did a mosquito land on your head during your morning walk? You won't notice these things in your brain, but your cells know. They just don't tell their friends. Or if they do tell their friends or the other cells near them, those cells aren't bothered. "It's not a big deal. It's normal, don't report it up the chain." This is because every system in your body has its own intelligence, deciding whether the things happening around you are worth talking about.

Imagine living in a home with a home security system, and at the very edge of your fence there are a bunch of different little sensors. If those sensors went off every time a squirrel tripped on one of them, you would never be able to sleep. In reality, there are trillions of squirrel equivalents scurrying around doing stuff that affects you that you don't consciously get notified of (thankfully).

Now imagine if you had to process every single detail in the world around you, even the insignificant stuff like the brand of shoes your neighbor was wearing this morning when you saw them get into their car. Not only that, but you also had to micromanage every bodily function, from regulating your heartbeat to controlling the opening and closing of valves in your body. Your poor human brain would probably implode within an hour. It's like asking your old-school box-shaped computer to run a modern-day program. It's way too complex for your brain to handle. Luckily, your body sorts this stuff for you so you can spend your energy on more important things.

REPROGRAM AND REWIRE YOUR BRAIN TO MAKE BETTER DECISIONS FASTER

In 2021, Jeff Hawkins, the cofounder of Palm Pilot, published a fascinating book called *A Thousand Brains*. I briefly worked with him at my first job in Silicon Valley when we bought Palm Pilot back in 2010. In his book, Hawkins makes a clear case that your brain predicts the future using "maplike structures to build a model of the world—not just one model, but hundreds and thousands of models of everything we know." This is why you can do a lot of things you can do. You don't think about catching a baseball. You tell your body to catch a baseball using these maplike structures. The body predicts where the ball will be before the brain. Then your hand has its own map and knows where to go. Then you take credit for it, even though you didn't think about the mechanisms to make the catch possible. "Let me flex my bicep and rotate my wrist twenty-five degrees." That doesn't happen. There's no time to think.

This goes back to the Bruce Lee example from earlier with the Ping-Pong balls. He learned to turn his brain off and let his body do what the body does. And his body was well trained. When you do the things in this book, you can train your brain to follow the body's signals. When you begin to cultivate awareness, you suddenly realize that when you walk into a room, there are all kinds of signals that your body has learned to ignore because it didn't have enough energy to pay attention. Now you're like a martial arts master, spotting every little nuance with laser-like focus.

The other thing that's going on here is that although you're incredible, your brain is stupidly slow (everyone's brain is), and if it tried to do everything the body does, you couldn't exist. Imagine if you had to consciously open the upper sphincter of your colon while simultaneously instructing your red blood cells to take in more nutrients and allow more synaptic interconnectivity between two neurons. You would flip out. It's impossible. These are your automated systems in the body or your ANS—autonomic nervous system. The ANS controls involuntary bodily functions. It has two main branches: the sympathetic nervous system (SNS), which prepares you to handle threats, and the parasympathetic nervous system (PNS), which helps you chill out and take care of business, like digestion and relaxation.

As you become more efficient in your thinking and expand your awareness because you've stopped spending energy on fear, food, and fertility (don't worry, you can still have sex; you're just not obsessing over it), what's left is this incredible ball of energy that's ever-expanding. You get to spend it on the fourth F: friends, relationships, and being of service to others, and the fifth F: forgiveness and evolving yourself.

That's why people who start a spiritual or meditation or awareness practice, whatever you want to call it, become more dangerous over time (in a good way). Because as you become more efficient, you have more energy to evolve even quicker. Despite all the doom and gloom we see in the news, we're collectively moving in this direction. We can now compare your unique brain to 1,500 other high-performing brains, know the spiritual states, and tune a computer to show you how to enter a specific state without drugs. That has never happened, at least in recorded history. Yet we're doing it at 40 Years of Zen. It's extraordinary.

| INTUITION: THE REAL INTELLIGENCE |

Before I dove into spiritual work, I didn't realize there was such a thing as intuition and that it was possible to deeply know something was true without hard data. There was no known signaling mechanism to hack; that's the logical part of the brain speaking. Believe it or not, solid scientific evidence shows that intuition is real and can be groundbreaking in decision-making.[15] Researchers at the University of New South Wales found that people can use their intuition to make faster, more accurate, and more confident decisions. They did a series of experiments where participants made decisions influenced by "nonconscious emotional information" from their body or brain. When exposed to positive subliminal images, participants performed better on tasks—proof that intuition isn't just a mystical feeling. It's your brain processing info on a deeper level. The feeling is evident to me now, but this was a foreign concept for a long time.

My path started at age thirty (roughly two decades ago), and it was not just to be smarter but to be in charge of my MeatOS, mainly the nervous system and mind. That's what the monks and shamans do.

You can learn the different brain states, and once you understand them, you can intentionally play them back. Some states are easier to access quickly, while others may take a few steps to achieve. Learning to get into new states takes work. And it's a heck of a lot faster with technology, like neurofeedback, than without it. You can train your brain to access these states in multiple ways.

At this time in history, we would benefit greatly from being profoundly peaceful, focused, or in a flow state. We need the capacity to feel love and gratitude effortlessly and be unprogrammable by anyone or anything, including a marketing company, a political campaign, or some government (or nongovernment) organization attempting to manipulate us with fear. There's enough negativity out there. We don't need to add to it. Instead, take a page from the playbook of the monks—understanding that true change starts from within. When you are steadfast in your beliefs and unshakable in your heart, that's when healing begins. Strive to be a beacon of positivity in a world that desperately needs it. When we get to this place, the world will heal itself.

This shift can't happen by overthinking or having slow, unproductive thoughts. Learning to focus and think more effectively is relatively simple; it's what 40 Years of Zen trains. Rewiring and training your brain isn't just about improving your cognitive abilities. It's also about mastering your nervous system and tapping into your full potential as a human being. After seeing all the esoteric, spiritual, and magical stuff happening worldwide, this really hit home. It sparked a deep curiosity about our potential as a species. This was all part of the genesis of 40 Years of Zen in 2013.

But I didn't just want to study the beliefs and behaviors of monks, shamans, and other spiritually enlightened beings. I wanted to understand how these differing beliefs and behaviors coexist, all with the same goal: peace. Peace is so much more than thinking positive thoughts. The plethora of global wisdom available and the pathways and desire to attain these states are more often about *choosing to be* a better, more compassionate human.

Many people come to 40 Years of Zen to train intuition and creativity. It's what some traditions call an "inner knowing," where you know in your gut that what you're feeling or thinking is true. And it turns out there's a quantitative and qualitative difference (that's measurable) and a felt difference between intuition versus ego versus thought.

Here's how to tell if it's **intuition**.

When you look at a situation, your intuition is the first thing you feel in your body. Then your emotions and programming will be almost right on top of that nudge (slightly delayed). This is where confirmation bias comes from. Your body knows the truth (intuition) before the programs in your head run (emotions) and do their best to either validate you or try to change your mind. This is the order of operations based on the timing of how our brains and bodies work.

Now the programs are running, and the memory of when you were two years old and someone dropped you pops up. Or when you were in elementary school, and little Suzy broke up with you. Or the time you got fired or got into a horrible car accident. Whatever your traumas are, the body quickly processes all those stored memories before deciding. This is all happening behind the scenes in your subconscious. It's like going to ChatGPT and asking, "Hey, ChatGPT, what's going on?" Then ChatGPT does its job and sifts through the entire internet, giving you its best and quickest response possible with the available information. This is what your intuition does instantly.

Your body reads the entire history of your existence and probably your ancestors through some weird genetic stuff. Based on all that information, in under a third of a second your body will tell you what to do based on its equivalent of AI, or what we know as intuition— the *real* intelligence. When you do the work to heal your traumas and the triggers they create, your intuition gets louder and easier to hear.

Then there's **emotion (ego)**.

This is the "I don't like that guy" (a judgment stemming from your intuition) followed by a sense of aversion, anger, or other negative emotions. Negative emotions are just your ego trying to protect and keep you alive. "Save energy! Save energy! Don't be in danger!" This is where your emotions take all the information swiftly processed by your intuition and decide what to do with it. The idea is that when you realize you can have enough energy, suddenly you don't have to worry about fear anymore because you're rooted in peace. This makes you dangerous in the best way possible. And as we like to say at Danger Coffee, *who knows what you might do?*

Having adequate energy equals less fear because you know you've got this. It doesn't matter if you do the hard or easy thinking because you have enough energy to move through the process with an upgraded, more efficient brain.

Next comes **cognitive thought**.

Many engineers, including successful Silicon Valley professionals and my own personal clients, often engage this part of their brain while quickly dismissing their intuition, if they even acknowledge it at all. They'll silence the pesky ego voice, saying, "I don't like that." Then they'll run it through their internal spreadsheet processing nodes and attempt to make the most logical decision possible. Or what feels logical, anyway. It's really just them justifying their initial gut feeling. They'll defend their decision tooth and nail, insisting it is the rational choice. I'm just speaking about my experiences with people I've coached and myself. It's called rationalizing. But since we know that everything in the world is processed through feelings first, all the rational stuff is a story about what you initially *felt*. And if you believe what you feel is true, your actions will be "rational" based on an irrational feeling.

But *feelings are not rational*. Why? Because they're feelings, they're not thoughts. So, yeah, it can get confusing. Just remember the order of events: intuition first, emotion next, and finally, the brain gets a say in the matter (or so it likes to think).

If you use your brain to squash your ego (where negative emotions come from), this is good. If you use your brain to squash your intuition, this is problematic. The goal is to follow your intuition.

The path we're talking about here is to be calm and have enough energy and efficiency in your brain for high performance and peace. When you've turned up energy and efficiency, it's like having an electric car that can go two thousand miles on a charge. This is what you want. With a more efficient battery, you'll use less electricity when cruising around. That's amazing. This is what you want your brain to do.

The practice is listening to and honoring your intuition when it says "no" and training your brain to be at peace with that decision instead of second-guessing yourself all day, which many people do. Or vice versa. If your intuition says "yes" and your logical brain says "no," the work is to get to where you trust your intuition above logic, so you do the intuitive thing anyway.

Learning to decipher intuition, emotion, and thought will reduce your energy expenditure dramatically because now you're running on more intuition than ever before, which is the most efficient way to operate. That cancels out negative emotions (ego) and thoughts, which are the real energy suckers.

When starting my mold-free coffee brand, Danger Coffee, the market size was zero. And for whatever reason, intuition said, *this is the time to start*. It was a visceral feeling in my bones. The logical venture capital MBA part of my brain was like, *this is the dumbest idea ever.* So I did it anyway because intuition trumps emotion. And now functional coffee is a $500 million industry category.

The same applied to MCT oil initially; the market size was tiny, but now it's also a multibillion-dollar category. The same with collagen. When I was running it, *Forbes* named Bulletproof one of the twenty most innovative brands in the country, which began on intuition, not because of thinking. Intuition spoke, and emotion and thought got tossed aside because of all the neurofeedback and brain training. The very things you're learning about in this book.

Your body wants you to be right, but then the skeptical part of your brain tries to slide in and prove that your intuition is wrong. As a former atheist and current agnostic, primarily focused on data and computer science, your skepticism is understandable. Hearing this would have previously sounded silly to my "broken" logical brain, except it's real and scientifically provable. There is a reason your body wants you to be right: to keep you safe (thank you, body). This safety cue is why people will stick to their story, even when it's wrong. You might think it's stubbornness, but something sneakier is going on behind the scenes. It's about getting out of your own way and trusting that change is possible.

MY EGO IS SMALLER
THAN YOURS

When you hear the word *ego*, is your first reaction a negative one, like ego is a bad thing? Most people would respond yes to that question. But what if I told you your ego isn't the villain here? It's just one of the many players in your body's orchestra. It's not all of who you are.

Before we get into the details, let's quickly recap the decision-making layers from the last chapter.

The initial gut feeling you sometimes get, the little whisper nudging you in a specific direction? That's your intuition, often brushed off or overlooked. Then, right on its heels comes emotion (or ego, if we're talking about negative emotions), followed by a flood of thoughts.

Imagine you believe your partner's out to push your buttons, even though their words don't mimic any sort of personal vendetta. You tell yourself a story about the negative emotions that arise and create a dramatic storyline, blocking your intuition. Maybe something like "My partner meant to piss me off," even though you know their response wasn't a personal attack. It just *feels* personal, likely because of your past experiences that felt similar. Sound familiar?

Keep in mind that your intuition is like the superhero of decision-making, minus the cape. It's also the MVP of energy efficiency and smarts among all the layers we just went over. This gut feeling knows what's up before your brain can put in its two cents. The downside of this inner knowing is that, despite having this superpower at your disposal, it's often met with the cold shoulder. You've trained yourself to find comfort in negative emotions and thoughts, adding unnecessary confusion when choosing what you know deep down is the right or better option.

YOUR EGO IS KIND OF AN ASSHOLE

If you've ever wondered where your ego comes from, you're not alone. Spiritual gurus and psychologists have pondered this puzzle for ages. After all of my cross-lineage training, here's my take.

Your ego isn't some villainous force constantly scheming how to ruin your day; it actually has a pretty crucial job—to keep you alive. But problems emerge when you give it too much power, getting triggered by things that should barely make a blip on your radar.

The ego isn't just some abstract concept; it's deeply intertwined with the very cells that make up your body. We're talking about those tiny powerhouses called mitochondria, spread throughout your entire being, playing a quantum dance that we're just starting to grasp. Every time your heart beats, the protons (positively charged particles) in your brain cells change the direction in which they spin. This proves that your brain and body are an intricate quantum duo. Without your ego, you wouldn't even have a physical form. It's like the cryptosystem that's both everywhere and nowhere at the same time. Your ego is there, even though you can't see it.

Your ego is like a wild animal, lightning-fast and primal. It's the puppet master behind your negative feelings and emotions. It doesn't want you to listen to or rely on your intuition because it wants to be in control. So it works overtime to override that deep inner knowing. It's like being stuck next to a toddler in full-on meltdown mode. Unless you've got some magical parenting abilities and have learned to tune out the chaos, it's a battle you're likely to cave in to just to get some peace and quiet.

Your ego is basically a collection of rapid, programmed routines whose main gig is ensuring your body's survival. As the first responder to reality, it processes everything in a flash. These programs don't care about your quantum-fast, instantaneous knowing—your intuition. And they don't care about you. They're all about their own agenda; unfortunately, it's not always aligned with what's best for you.

Your ego is kind of an a-hole, and it's also pretty dumb. Because it operates from fear, the most energetically expensive response in the playbook, it tends to jump the gun in ways your intuition shrugs at—unless you've mastered keeping it in check, allowing your intuition to take the wheel.

Your ego is your own personal emotional roller coaster, dishing out negativity left and right. It's masterful at sweeping things under the rug, especially if they're too scary or too painful to face. It makes you see phantom threats and muffles stuff you really need to hear. It does all this from fear to protect you, not because it's evil or conniving, although it sometimes seems that way.

You might believe you should have compassion for your ego. But every time you give your ego an inch, its instinct is to take a mile. Your best bet is to recognize and accept that it exists and that it's not going anywhere. Then, learn how to manage it so it doesn't run wild.

Your ego will always try to lead you astray. It'll twist the truth, make you dig your heels in during an argument, or tempt you with a pint of ice cream instead of hitting the gym. It has a knack for whispering those not-so-nice things in your ear, telling you you're not enough or worthy or capable. And while that sounds "bad," understand that it's doing all of this to protect you in the only way it knows how. To your ego, its reaction is a safety and survival instinct; everything else takes a back seat.

When dealing with your ego, it's all about training it like you would a wild animal. It's the unruly critter in your very own mental zoo. I'm not a fan of putting animals in cages, but when it comes to taming your ego, bring it on. Remember that if left unchecked, your ego will wreak havoc when you're not looking. As a good zookeeper, your job is to keep a close eye on it and practice constant vigilance through curiosity, keeping tabs on its every move.

In Byron Katie's self-inquiry method called "The Work," she uses four simple questions to help diffuse the chaos your ego and mind create so you can return to reality.

Is it true?

Can you absolutely know it's true?

How do you react; what happens when you believe the thought?

Who would you be without the thought?

These questions sound simple because they are. They're also highly effective.

When you feel triggered, instead of taking the bait, which is your ego trying to control your reality, look at the situation with curiosity—"Isn't that interesting? I'm feeling triggered right now. I wonder why?" When you do that, you realize it's funny because your ego almost won. You *almost* cussed a guy out on the freeway for cutting you off when he wouldn't have heard you through the glass anyway. You *almost* sabotaged your relationship by picking a fight because you feared rejection or being wrong instead of leaning into vulnerability to fix the problem together. But because you took a moment to pause and laugh at yourself, the ego quiets down, and the trigger shrinks. You respond instead of reacting, which is a valuable shift.

Here's the golden rule: When your ego acts up, pause and be curious. Ask yourself Byron Katie's four questions, then sit back and laugh at the ridiculousness. It's funny that your body pranks you constantly. It's okay to laugh at yourself. Humor solves more made-up problems than we give it credit for. And hey, if you're easily offended, learn to laugh at yourself regularly. Life doesn't have to be so serious all the time.

| HUMOR AS A TOOL FOR EGO MANAGEMENT |

Not too long ago, I attended a longevity event surrounded by top-tier doctors, billionaires, and big-shot investors. I stretched out in the chair during one of the speaker presentations, and just like that, I was flat on my back, legs in the air, unable to move, and laughing uncontrollably in front of seventy-five people.

It would have been really easy to get embarrassed or feel a wave of judgment, but instead, what came up was how absurd this must look. Seriously, who falls backward in their chair in a room full of VIPs? But there I was, laughing while everyone asked if I was okay. And the laughter just kept pouring out. What could have been an ego-driven moment turned into a reason to laugh because, let's face it, it was really funny.

Speaking of absurdity, another trick to kick your ego to the curb is to point it out. Imagine everyone's having a good laugh over something that happened, and suddenly, Mr. Ego decides to crash the party. You can feel the tension rise as he starts to take things personally. Instead of getting all worked up, take a step back and tease yourself a little. "Oh my God, this reaction I'm having is ridiculous," you might say with a smile. And just like that, anger leaves the body, and the ego loses its power.

While traveling for work awhile back, I posted a video on social media reminding everyone about the benefits of getting outside for their circadian rhythm. In the background? My girlfriend, soaking up the sunset in her bikini. It was hilarious, and it was completely her idea. There was nothing shady or shaming about it, just some good, lighthearted fun to boost everyone's sleep, mood, and overall health.

Of course, like clockwork, someone had to rain on the parade with a snarky comment: "Absolutely disgusting! I can't believe you would post that." Talk about a buzzkill. But instead of letting the ego go into defense mode, I let my sense of humor respond: "I can't believe you practice body shaming. I think she's beautiful."

Now, clearly, this person thought it was disgusting that my girlfriend was in a video in her bikini. But I don't think she's disgusting. I quite like her. So, instead of getting defensive, I turned the snarky comment on its head, showing a different perspective. And it worked. The person replied, "Okay, that was a good response." Hopefully they laughed about it because it was an innocent video meant to be funny, not misogynistic.

I'm not saying to constantly poke fun at people's egos. In some cases, it can be dangerous to poke the bear. They could punch you, or worse, right? But if you can make fun of yourself during an ego attack, your ego has no choice but to chill out. When you can laugh at your mistakes or the absurdity of a situation instead of shutting down, you free yourself from the seriousness we tend to place on being human. It's liberating.

I've stood onstage in front of thousands of people and made mistakes more times than I can count. How many people know about those mistakes? No one. Instead of crickets chirping out of vicarious embarrassment, the crowd is usually howling with laughter, like it happened exactly as it was supposed to.

People always ask if I get nervous speaking to crowds. But my heart rate doesn't change when I go onstage. Peace is the default setting. It wasn't always this way, though. Before I did all this work, panic used to take over. Heart racing, sweat dripping—total meltdown mode. But you know what saved the day? Training the ego and nervous system toward peace using gratitude.

By focusing on being grateful for the opportunity to share something meaningful with the audience, that panic turned to peace. So, even if there are thousands of people and I do something stupid now (which happens often), self-deprecating humor swoops in to save the day. And not in a "cover up the ego; I'm so embarrassed" kind of way, but with a genuine appreciation for the absurdity of life and these little moments we all experience.

Embracing your imperfections is the ultimate ego-buster. And it diffuses stress for yourself and everyone around you, translating to more relatability, authenticity, and integrity. Nobody is perfect, so why sweat the small stuff or the things you can't control? Trust me, people dig that.

There's something called the pratfall effect[1] in social psychology. Turns out, making mistakes in front of others makes you more likable, not less. It's science. So be a nerd, mess up, and fall on your face. And laugh—a lot.

Laughing at yourself is one of the easiest ways to tame your ego. If you make fun of your ego, it might puff up for a minute or two. But when you laugh at the absurdity of it all—like when it thinks you'll die if you don't scarf down tacos ASAP or when it tells you to freak out about the person who cut you off in traffic—life feels lighter.

In my twenties, I was driving down the highway, minding my business, and accidentally cut someone off in traffic. Whether it was an honest mistake is irrelevant; the guy in the other car was furious. Instead of escalating things and playing into his overreaction, humor jumped into action. I started making highly exaggerated gestures and acting like a monkey. This guy's fuming, flipping me the double bird, and I couldn't help but monkey around. The distraction worked like a charm. After a few seconds of that impromptu monkey act, the guy couldn't keep a straight face. He put his hands down, busted out laughing, and shook his head like, "All right, you win." He could have tried to run me off the road, but it was so stupid that it was funny and defused the situation.

Life is one big laughable adventure, no matter who you are or your status. We'll all mess up, and our egos will try to be the hero (even if they come off as total jerks). You've got a choice: you can fall into the trap and let the ego take charge, or you can ask it to sit down and laugh at yourself. No matter how badly you screw up, it's never the end of the world. You might stumble, but that doesn't make you a bad person. So own your mistakes, apologize when necessary, and move on. Life is too short to dwell on the past.

Next time something happens that would usually piss you off, use humor for a change and see what happens. Don't let your ego steal your energy any longer. It's about flipping the script on the expectations you have of your ego and realizing that it's just doing its job. Once you've nailed down how to put your ego on mute and operate from a place of peace (most of the time anyway, you're still human), things just don't affect you like they used to. It's a magical feeling.

| YOU ARE NOT YOUR EGO |

There's a book by Ryan Holiday called *Ego Is the Enemy*. It's a well-written book, no doubt about it. However, I would argue that ego is not the enemy—it's more like an unreliable friend you can't count on. That's why you've got to pay attention and stay curious.

Think of your ego like a piece of software running in the background—it's there, but it's not the whole package. The good news is, with a bit of practiced awareness, you can train your ego to behave itself and not act out. Eventually, the easier it is to notice when it does act out, and the less power it will have to control you. That means you have more energy to be happy and express yourself. Plus, you have extra energy left to keep yourself looking and feeling young instead of wasting it all on ego-driven antics.

Okay, so your ego is not your enemy. But it's also not your friend. It's simply a hyperactive, not-too-bright consciousness that is desperately trying to keep you alive (you will hear this repeated because it's that important). It's got your back when it comes to avoiding scary stuff (fear), chowing down (food), and keeping the human race going strong (fertility). And, of course, finding a tribe (friends) and attaining peace (forgiveness)—as long as you're not already wasting all your energy on fear and food. But in the long run, it's willing to sacrifice your happiness, your longevity, and your soul. Not exactly in your best interest now, is it?

So much of the stress, struggle, and sense of failure and limitation that people are experiencing today comes from the fact that they believe they are their bodies and, by extension, their egos. It's important to remember, though: you are not your ego. So why on earth would you listen to everything it says? Why let it drag you down with self-doubt and intrusive thoughts?

Well, here's a more accurate perspective. Those intrusive thoughts that keep popping into your head? They're not some random glitch in your mental matrix. Those sneaky thoughts are courtesy of your ego, working hard to distract you from everything.

When people sit down at 40 Years of Zen, we attach electrodes to their heads to monitor their brain waves. It's like a sneak peek into the inner workings of the ego. The moment they sit down and attempt to focus or quiet their mind—BAM! The ego kicks into high gear. Suddenly they feel itchy, too hot, too cold, thirsty, nauseous—the list of distractions continues. And some people would rather throw up than face the truth that their ego exists and it's running the show. The ego is capable of just about anything you can imagine. Even things you haven't thought of.

During a particular session at 40 Years of Zen, there was a high-powered executive, sharp as a tack but struggling with some serious ego moments. She was grappling with these intense, irrational feelings toward a family member, and it was like her ego had a stranglehold on her emotions. She was about to discover something true, and her body didn't want her to know it.

So, the facilitator steps in and starts asking her the same question over and over: "Where is the feeling coming from?" But instead of getting to the heart of the matter, she keeps circling back to her past experiences, dodging the real issue like a pro. It was clear to everyone in the room that the woman couldn't hear his question because her responses were about her experiences, not her feelings.

The facilitator asked everyone to jot down the question and the answer on a Post-it note. So we all wrote down, *Where is the feeling coming from?* And the answer was *the ego.*

Cue the meltdown. Usually poised and polished, this executive woman lets loose a string of expletives, throws the papers to the ground, and storms out in tears. Five minutes later, she's back, apologizing profusely for her outburst. And when the facilitator gently asks her what set her off, she nails it: "My ego."

It's a humbling moment, for sure. But who hasn't been there? Sometimes it takes a little tantrum to put things into perspective and realize who's calling the shots. Then we can get curious, change gears, and refocus our energy toward more important things.

As an executive myself, sitting across from a board member years ago, he drops a truth bomb that hit like a ton of bricks. "Dave," he says, "you're about to break your company. You have two hundred products, and it's way too many for the size of your team. People are stretched too thin, and you're focusing on products that aren't moving the needle. You need to pump the brakes—now."

You'd think I'd be grateful for the heads-up, right? But instead, frustration bubbles up, and I fire back, "Why didn't you tell me this sooner?" That's when reality hits. "We've been screaming this at you for the last six months!" he shoots back, with a look that says, "Are you even listening?"

It was a wake-up call, for sure. It was obvious that my ego had been in charge all along. I couldn't hear the feedback until it was almost too late. The pesky ego wouldn't let me hear it because I believed that it was necessary for the company's survival to keep making products, even when the evidence pointed elsewhere.

When you understand the nature of the ego, you hold the power to change the narrative. Untrained, the ego will make you think you saw or heard something that didn't happen as you thought it did. This is why being curious is so valuable. Curiosity turns off fear, and fear is what triggers your ego.

For example, let's say you see a snake in your path. Your knee-jerk reaction might be to bolt and scream bloody murder—classic ego move. But what if you got curious instead? *The snake is far enough away, so I'm not in danger. I wonder what kind of snake it is?* Then you might think, *It looks like it rattles, and it's coiled. It's a good thing I'm not too close to it. I guess I'll take another route.* You might feel fear at first glance, but by facing a fearful reality with curiosity, you rewire your brain and nervous system to be peaceful, even when the stakes are high. So, the next time you feel panic rising, remember: it's just your ego throwing a tantrum. You've got this.

| YOU'RE NOT LITERALLY GOING TO DIE |

The ego is a tangible part of your body's survival tool kit, made possible by billions of mitochondria running the same F-words repeatedly. And while it's fast, it's as smart as a bag of rocks. It doesn't understand time, context, relationships, abundance, or basic hunger cues. Imagine having a drama queen living rent-free in your brain. Well, you do. It's called your ego.

In my corporate days, my ego had me in a headlock of hunger. It was nearing lunchtime, and while leading a meeting with a stomach growling like a bear, all my brain could think about was food. Without thinking, going purely on emotion, I said: "You know what, guys, we're going to end the meeting early. It's almost lunchtime, and I'm so hungry that I will probably eat one of you if we don't end the meeting now. So, if you want to talk, let's take this conversation to the cafeteria." And I made a beeline for the door.

Continuing the meeting felt impossible because of my ego's voracious hunger and visceral response. In reality, death was not imminent by waiting fifteen more minutes to eat. It takes at least sixty days to die of starvation. That's the reality.

Ever notice how often your mind wanders to thoughts of food? Turns out, roughly 30 percent of your daily mental chatter is about chowing down. You're spending a third of your time thinking about tacos because of your ego. You can train your ego to stop telling you you'll die when you're hungry, just like you train a dog not to bark when someone comes to the door.

You can train your ego to say, "I'll be okay if I don't eat within the next few hours," without fear or stress. You can teach it to stop telling yourself that speaking onstage to a large group of people is terrifying and people will judge you for eternity. It's about rewiring those background processes and getting curious about why your brain is pulling these stunts in the first place. And a good laugh never hurts, either.

The thing is, though, it's scary. Your ego's going to fight you every step of the way. It's probably already tried to erase parts of this chapter from your memory just to stay in control. Because its biggest fear is that this other person (you), who lives inside the same MeatOS as it does, might gain control. So, if you catch your-self forgetting or resisting what's in front of you, know that this is the ego doing what it does best: messing with you. This is your sign to pause and regain control.

Even at 40 Years of Zen, where clients have incredible break-throughs, the ego tries to take over in real time and make them forget things. I witnessed this with a client who had an enormous breakthrough during the Reset Process (this is our potent experien-tial process we take clients through—more on that in Part II). She had this lightbulb moment about her parenting patterns, and sud-denly her whole life made sense. As we continued discussing other things, barely five minutes later, she completely forgot her massive breakthrough. And it was a big deal!

This forgetfulness is a perfect example of the ego playing tricks on an unassuming, well-meaning person. Your ego will always try to make you forget your wins because it's too busy scanning for threats. Become aware of these interruptions to your reality, and don't let your ego win.

We do some things at 40 Years of Zen to help ground these "aha moments" into the brain and body because, honestly, while it's powerful work, it can be a lot to manage. We record our facil-itations and take notes with AI. This way, people have a summary of everything discussed so they can't forget it. After five days of intense work, we ask our clients to record a video for themselves that we email to them six weeks later, reminding them of the work they just did. Because when you do ego work, it's easy for those big breakthroughs to fade. But at 40 Years of Zen, we think they should be remembered and celebrated.

It's possible to fully resolve the ego in one area so it's no longer triggerable in that space. But what tends to happen is that you tell yourself a story like, "Oh, I was never triggered by (fill in the blank). I've always been cool as a cucumber." Until you ask your spouse or a friend, and they tell you the truth: "You're way calmer now than before. I can see a positive shift." But in your mind, your upgraded reality is how it's always been. Again, that's the ego editing your memories so you're unaware of its constant presence and the fact that you used to freak out over silly things. Don't worry. We've all done this at some point.

Your ego makes you forget things and gets you to avoid things to protect you from perceived threats. Let's pretend you've got an upcoming doctor's appointment to review recent lab results. You feel anxious and don't want to go because you have a sinking feeling in your gut that something's wrong. Then, as you're getting ready to leave the house, your car keys are nowhere to be found. In a panic, you tear the house apart, but those elusive keys play hide-and-seek. You end up missing your appointment. *I guess the news will have to wait*, you think. And just as you call the doctor's office to reschedule, you spot your keys hanging innocently by the door right where you left them. Your heart skips a beat as you realize your ego had you convinced you'd already checked there, all because it was terrified to face reality at the doctor's office.

SIT, STAY, GOOD DOG

Your ego leads all self-sabotage, hiding behind your emotions and pulling strings like a puppeteer. It's the mastermind behind all those cravings, repulsions, and greedy impulses—basically, *every negative emotion*. And it feels irresistible.

This is your brain's way of desperately trying to make sense of reality. The problem? Your ego is manipulating reality, sabotaging your efforts toward the thing it's avoiding.

Some argue that the ego is in the brain, but it's not. It's like the CEO of your MeatOS, bending your reality to its will to keep you alive and kicking. Once you see through all the smoke and mirrors, you can have compassion for yourself for mistakenly believing that you are your ego: a separate intelligence with its own set of goals. These parts of you have been playing a game of tug-of-war, and because you assumed you were the same, you didn't think you could train it.

That's where this book comes in. It teaches you the tools, techniques, and technologies that allow you to reduce the influence of your ego. You will become aware of when it's manipulating you so you can get it to behave like a good little dog instead of you being yanked around like a puppy on a leash. It's time to show the ego who's boss.

Teenagers are the poster children for ego in action. They'll argue their point to the ends of the earth, even when they don't know what they're talking about. Somewhere along the line, we adopt the belief that being right equals being lovable. And from an ego's standpoint, this belief makes sense. Being right means being respected, which means more access to food, shelter, and sex—basically, better chances of survival. And according to your ego, that's the most important thing in the world. So, when you see someone hell-bent on being right, just know that it's the ego doing its thing. Then, laugh about it.

The ego's irrational fear of death is also enough to justify lying. When you come across someone who is a chronic liar, that's them listening to their ego and avoiding the truth to remain safe. It's so important to them that they're right that they'll spin a wave of lies just to keep their story intact. It's the belief that their story is the correct one, and they won't let anyone say otherwise.

This justification and unwillingness to be wrong are breeding grounds for narcissistic behavior. It's just the ego saying, "If my story isn't right, then who am I?" It's a threat to their very existence—or at least that's how the ego sees it. Narcissism is like a wrecking ball swinging through relationships and people's lives to destroy anyone who sees through the facade and challenges their behavior. It's the ego's last stand to protect its fragile sense of self.

This discussion about your ego can be unsettling, especially if you haven't dabbled in ego work. Realizing that you've been living a version of reality that is not exactly as it seemed can be a hard pill to swallow. But that's the truth of it. You're living in a house of mirrors—filled with distortions and illusions crafted by fear and the ego's desperate need to survive. That is, until you choose to break free.

Once you wrap your head around this reality check, you'll realize that you are, in fact, in charge, not your ego. Sure, it will try to tell you a different story, but deep down, you know the truth. That's your ticket to freedom. The possibilities are endless; once you understand this, you can train your ego to work for you instead of being its slave.

Your ego is a self-centered creature and will always prioritize itself above everything else. That's why it's crucial to train it to be less reactive and train yourself to know when your ego is messing with you. It takes practice, so don't beat yourself up if you haven't mastered it yet. You didn't learn to ride a bike on your first try. Stick with it.

Let's pretend you're feeling utterly enraged because you're already running late for a date when the lady at the flower shop hands you yellow flowers instead of the red ones you ordered. You're about to lose your mind, but under the anger, a tiny voice—maybe just a whisper—finds the situation amusing. It's like, *Really, this is what's setting you off?*

Embrace humor and curiosity. Give yourself permission to laugh at yourself for having such a mismatched reaction to this innocent mistake. It's okay to find humor in your over-the-top response. Take a deep breath and acknowledge that the urge to unleash your fury like a toddler denied their favorite toy is not you. It's your ego having another tantrum.

The woman who made an honest mistake is not Satan. She's just a florist who screwed up your order. You don't have to be happy about it, and you don't have to settle for the wrong flowers. You can calmly assert your boundaries and decline to pay for the mistake. Then you can carry on with your day without letting the incident ruin your mood or occupy your thoughts for hours, which is what most of us do because we're humans with untrained egos.

| TAMING THE BEAST |

The idea of "letting go" of your ego might sound enticing, but it's impossible unless you let go of your body, and that's called dying. Your ego is an omnipresent competitor, constantly vying for your attention. It's an integral part of your body, whether you like it or not, making it impossible to eliminate. Instead, the goal is to *own* your ego and understand that it's working precisely as designed— until you train it otherwise. To own your ego, you have to understand how it manifests. Ego manifestations are diverse but easy to spot when you know what to look for.

Perfectionism is a classic example of the ego gaining control. It makes you feel anxious, unsafe, or uncomfortable when things don't unfold flawlessly. However, the ego doesn't understand that perfectionism is an unattainable standard.

Going out to dinner with a group when you're a well-known nutrition expert is often an interesting experience. "Dave, what are you going to eat? What's the perfect meal?" When the waiter comes, ordering food unfolds like a comedy sketch: "I'd like a steak; is it grass-fed?" "Yes, it is." "How about grass-finished? Locally sourced?" "Oh yes, it's from a farm right down the road." "Was it raised by monks?" This is usually where they've caught on to the act, and we begin to play the audience together. "Oh yes, absolutely."

"Great, were they left-handed monks?" "Oh yes, it was also blessed with holy water and angels." This banter continues until the orders are in. It's fun and *funny* when we do this with a waiter. But it isn't funny when your ego always does this to you.

These are the "you're not enough" type of conversations you have with yourself in your head. But you will never be enough if you listen to your ego. In reality, you're way more than enough, and asking to *be* enough is a giant waste of time. The ego limits your belief in what's possible in the world around you and for yourself.

Your ego fears being wrong, bad, or "less than" because it means ostracism, which inevitably equals death. It's a subconscious program running in the background, manifesting as toxic perfectionism or deflecting blame onto others to preserve your sense of worthiness. The ego believes you're less worthy if you do something wrong. You're less lovable. But when you know the ego's role in your behavior, you can break free from its grip and take ownership of your actions, even if it means admitting fault and offering apologies when necessary.

Consciously, apologizing when you're wrong seems like a good strategy, but your ego and your unconscious say, "No, no, that's not it. Don't apologize; they don't deserve it." Your aversion to apologizing is just another programmed response. Think about a three-year-old— they can apologize, and it's not painful. But as adults, we've wired our systems to be hypervigilant and self-protective to avoid perceived threats so we don't die or end up alone. This is your ego at work, doing its best to manipulate you and serve its own agenda.

Consider when you see an aggressively toxic political ad, and your initial reaction is anger toward "woke" people, conservative factions, or whatever narrative you've adopted. That's proof that the ad's creators have played your ego, and they played you masterfully. But if you're aware of your ego, you can shift your internal dialogue to something more constructive. You might think, *Hmm, that's interesting. I believe one of these sides is making mistakes and potentially harming society. Regardless of my stance, I don't have to be mad about it. I can choose to take action or decide it's not where I want to direct my attention.* You become unaffected by the political ad because you're no longer programmable.

The number one question for detecting the ego is: Am I feeling negativity toward something? If the answer is yes, that's your ego, period. Once you have a clear answer, you can shift to the most effective tool for halting the ego: gratitude. If negativity comes up, find something to be grateful for instead.

For instance, let's say someone rear-ends your car, resulting in repairs and neck pain. Dealing with insurance and repairs can be frustrating. But instead of succumbing to the negativity, tune into your body (aches and all) as soon as you can and decide to find something to be grateful for. You didn't die, you have insurance, and you can get a new car—it's just a material object, anyway. This time, you'll get a car in the color you want. See how that works? It's not magic. It's just awareness and reframing your mindset.

This isn't about adopting a simplistic "glass half-full" or "glass half-empty" mentality or being a Pollyanna. It's about consciously choosing to turn on the physiological response of gratitude, which can help your body break out of a negativity loop, even in the face of trauma. When you learn how to do this, you'll recover much faster, even from physical injuries like whiplash.

Instead of acting impulsively and yelling at the person who hit your car, possibly getting in a fight with them, or saying something that will get you in trouble, practice being calm. Acknowledge the situation: "Oh, man, that sucked. I didn't want that to happen." Calmly suggest exchanging insurance information to deal with it. Then, go about your day. This sense of freedom comes from practicing gratitude, making it a core part of daily ego awareness. You can't be fearful or angry and grateful at the same time. So, you might as well choose the best feeling state: gratitude.

START YOUR DAY WITH A GRATITUDE LATTÉ

One of the practices I have been teaching ever since I started the biohacking movement is to write down three things you're grateful for before you go to bed and another three when you wake up in the morning. It's not a new concept, but it's incredibly powerful. I've done it with my kids since they were young, and it's always a cool bonding moment for the family.

My friend Dr. Barry Morguelan, one of nine living grandmasters of Lao Tzu's lineage, teaches a variation of this practice. (If you're unfamiliar, Lao Tzu is essentially the traditional Chinese equivalent of Buddha or Jesus.) Instead of limiting yourself to three things, he encourages you to see how many things you can be grateful for and jot them down each day. Initially, finding three things to be grateful for may seem easy, but aiming for fifty or even one hundred can feel almost impossible. However, over time, it's incredible to see how many positive things happen each day that we simply forget about. This practice brings about a profound recognition of how the ego can hide the good things in our lives and focus on fear instead.

One night, while sitting down at the end of the day and racking my brain for good things to write down, eight or nine things came quickly, so they went on the list. I expressed gratitude for waking up feeling good and enjoying dinner with the kids, among other things. Yet, amid these reflections, I forgot a massive piece of news.

Earlier that morning, my editor called to say that *Super Human* had landed on the *New York Times* list. And not just any list, but the monthly science bestseller list—a remarkable achievement that's hard to attain. Yet, while writing everything I was grateful for at the end of the night, this significant accomplishment had already been removed from the mental list of good things that happened. The sneaky ego had subtly shifted the focus away from positive news and toward the potential negative aspects of the day. This kind of subtle manipulation by the ego is happening all the time, behind the scenes, hoping you don't catch on and do something about it.

This is why practicing gratitude, at least three things daily, is so important. The physiological impact of gratitude resonates throughout the tissues in your body, temporarily quieting the ego or reducing its influence. Gratitude is the easiest way to turn down the ego when you feel an ego attack coming on. The problem is that it's incredibly easy to think you're grateful for something without letting it sink in. The work is to *feel* it. Thinking about it is simply not enough.

Now remember, thoughts are not feelings; *emotions* are feelings. You have the incredible ability to replay any emotion you've ever experienced, like your Spotify playlist. All you have to do is sit down and ask yourself, *What did that emotion feel like? Did the hairs on the back of my neck stand up? What did it feel like on my skin, in my body? Was my heart beating faster? Was I sweaty? Was my stomach clenched? Was there a heart-open, glow-y, warm feeling? What color was it?* Use all your senses and get curious.

To tap into profound gratitude, replay the multisensory feelings associated with deeply meaningful experiences. How you get there isn't as important as the outcome. Think about puppies. Think about the first time you held your newborn child, the first time you fell in love, or when you landed your dream job. All of the feelings associated with those experiences can be revisited and reexperienced with some effort. When I tell you to practice gratitude, it's imperative to write down what you're grateful for and then connect with *how your body feels* in response to those thoughts. When you take this step toward full-body gratitude, your ego will lie down in Savasana, and you can be free.

| DROP THE MASK |

Have you ever been in a conversation where you're already plotting what you'll say next, and suddenly, the other person's words start to sound like Charlie Brown's mom—"Wah wah, wah wah"? If you're nodding along, thinking, *Oh yeah, been there*, guess what? That's your ego in charge. We've all had those moments, right? The brain plays defense, ensuring you don't accidentally say something stupid to maintain your spot in the tribe. This is the ego in full-on self-preservation mode, doing its best to save you from social disaster.

When you genuinely tune in to someone else, your ego shuts up. There's no inner monologue rehearsing your next witty comeback. Instead, you're fully there, soaking in what they're saying. You're curious, and the other person can feel your presence. Their intuition tells them that you are a high-integrity person. They feel understood and valued. In those moments, the noise fades away. You're not wondering what to say next. You're not judging their words or feeling triggered. Instead you're intently listening, like, really listening. We can all agree that being on either side of that connection feels great. Do your part to ensure that happens.

If you notice yourself falling prey to your ego and feeling any sort of way about a conversation, you can laugh at yourself. *Oh, look at me, not listening to the other person. I'm making up a story about what to say next.* Then, return to the present moment and reengage with the person before you.

One of the best places to practice this is with little kids. Watch the way a little kid is present with their favorite toy. It's like nothing else exists in the world. Or if you sit down with a five-year-old, they acknowledge your presence through their eye contact or words. Leave your phone in another room and tell yourself that you will be fully present with them for the next ten, fifteen, or thirty minutes. You will see a considerable shift in their behavior because they feel loved and cared for. They feel safe.

Mastering presence is simply telling your ego to hush while you pay attention and practice curiosity instead of the need to be right. When you do this, you'll find that dating isn't difficult anymore. Making friends feels easier. Finishing tasks takes less effort. Because as your ability to control your ego expands, so does your ability to stay focused.

| MASTER YOUR INNER GAME |

With tools like neurofeedback, breathwork, and meditation, you can hit pause on a lot of your mental programming, at least temporarily. This opens up a whole new world of sensory experience. It feels expansive and galactic, as if you've melted into the universe and are one with everything, without drugs. This is what it feels like to sense the world the way your body does, outside of logic (thought).

Like most people, you probably don't realize that your body constantly runs these background programs. Some are in your brain, but most are in the body itself. And there's solid evidence to back this up.

Take somatic therapy, which is all about tuning in to your body's sensations to heal emotional wounds and release stress. Instead of just talking about your feelings, you feel them in your body and use techniques to release stored trauma. It's like hitting the reset button on your nervous system and biohacking your emotions. Or people who swear by bodywork or deep tissue massage. You've likely heard stories of people getting emotional during hip massage or stretching, especially women. That's because the issues are in the tissues, and it's well-known that we store emotions in our hips.

Bessel van der Kolk is a psychiatrist, neuroscientist, researcher, educator, and author of the brilliant book *The Body Keeps the Score*.[2] In his book, he discusses how our bodies hang on to emotional baggage from trauma, whether remembered or not, and how that baggage shapes how we operate, think, and act.

Your body is like a vault for all those emotions. It *does* keep the score, and that's okay. The key is not to get stuck in those heavy, energetically depleting places. Your ego is part of your body, just like your hardworking heart that pumps your blood and keeps you alive. Or your legs that carry you miles and miles without expecting anything in return. Think of this dance as a team effort, and accept that you're on this journey together. Otherwise your life will feel much more difficult to manage, and challenges will feel impossible to conquer.

Your ego can either be your loyal sidekick or your ruthless dictator. By default, it loves to boss you around and stir up unnecessary drama in traffic or at home. You're likely to give in if you haven't trained your ego—like snacking on a bag of cookies when you're not even hungry, and you know sleep is the better option. Is it enticing and delicious? Sure. But healthy? Not so much.

Your ego is what makes you pick a fight with your partner when you're in a bad mood, act like a jerk to your friends because you're tired, or yell at the checkout person when the store is out of your favorite grass-fed butter.

Your ego will always prioritize fear to keep you in your comfort zone so you don't take action and evolve. This fear factory will make up silly reasons why you shouldn't take risks or try new things— saying yes to a new job, asking your crush out, moving across the country, traveling the world for a year, getting a pet, or starting a business. You name it, and the reason you haven't done it yet may very well be because of this three-letter word you're giving way too much power to—your EGO.

Your ego isn't all bad. Think of it as your personal security system and cheerleader combined. Training your ego helps you recognize opportunities, focus on your goals, and navigate social dynamics. It's about balance: harness the power of your ego to boost your confidence and drive without letting it control you. Use it as a tool to thrive, not just survive.

IF YOU CAN BE
TRIGGERED,
YOU'RE HOLDING A
LOADED GUN

Think of all the incredible things happening around you that you never even notice. It's crazy to realize how much is going on behind the scenes, completely automated, that we're unaware of. Take bugs, for instance. Did you know that some of them can see a whole rainbow of colors that we humans can't even fathom?

But it's not just bugs. Humans are diverse, too. There are people we refer to as "supertasters" who taste things like they're experiencing flavors in HD. And then there are those with synesthesia, where their senses get all mixed up in the most mind-blowing way possible. Imagine hearing colors or smelling the truth—yeah, it's wild, but it's real.

I have a friend who's wired like that. He can sniff out the truth like nobody's business. Literally! He has a uniquely wired brain, letting him smell whether something's legit. At first, this seemed made up. *How can that even be possible*, I thought. But after getting to know him, it's clear that his strange way of interpreting information is 100 percent real. It's odd but also really cool.

So, what's the connection between bugs, supertasters, my truth-sniffing friend, and our primal survival instincts? It all comes down to our brains being these incredible, adaptive machines. Just like my friend's brain can decipher the truth, our uniquely wired brains keep us safe in a world full of mystery.

When we're young, our bodies are like little detectives, always looking for danger. If something seems scary, your body wants to make sure you know it ASAP, and your survival instinct kicks in. It will inevitably make mistakes, and that's okay. The point is not to make the same mistake twice. There's an old saying by Winston Churchill: "You cannot reason with a tiger when your head is in its mouth." You might be able to survive and recover from a single tiger bite, but when you mess up multiple times and the tiger has you locked in its jaw, you're probably not going to make it out alive. Being jumpy and cautious, you'll probably stick around long enough to pass on your genes and keep the species strong. Your ego—that cautious voice inside your head—wants to keep you safe. It will do whatever it has to, even if it means jumping at things that aren't a threat. You know, just in case.

Now, here's where it gets really interesting. As we grow older and our environments change, those survival instincts don't just disappear. They're always lurking in our subconscious, ready to pounce at the slightest hint of danger.

Think about a deer in the wild. Have you ever noticed how a deer will freeze at the slightest noise? They're on high alert and ready to bolt at any moment. If you think about it, we're not that different from deer regarding our safety responses.

You might not spook at every noise in the forest (unless you're alone at night, in which case flight would be a reasonable response). But listen to a sneaky ad telling you you're not good enough unless you buy some fancy endocrine-disrupting body spray, and it will push your buttons. Your brain learns to respond to specific triggers, especially when it comes to feeling inadequate or insecure—essentially, anything that puts you at risk of being alone or dying.

The good news is that we don't have to be slaves to our primal instincts. We can train our brains to distinguish between real threats and mere shadows with awareness and strategic biohacking. It's all about rewiring those neural pathways, priming your mind for high performance, and quieting fear so you can take action on the things that matter.

YOUR TRIGGERS ARE HOLDING YOU HOSTAGE

Have you ever been triggered by a nasty comment or felt alone in a crowded room? Maybe someone throws a jab at your weight and it really hits you hard. You feel yourself shrinking, wishing you could just disappear. As a former fat person, I know this sucks.

But here's the deal. If something can rattle you, it's like you're walking around with a loaded gun, ready to go off at any moment. It's up to you to unload the gun so triggers do not consume you. Because if other people can push your buttons, they're calling the shots, not you. And let's face it, nobody wants that. Asking you to stop being triggered is a big request. Almost everyone gets triggered, right? But with practice, you can train yourself to respond differently and regain your power.

You don't have to stay trigger-happy forever. That's the good news. Once you understand how your ego works and put into practice the tools from this book to keep it in check, you'll find that those triggers start losing their charge. You're no longer so easy to control. Because if other people's words and actions don't affect you, you become the captain of your ship. And it becomes nearly impossible to be triggered, which means you're impossible to control and manipulate.

Do you want to be free? Be untriggerable. Do you want to be happy? Be untriggerable. Do you want peace and joy in your life? Be untriggerable.

Hearing all this might stir something up inside you. That's fine.

It means you're tuned in and paying attention. You can be upset, or you can get curious. Curiosity tends to be a more productive option, but that's really up to you.

Your body is an intricate machine complete with a built-in trigger system that you can control or let control you. Your response is ultimately your responsibility. Your "buttons" make you susceptible to triggers and are often rooted in childhood experiences, including your environment while in your mother's womb.

Maybe you had a strict teacher or a relentless bully who loved to pick on you at recess. Maybe your parents dropped the ball a few too many times, leaving an imprint on your subconscious. They're human, too. It's all part of the journey.

There are also the potential effects of generational trauma—stuff passed down from your ancestors, shaping your thoughts and actions. Your great-great-great-grandmother's fear of being eaten by a lion, which was a real fear back in the day, is now your irrational fear of being devoured by a wild animal even while living in suburbia. And let's not forget about past lives! I used to roll my eyes at that but then decided to be curious about it.

Believe it or not, embracing the possibility of things you can't fully explain simplifies life. Even if you're not 100 percent right, just entertaining the idea can open up a new world of understanding. We all carry our own set of triggers from our past, but they don't have to rule our present-day experiences. The more you learn to disarm them, the more freedom and joy you can invite into your life.

You've probably had times when you're going about your day and suddenly find yourself doing something without knowing why. You're operating on autopilot, just going through the motions because it feels natural. And it is, kind of. It's how we learn to navigate society. But sometimes we learn and internalize things that aren't helpful—like how to be triggered.

Having an angry voice in your head constantly chattering away is not fun. Letting other people get under your skin because you don't know better? Also not fun. These things make you feel like you're pushing through quicksand while trying to get stuff done. They're distractions and make you procrastinate or, worse, say you'll do something, and you don't do it. This misalignment puts a kink in your integrity, and if you do it enough times, people stop trusting you. This kind of damage is hard to correct. You don't trust people whose words don't match their actions, do you? Exactly. That's why being aware of how you show up and who you let control you matters so much. Being in charge of yourself is easier when you focus on what's real. You make better decisions that align with who you know you are—not who you think you should be.

A prime example of this is asking someone on a date. It can be nerve-racking unless you train yourself to be present with reality instead of listening to the made-up stories in your head that tell you all the reasons to run the other way. For many people, there's a big fear of rejection, something we've all experienced at some point. You can hear your ego screaming, *Don't mess this up! You have to reproduce, or else you'll die alone!* It's a complete overreaction but remember that fertility is one of the F-words. Your ego is on a mission based on fear and not reality.

Let's say you're at a coffee shop or Burning Man, and an attractive person catches your eye. You psych yourself up, like, "All right, I'm gonna do it. I'm gonna go over there and talk to them." But then you freeze. It's like someone hit pause on your courage, and your feet are stuck in dried cement.

Maybe you're like Stan from *South Park*—every time he talks to a girl, he ends up tossing his cookies. There are a ton of people who feel exactly like that. It's scary, but you're willing to push through that fear and see what happens.

It takes you a while to approach them, but you finally do it (and don't throw up). And you ask them the big scary question, "Can I take you out sometime?" and they say, "No." Ouch, right? Now you've not only missed out on passing down your genes, but your ego is whispering in your ear, *You're unlovable; nobody wants you.* In ancient tribe terms, being unlovable meant getting the boot. And getting kicked out of the tribe meant game over—hello, starvation, and becoming lunch for a predator.

Although your ego might scream all these negative things, you don't have to listen or believe its lies. Your worth has nothing to do with whether someone wants to make babies with you, regardless of what your ego wants you to think. The tricky part is that you already felt the feeling. Now reality, along with your pride, is hidden behind the lens of lies.

Just because you feel like you'll die from embarrassment doesn't mean you will. Your body treats rejection as a life-or-death situation when it's not. It might sting, but you won't die. (The ego can be so dramatic.) You can press pause on that fear, rewrite the script, and step into your worth, one awkward encounter at a time. Just remember Byron Katie's four questions: *Is it true? Can you absolutely know it's true? How do you react; what happens when you believe that thought? Who would you be without that thought?*

Begin to create an awareness around the stories you tell yourself versus the reality of the situation. Notice all the ways you make stuff up that isn't true—all there to convince yourself not to change. "Don't grow; the unknown is terrifying!" When you see these voices for what they are—well-meaning safety signals—you can release them with love and go about your life instead of allowing them to control your life.

This warped sense of reality is the human condition. But the more you work on your ego, the more humor and laughter you inject into your reality, and the more gratitude you sprinkle in, the less daunting these situations become. Because truth be told, asking someone out, taking a new job, or moving across the country isn't scary—it just feels that way. Thanks to all these factors, your body is excellent at fibbing to you. It uses you against yourself to hide reality so you don't have to grow, change, and ultimately evolve.

Walking up to an attractive person becomes a breeze when you are untriggerable. You can casually initiate a conversation and invite them for coffee without pain or fear. When you do this fearlessly, they're more likely to sense your confidence and feel at ease. And you become a magnet for everything you want to find you.

The mere idea of someone showing interest can trigger some people. Maybe they've experienced sexual or other forms of intimate trauma, and your interest brings everything to the surface. That's okay. You simply take a step back, no fear, no fuss. And you try again with someone else. Your goal is to be so untriggerable that even if someone else gets triggered, you don't get sucked into their drama. As long as you're not being a creepy stalker when you approach them, remember not to personalize the rejection. It likely has nothing to do with you. You won't be for everyone, but that doesn't make you less of a person. It just means there's another opportunity to discover.

By the way, this works in personal and professional situations that feel scary, not just dating. The more confident and untriggerable you are, the more at ease everyone feels. And the better you become at exiting questionable situations without personalizing them, the better off your nervous system will be.

Some people have built their whole identity around being triggered. They think it's everyone else's job to tiptoe around them. If that's you, you're probably feeling triggered right now. That's fine. Go back to the beginning of this chapter, or maybe even dive back into Chapter 3 on ego, and practice the tools and techniques laid out for you. Remember, the ego wants you to be triggered. But also important to note: you are not your ego.

It's not anyone else's responsibility to tiptoe around your triggers and cater to your every whim. You are responsible for managing your triggers so others can have the freedom to be themselves around you. Using your triggers as a tool to bully other people into changing their behavior isn't cool. It's foolish and disruptive to society.

One of the most famous triggers is "your mom." Yep, those seventh-grade jokes we all know and love. When trolls come at me with their nonsense on social media, a mom joke is often the default response. And if I've ever used a mom joke on anyone reading this book, sorry, not sorry. Because I don't mean to offend you, except I kind of do to help you. It's not out of a desire for harm or revenge but to highlight your blind spots and support your growth. And because it's funny, and humor is okay, even if it's at your expense.

If you get triggered, expect a little teasing. That's just how it goes. And if reading this triggers you, well, good luck out there. Because these kinds of things will happen repeatedly in the real world, and you don't want someone (or something) else to be in charge of your life.

TRAUMA TRIGGERS AND EMOTIONAL FLASHBACKS

Trauma is anything that leaves a lasting imprint on your nervous system. So, when something triggers the same sensations you felt during your original trauma, your body jumps into action before your brain even catches up. Remember, your feelings take the wheel before your thoughts even get a chance to buckle up (thanks to that sneaky third-of-a-second delay). You'll feel the emotion first, and then your brain will scramble to find a reason, even if it's a lie.

A lot of people hear the word *trauma* and automatically think of abuse. And yeah, that's a major form of it, no doubt. But there are many faces of trauma you can acknowledge and rewire. Trauma might look like losing money, being kicked out of your country, sexual assault, divorce, near-death experiences, car wrecks, or even the heart-wrenching premature loss of a loved one to disease or an accident. The list goes on and on. And the healing journey looks different for everyone.

Childhood traumas are like buried treasure chests, hidden so deeply that you don't even realize your reactions are coming from fourth grade when little Billy broke your nine-year-old heart. Or when Carly, your first love, shattered your trust. Or when your science teacher teased you in front of the whole class.

One of the fastest ways I've found to shift these forgotten or buried traumas is EMDR (eye movement desensitization and reprocessing) therapy, two to three times a week. Or, if you're feeling adventurous, sign up for 40 Years of Zen and experience five days of intense brain training using neurofeedback, deep ego work, and forgiveness to rewire those old scripts.

Many of the most successful people out there are driven by some sort of childhood trauma, using it as rocket fuel to prove themselves. That was undoubtedly me in the beginning. When you've learned that failure equals death, you will do anything, spin any story, even if it's a tall tale, just to keep that fear quiet.

One person who underwent the 40 Years of Zen program runs a 1,200-person company. He had a significant lightbulb moment during the program when he realized that his entire success story stemmed from experiencing painful bullying back in seventh grade. "I am still trying to prove that I'm good enough," he admitted. As someone who faced bullying as a kid, this hit home.

Those early childhood experiences shaped so much of my life until age thirty. The first $6 million I made at age twenty-six was mainly about proving I was worthy and "enough." Then, poof, it vanished into thin air two years later. Had I listened to the ego, that could have been all the "proof" needed to confirm the long-standing fears of unworthiness and not-enoughness. Thankfully, I had the tools to move through the pain of the experience and keep climbing toward future success—a redemption of sorts.

This negative chatter from the ego isn't supportive or healthy. It's a trauma loop that puts you in a perpetual state of fear because you never truly feel safe. Fear can be an incredible spark capable of igniting real change in your life. It's a little nudge that says, "Hey, something's not right here. Time to shake things up." Unless you change, your life will remain a constant striving for approval and validation, and that takes a ton of energy to manage. If you let fear take the wheel, it'll burn you alive. Lighter fluid is handy to get things moving, but relying on fear alone is a recipe for disaster.

Instead, use fear to light the fire of *transformation*. Feel it coursing through your veins, and instead of succumbing to it as a way to remain stuck and the same, do something productive with it. Use it to transform yourself, make a positive change in the world, and let that fear go. If you need to forgive someone or something to make that all possible, do that, too.

Real change doesn't come from shaming others or shouting opinions from the rooftops. It's not about bullying people into submission. Take Greta Thunberg, for instance. She's all about climate change. But her approach points fingers and shames people, which breeds resistance, not progress.

Commit to focusing on transformation through understanding and empathy. Listen, learn, and find others who want to work together to create lasting change. When fear becomes a tool for growth, magic happens. That's how we make a difference—not through ego-driven complaints but genuine compassion and aligned action.

| THE NARCISSISM PYRAMID |

If you've ever felt trapped by your triggers, like you can't escape the knee-jerk reaction you have in certain situations, listen up. You might feel like you can't control your response. Maybe you even say, "It's just who I am." But rest assured, playing the victim and identifying *as your* triggers or your ego is a dangerous place to be. It can be really easy to fall into that trap, especially if your ego is running the show.

This kind of behavior isn't just your run-of-the-mill ego trip. This strong tie to your triggers is when you get into narcissism territory. Before you get all huffy-puffy and throw this book out the window, know that being a narcissist and acting out narcissistic behavior are not the same thing. This explanation is not about labels but about understanding your patterns or the patterns of the people in your environment so you can change course as needed. It's about being better than your ego so you can squash your triggers instead of being consumed by them.

Narcissists aren't your textbook villains. They truly believe with every ounce of their being that they're right. These people are convinced that their version of reality is the only one that matters. They'll bulldoze anyone who disagrees, without batting an eye. Narcissists have crafted their version of reality where they can do no wrong. No matter what they do, they believe they're great. That's the most classic example.

The worst part? They don't even realize they're doing it. In their minds, they're just asserting the truth. But you don't have to buy into it. Your job is to remain present in reality without getting swept up in their fantasy world because the havoc they wreak while immersed in their own little world is no joke.

We've all crossed paths with them—maybe in the office, maybe in relationships—and man, do they mess with your head. If you've ever been in a relationship with one, you probably carry some triggers yourself. Or maybe, if you're brave enough to admit it, you've been the one doling out narcissistic behavior, and it's cost you considerably. Doing the ego work to keep those triggers in check is key. Otherwise you risk letting them consume you and override your reality. And suddenly you identify as your trigger or ego instead of a loving human with autonomy and the power to change.

My friend Dr. Scott Barry Kaufman is among the top 1 percent of the world's most-cited scientists for his groundbreaking research on intelligence, creativity, and human potential. Scott's work is like peeling back the layers of an onion—it's deep, a little spicy, and fascinating.

In an interview on *The Human Upgrade* podcast, Scott talks about different levels of narcissism, and it's a real eye-opener. First up, you've got your **grandiose narcissist**. These people walk around like they own the place, thinking, *I'm so great. I deserve the world on a silver platter.* And if anyone challenges their greatness, watch out. They'll unleash a storm of lies and emotional warfare without realizing they're doing it. They're so far removed from reality that they can only see the stories they've created based on their inflated beliefs about themselves.

Then there's the **victim narcissist**. These are the ones who've been through some serious stuff—chronic medical conditions, torture or abuse, near-death experiences—you name it. Instead of rising above their struggles, they get stuck in the cycle of entitlement for enduring all they have. But that kind of mindset only plants a big trigger in your brain. It keeps you stuck in an unhealthy pattern of expecting the world to hand you what you think you deserve simply because you believe you deserve it.

Scott also discusses the newest kid on the block: **group (or communal) narcissism**. These people think they're all that just because they're part of a particular group. They believe they are special or better than others because of their status. But guess what? All of these flavors of narcissism stem from lies. They all scream, "I deserve XYZ, not because of anything I've done, but because of who I am or what I've been through." It's somewhat funny if you think about it.

True deservingness is not about your ego or past; it's about what you do and your contribution to the world. Being deserving is earned. Entitlement is an expectation. It's probably more accurate to say that narcissists feel entitled to get what they want when they want it. Deserving has nothing to do with how they operate, although that's the language their brain uses.

Something to highlight is that we all have narcissistic tendencies. But you're in charge of keeping them in check. Once you learn to spot reality (what's actually happening versus the story you're making up), identify your triggers (where is this reaction coming from?), and turn your ego way down (the narcissistic tendencies love the ego), you'll have better access to peace.

Achieving this calm state is possible for everyone. You cultivate it through practice, conscious awareness, and being okay with laughing at yourself when you notice you're not present and you're playing story time in your head again.

| FOUR KINDS OF PEOPLE |

If you've ever wished you had a cheat code for understanding people, you're in luck. Another friend, Dr. Barry Morguelan, has laid out four distinct types of individuals you have most definitely encountered in this crazy world. He learned this "typing" in a monastery and shares this information openly with business leaders. I've found it to be an accurate representation. Get ready, because human interactions are about to make a whole lot more sense.

It's easy to slap a quick "jerk" label on someone who rubs you the wrong way. Sometimes it's warranted. But it's not always that simple. Knowing which category someone fits into is like having X-ray vision of the soul. It makes uncomfortable interplay more tolerable, and you stop taking things personally because now you can see the bigger picture.

These categories aren't just some theoretical, hierarchal system. It's become a cornerstone of my vetting process, personally and professionally, because it's that impactful. Putting this knowledge into practice shifts your energy expenditure. Instead of feeling depleted when dealing with someone who falls into an "energy sucker" category, you begin to notice *more* energy because you learn to move on faster. You are in control of your environment in a brand-new way, and it's freeing.

Category 1 People: Win-Win

These people are in a league of their own, making up a small percentage of society (around 5 percent). They're like Jedi masters of win-win situations.

Whenever they're in the mix, everybody comes out on top. They're all about ensuring that you win when they win, too. They're not playing a zero-sum game where someone has to lose for them to be victorious. They are genuinely in it for the greater good.

These people have put in the work—whether through meditation, personal development, or just marching to the beat of their own drum. These are the people you meet, and you know they're the real deal. They're the ones who always lend a hand and don't seem to have a deceitfully selfish bone in their body. They make the world a better place just by being in it. Hopefully, you have at least one of these rare people in your life. Or maybe you're one yourself. And if so, can we be friends?

Category 2 People: Win-Win

These people are the backbone of society, around 60 percent, making up the majority of the population. They aim for win-win scenarios, but hey, they're human, too. They slip up sometimes.

The beauty of category 2s is that when they slip up, and you call them out, they have no problem owning their mistake. They don't try to make excuses or deny it. Instead they're in the "let's fix it together" camp. Their ego might rear its head occasionally, leading them to do something out of character. But when they realize it, they're quick to make it right. They're willing to learn and grow from their mistakes—you want these people in your corner.

Within category 2, there's some variation. You've got your higher-level 2s, who tend to get it right more often, and your lower-level 2s, who might mess up more but are always happy to course-correct to make things right. They're on a never-ending journey of evolution, always learning and improving.

Category 3 People: Win-Lose

This is where things get a bit dangerous. Category 3s are people you're better off steering clear of. They play a win-lose game and don't even realize they're doing it. They'll lie, cheat, and steal if it serves their agenda. And they'll believe their lies. These are the narcissists of the world.

An extreme example of this would be walking into a room and seeing them covered in blood, surrounded by dead bodies. You confront them, and they look you in the eye and say, "It wasn't me. I'm a good person." And they'll believe it while holding a knife, with blood on their hands, and footage proving they're guilty. They'll deflect blame and paint you as a "bad guy" for suggesting they could do such things. They will make you question your sanity, gaslighting you into doubting what you know to be true. They're masters of manipulation and will stop at nothing to protect their fragile egos.

I've had my own run-ins with these characters. I once had an employee who was so deep in grandiose narcissism that she couldn't even fathom the idea of failure. She cost my company millions while insisting she did nothing wrong. When the truth finally came out, she dared to demand more stock options simply because she believed she deserved them. When I refused, she disappeared without a trace.

Sadly, we're increasingly seeing category 3s, thanks to social media, parenting styles, politics, and who knows what else. They make up around 30 percent of the population. That's a big chunk of humanity walking around with their own twisted version of reality.

Category 4 People: Win-Lose

These people are playing a different ball game, and they know it. They're not like the category 3 people who stumble into win-lose situations. They're the ones orchestrating them with a sick sense of satisfaction. These are the sociopaths and psychopaths.

They have no problem looking you straight in the eye and telling you exactly what you want to hear while plotting their next move. They enjoy manipulating your emotions, and the scariest part? They don't feel an ounce of empathy for your pain and anguish. If you call them out, they'll gaslight you into oblivion and make you question your reality. They're masters at their craft and can weave a web of lies so intricate you start to doubt what you know in your heart is the truth.

Category 4s are dangerous. They'll do whatever it takes to get what they want and leave a trail of destruction in their wake without a second thought. They round out the rest of the population at around 5 percent.

Here's a quick test: If you find yourself immediately drawn to someone more than usual, it's a red flag. And if you feel like you can't live without this person, it's another warning sign. Of course, there are always exceptions. But in my experience, this rings true nearly

100 percent of the time. This information comes from Robert Cialdini, a professor at Arizona State University, who wrote a famous book called *Influence*. In normal, healthy relationships, getting to know someone and really liking them takes time. So just be aware.

These people prey on your vulnerabilities, so spotting these patterns and tuning in to yourself first is important. You know whether someone is good for you, so be vigilant and choose peace. Trust yourself. You don't have to explain your decision. The fact that it doesn't feel right is enough.

With awareness comes power. Understanding these categories and doing the inner work to master your ego will help you spot the manipulators and protect yourself from their toxic influence. It's not always easy or comfortable, but it's worth it. I've faced these challenges head-on, and it's come at a cost. Now spotting reality so I'm not easily triggered is second nature. And when meeting new people, putting them in categories is easy. I don't do this from a judgmental place but from one of protecting the peace. It's been beneficial in many ways, personally and professionally, not to mention the sanity upgrade that comes from trusting your intuition and putting the ego aside.

This is where it gets interesting. Studies in game theory show that when you have a bunch of people practicing win-win (category 1s and 2s), you create something close to utopia. But throw in just one win-lose player, and it's like tossing a wrench into the gears—they wreak havoc and grab power in the process.

Now for a taste of humble pie: If you're acting from your ego, you might unknowingly be taking from others (yes, even you, a well-meaning, thoughtful person). But if you use the teachings in this book and learn to spot these categories and curate your circle wisely, you'll be a much happier contributor to society.

You're bound to encounter category 3 and 4 people. These are the ones playing the win-lose game who believe they deserve it all.

It's a recipe for chaos; even the most enlightened aren't immune. That's why knowing what you're up against is so essential. When you spot them, you can say, "No, thank you," and move right along. No harm done.

Don't worry. There's a high likelihood that you're a category 1 or 2. (Category 3s and 4s aren't willing to see and admit they're one anyway.) As a 1 or 2, you are more susceptible to falling prey to the lies and manipulation of category 3s and 4s. When you meet new people, consider this an opportunity to practice discernment. If your intuition is telling you one thing but your ego is trying to tell you something else, and you can't seem to reconcile the difference, look at reality instead. Then tune back in to your intuition, where truth lives, and choose from that place.

I've had to clean up the mess from narcissists in my company not once, not twice, but four freaking times—costing me $100 million. But hey, at least you get to learn from those mistakes so you can dodge the same expensive bullets. Trust me, every big-shot exec I've swapped war stories with has a similar tale to tell. It's tough when you're flying blind, but now that you know better, it's time to become aware and ditch the category 3s and 4s that are sucking your energy. Your circle is your responsibility.

If you ever find yourself knee-deep in a mess like the ones I've waded through, grab yourself a book on narcissism, pronto. I like *Escape* by H G Tudor.[1] It's like a crash course in dodging manipulation land mines. Or better yet, find a therapist who understands how to navigate the whole narcissism scene. Realizing they played you like a fiddle is a tough pill to swallow, but it's the first step to reclaiming your power.

Over the past fifteen years, there have been more "wake me from this nightmare" moments than I care to admit when dealing with narcissists. As a trusting guy by nature, it hasn't always worked out in my favor. I wasn't even remotely aware that these different categories of people existed until I learned about them from Dr. Morguelan.

But when I did, the clouds parted, and the sun shone. Doing the ego work is like putting on a pair of glasses that let you see through all the BS. It takes discernment, which is a practice in and of itself. Since diving deep into the practices outlined in this book, peace and gratitude have become trustworthy wingmen 99 percent of the time. But hey, I'm only human—there's still that rebellious 1 percent that likes to stir the pot just to see what's out there.

Your job is to crank up your awareness dial to 11. And who knows? If you put in the work, you may reach category 1 status, where spreading peace and positivity is as natural as breathing. You might never know you've hit that level because you'll always have your eyes peeled for slip-ups. I identify as a category 2 and strive for win-win scenarios in every interaction. Sure, I make mistakes occasionally, but that's where my carefully cultivated crew comes in, keeping me honest and helping point out the blind spots. Because at the end of the day, that's where true freedom lies: doing what matters most to you and making waves that ripple into the world.

| REALITY TRAINING |

In a world filled with distractions, distortions, and downright delusions, it's easy to lose sight of what's real and instead see what appears to be more like the reflection of a funhouse mirror. This book is a guide to take you through the labyrinth of the mind so you can strip away the layers of illusion and uncover the truth hidden beneath.

Reality is a malleable construct shaped by your thoughts, beliefs, and experiences. Many interventions are designed to transform your perception and elevate your consciousness. It takes work to make the necessary shifts and create a new reality, but anything worth having usually does.

Being stuck in a perpetual fight-or-flight state is one of the biggest gaps in presence. This usually happens unconsciously and is deeply rooted in an unregulated stress response, environmental or dietary toxins, lack of sleep (or poor sleep habits), never-ending to-do lists, ruminating thoughts—anything that leaves you tired and wired or constantly on high alert. This fight-or-flight state causes you to over-react, override your intuition, and follow your ego's signals to do whatever it takes to survive. You might feel like you're drowning when it's just your nervous system telling you it's out of whack and needs your help. Thankfully, there are some great tools to get your body out of fight-or-flight mode, calm the nervous system, and re-turn to reality with a clear mind. And, no, they don't have to cost a million dollars and they don't require you to hibernate in nature for a week alone without distractions. You can do most, if not all, of these hacks from your home.

Red-light therapy: Light is a massive signal for the brain, the skin, and every cell in your body. Think about how you feel after a day in the sun. Your soul feels energized, your mind and body are relaxed, and you feel like you hit the refresh button, ready to step into life as a new human.

Red-light therapy works kind of like the sun but without the UV rays. In this case, you're soaking up red and near-infrared wave-lengths that penetrate deep beneath your skin and into your cells. This type of light helps your mitochondria make energy more effec-tively, so your cells work better. As a result, you have more energy and less stress. Red and near-infrared light reduces inflammation,[2] accelerates injury recovery, and stimulates collagen production.[3] Collagen keeps your skin youthful, so if you want to age gracefully, red-light therapy is a great tool to have in your toolkit.

Red-light therapy is super easy to use and incredibly effective. Here's how you do it:

First, you'll want to choose a high-quality red-light device. My company, TrueLight,[4] makes light therapy devices with the most beneficial, scientifically proven wavelengths to upgrade your cells. All you have to do is place the device a few inches away from your body and relax.

Once you have your device, you'll need to expose the area of your skin that you want to treat. This could be your face, back, joints, or any other part of your body that needs healing or rejuvenation. Make sure the skin is clean and bare to allow the red light to penetrate effectively.

When you're ready, set the time for your session. Typically, red-light therapy sessions last about 10–20 minutes. Follow the manufacturer's guidelines to ensure you're using your device correctly.

Position the device about 6–12 inches away from your skin, depending on the device's instructions. Sit back, relax, and let the red light do its work. The key is to use it regularly—a few times a week for the best results.

For the ultimate experience, visit Upgrade Labs and try our state-of-the-art red-light therapy beds. These beds cover your entire body, taking your biohacking to the next level.

Vibration training: Not only do our cells respond to light, but they also respond to movement and vibration. There are many options for vibration hacks, and I share them in *Smarter Not Harder*. But to highlight some of my favorites, let's start with the lowest-hanging fruit: rebounding. You know those mini trampolines that were all the rage in the 1980s? They look like they're for children but are great for all ages. And they're fun! Plus, they don't take up a ton of room, and they won't break the bank.

To start, jump on it for 5–10 minutes, 2–3 times weekly. Then increase your time as you build strength and endurance. It doesn't sound like much, but you get fantastic benefits. As you jump, the vibration works its magic on your muscles, making them contract superfast. The vibration helps with flexibility, circulation, and boosting your mood.

Then there are vibrating foam rollers and balls that offer a unique approach to self-myofascial release (SMR). The vibration helps increase blood flow to your muscles, allowing you to recover faster after exercise. It can also help with muscle soreness and stiffness.

Combining foam rolling with vibration can help release tight muscles and fascia to improve flexibility and range of motion. These devices tend to calm the nervous system, so you feel relaxed afterward. This can be great if you've just completed a challenging workout. If you want to boost your performance and prevent injuries, do this.

If you're serious about leveling up, consider a whole-body vibration device. It is a bigger investment but beats leaving the house whenever you want to shake your booty. I mean, body. These plates work wonders by vibrating at the right frequency to simultaneously fire up your whole body, including your hormones, heart, and lymph and nervous systems. Different machines have different vibration frequencies, but the most effective for most people is a constant 30 Hz.[5]

At 40 Years of Zen, we have The Vibe Plate™ on standby for our clients. Start with short sessions, like 30 seconds to a minute, and slowly work up to 15 minutes. You don't want to overdo it. The benefits are priceless and include hormone balancing, fat loss,[6] increased bone mass and mineral density,[7] improved blood circulation, proprioception, and balance.

Pair one of these vibration hacks with red-light therapy to give your body a VIP treatment.

Functional movement: If you're like most people, you're probably walking around with hidden patterns that have been invisible to you for years. Maybe you have a slight tilt to your pelvis when you walk, or because you hunch over your computer all day, you have back, neck, and shoulder issues that have manifested in how you physically carry yourself.

Functional movement focuses on improving mobility, stability, and strength in the body, which also supports your nervous system. By releasing tension in the body, these techniques help reduce stress. A good functional movement expert (you can find one near you with a quick internet search) can help you quickly identify inefficiencies and improve your movement patterns. Mindful movement practices like yoga or tai chi can further strengthen your mind-body connection.

Therapy is the ultimate reality check. It's more than sitting on a couch and talking about your feelings (although that's cool, too). We're talking about an entire spa session for your brain.

Therapy is about getting honest with yourself, digging deep into your thoughts and feelings, and coming out on the other side feeling better than ever. It's going to be uncomfortable at first, but that's temporary.

EMDR (eye movement desensitization and reprocessing) therapy is one of the best—and fastest—ways to rewire your system. In an EMDR session, your therapist will move their finger back and forth in front of you and have you track the movement with your eyes.

At the same time, the therapist will ask you to think about the traumatic event and the feelings and bodily sensations that accompany it. The therapist will guide you to replace these painful thoughts with more positive ones throughout the session or several sessions. It sounds unbelievable, but plenty of controlled studies prove EMDR works for resolving trauma.[8, 9]

Changing your lens on reality and reaching a higher level of enlightenment requires extreme commitment. Buddha didn't just wake up one day as a Zen master. Or maybe he did, but you know what I'm saying.

The goal is to be able to remove the lenses and filters on reality that aren't serving you well, anything preventing you from being kind and forgiving. And to replace them with lenses that expand your mind, body, and soul so you are full of love instead of being full of shit.

PART II

IMMEDIATE UPGRADE

BRAIN STATES 101

By now, you probably realize that your brain is a stealth operator, hiding truths and complexities behind the curtain of consciousness. But it's not all smoke and mirrors. Your brain has a good reason for playing hide-and-seek. You just don't want it to hide the good stuff.

Your mind has a knack for sweeping massive chunks of reality under the rug. We're talking about the microscopic details that would make your head spin—automated stuff like the angle of the sunlight hitting your eyeballs or the intricate dance of neurotransmitters in your brain. Your brain has bigger things to do than sweat the small stuff.

But behind the scenes, someone's controlling the system. And it's not you. You're not exactly an Olympic sprinter when it comes to brain speed. But you do have the power to change your state using your mind and body. When you do this, all the systems will change and do what you want them to do.

Changing your mind alone isn't enough, though. Your body is a necessary player to help change how you feel, which is a thing you can choose. Remember, choosing the state of gratitude, forgiveness, or compassion is not a thinking state; it's a *feeling* state.

Now that you know all about ego, triggers, and deciphering what's real and what's not, let's discuss altered states and how everything is connected. Humans have been tapping into these states of being since, well, forever—states like ecstasy, oneness, and flow. These aren't just idle daydreams, either. They're tangible, achievable states, available to you at any time with some effort.

If you're wondering how to dip your toes (or dive headfirst) into these otherworldly realms, you're in the right spot. Monks, gurus, and spiritual seekers have pondered these questions for centuries. And as you've probably figured out, there is no shortage of paths to enlightenment. I've shared some of those paths in other books. But here we're going to take it a step further. We're going to look through the lens of brain waves: how to access certain states using ancient and modern tools and technologies.

These paths have something in common: they converge on the same destination but take different scenic routes to get there. Whether you want to dive deep into meditation, lose yourself in ecstatic dance, expand your consciousness with psychedelics, explore your sexuality with tantra or conscious kink, or surrender to the flow of life itself, the goal remains the same: to transcend the confines of the mind and experience an internal state of peace-on-demand.

If you're interested in studying altered states, there are many different methods to explore. Start by asking yourself, *How do I feel?* Then take a minute to really sit with what comes up. So often, we hear this question and shoot back with a generic answer like, "I'm good." But what does "good" feel like? Tap into all your senses and learn to feel the feelings before you respond. A bit of silence while you feel into your answer won't kill you, although it might feel awkward given all the distractions surrounding you each day. This discomfort is a good thing; it's growth. If you're feeling a bit more adventurous, veer off in the direction of esoteric topics like measuring the light emitted from your light body. Things just got weird but stick with me.

Your DNA and cells emit tiny amounts of light called biophotons. These light emissions are crucial for cellular communication and metabolism regulation. It's like your body's own internal light show, happening on a level too faint for the naked eye to see. Studies show that you can measure biophoton emissions in real time, and they can change with stress and temperature.[1] Your mitochondria are like little light factories, while your gut bacteria practically glow with bioluminescent brilliance. You have your very own cosmic light show happening inside your gut. Pretty cool, right?

Having some guidance is helpful if you want to fast-track your journey into these states. Understanding the basic states your brain can slip into helps to lay the foundation for mind-bending exploration.

Don't let the terminology scare you off. It's much simpler than it sounds, I promise. Maybe you've heard of the states—delta, theta, alpha, beta, gamma. Or perhaps this is all new to you, and that's okay, too. The reality is that, even when operating higher in any of these states, you're constantly oscillating between all the states to some degree. Think of these states like a symphony, each acting like a different musical note to create a beautiful composition of consciousness.

Now imagine that all the different parts of your brain are playing the same note simultaneously, which could be cool. But if you think about it, you'd probably get sick of hearing the same sound constantly, with no change in tone—like a hum in D4 all day. Depending on your musical taste, it would be predictable and possibly soothing or irritating, but it would also be boring.

What's really happening is way more interesting. This rhythmic symphony unfolds within your consciousness, composing a song complete with its own unique melody and pattern. Some people refer to this as a "symphony of the mind." Different parts of your brain aren't just playing the same instrument; they bring their unique sound to form the world's most eclectic band. And it's all happening inside you. Think about that. You have a full orchestra assembled inside your skull. Like, what? That's so cool!

I want you to picture this because it's a miracle that your brain does this without conscious effort. So, let's say you're organizing a concert in your mind, and you realize that to create something totally amazing, you need the guitar and saxophone to play in harmony. The magic isn't having them play the same note constantly. That would be like listening to a broken record. What makes music so captivating is the interplay between different notes and different melodies coming together in perfect harmony. And when you venture into the altered states of consciousness, the possibilities for expansion are endless.

It's like stepping into a new world when slipping into these altered states. You're not just flipping a switch; you're conducting a delicate dance of brain activity. You turn off the filters that usually keep your reality in check, and suddenly you find yourself in uncharted territory. This is gold. It's like discovering a hidden gem buried deep inside your consciousness, just waiting for its moment to shine. It's been there all along, patiently waiting for you to give it the green light and let it come out to play.

| INTRODUCTION TO BRAIN STATES |

Okay, let's get nerdy for a minute. Pay close attention because this is important. The brain is made of millions of neurons, and their patterns of electrical activity are called brain waves. Brain waves are like the brain's language that dictates how you think, feel, and behave. Every experience you have, from the mundane to the extraordinary, leaves its mark in the form of brain wave patterns. These patterns, detected using sensors on the scalp, reveal a lot about what's happening inside your head. They range from slow and steady to fast and frantic, each frequency telling a story about your state of mind. The speed of the brain waves is called frequency, measured in a unit called hertz (Hz). Hertz tells us how many cycles occur within one second.

We can hack into this brain wave symphony with neurofeedback and fine-tune it to perfection. At 40 Years of Zen, we don't just help you understand your brain waves; we teach your brain how to dance to its own beat. By amplifying specific frequencies relative to others, we can unlock the door to a new level of consciousness filled with presence, focus, and inner peace.

There are technologies available and designed to enhance these states—everything from meditation practices to breathwork techniques to cutting-edge biohacking tools. Don't worry; we'll get into many of them in this book. Remember, it's not just about how deep you can go. It's about asking how deep you're *willing* to go and then training your brain and body to dive in and fearlessly explore those depths.

So, imagine you're at the beach. The waves are rolling in with perfect precision, cresting at just the right moment, one right after the other. It's a surfer's paradise. Now, imagine if those waves were one hundred feet tall instead of a foot tall. You'd have a very different experience—surfing a tsunami instead of riding a gentle ripple.

Your brain is a lot like those waves. It's constantly ebbing and flowing, with peaks and valleys that shape your consciousness in ways you might not even realize. But what if you could teach your brain to create bigger, more powerful waves? Waves that crash with the force of a hurricane, leaving a wake of transformation in their path.

This is where brain training comes into play. You can learn to dial up the power and amplify your brain waves for high performance. But size isn't the only thing that matters—it's about making them cleaner, more precise, more refined. It's like having a conversation with the universe and asking it to craft you a series of perfect waves—ones that break just the way they're supposed to, every single time.

Now, you're probably thinking: *How do you even begin to tackle something as complex as brain wave training?* Well, it starts with understanding the basics laid out for you in this book. The truth is, we know a lot about brain states. At 40 Years of Zen, we've looked at the results of over 1,500 brains, each unique and intriguing in its own way. But in the grand scheme of things, we're only scratching the surface of what's possible.

So, let's examine the five main frequencies in the ranges we focus on at 40 Years of Zen: delta (1–4 Hz), theta (4–8 Hz), alpha (8–12 Hz), beta (12–38 Hz), and gamma (38–100 Hz).

We'll start with **delta**. Delta brain waves have the greatest amplitude and slowest frequency (1–4 Hz). This is the deep, dreamless sleep state where you're completely unaware of your surroundings. Time escapes you, and you lose yourself in the abyss of your mind. Delta is the king of relaxation. Scientists recognize this as the slowest brain wave, but there are much slower brain waves than delta. For instance, there's one wave in your brain that happens about once every twenty seconds, called **slow cortical potential** (or "subdelta" brainwaves). And just like delta, slow cortical potential is trainable. You can fine-tune your neural symphony to perfection using your very own mind-mixing board. You can dial in the purity and clarity of the tones, making them crisp. Or you can adjust the volume, cranking it up to amplify the effects or dialing it down for a more subtle experience.

After studying all these brains, we found that something interesting happens when people enter states of healing, peak performance, or spiritual enlightenment. Instead of investing their energy into these deep, unconscious waves—the kind typically associated with nondreaming sleep, where the body performs its essential maintenance tasks automatically—they start diverting energy elsewhere.

For this example, your brain has a limited energy pool to draw from—say, 100 energy units. Now, if a major chunk of that energy is being used to generate these slow, unconscious waves and not even doing a particularly good job, you've got a problem. It's like having a leaky bucket; you're losing precious energy that could be better used elsewhere.

So, what do you do? You reallocate energy resources, shifting your focus away from the sluggish unconscious waves and redirecting it toward states more aligned with your goals and aspirations. This strategic reallocation of resources upgrades your brain's energy output for maximum effectiveness.

It's like flipping a switch when people achieve these spiritual, emotional, or psychological breakthroughs. All of a sudden they are able to redirect the sluggish, dirty waves to clean, pristine ones. Think of it like unclogging a drain, and everything begins to flow effortlessly. This frees up a lot of energy to do other things. They move into the next bucket of brain waves during this shift: **theta**.

Theta is another slow state (4–8 Hz). This is where creativity and intuition run wild, daydreaming and fantasizing know no bounds, and memories, emotions, and sensations bubble up to the surface. The boundaries between imagination and reality blur as you drift into the theta state. Your creativity flows, and breakthroughs come out of nowhere as you tap into your inner genius and unleash your full potential.

Take James Watson and Francis Crick, for instance. They weren't sitting in a lab crunching numbers when they stumbled upon the structure of DNA. They were dreaming—literally. It was a moment of clarity that emerged from the depths of their subconscious minds, paving the way for one of the greatest discoveries in modern science.

Or consider Thomas Edison, a master of innovation. He had a knack for tapping into the theta state, using an unconventional method called "the Edison nap" to boost productivity. He would sit in a chair holding a metal ball in his hand, hovering it over a metal plate. When he would start to doze off, the ball would drop, hitting the plate and waking him up. It was an easy way for him to take power naps and recharge quickly while tapping into his creativity and the collective consciousness for inspiration. What works for one may not work for others. But there's always a path to get where you want to go.

Not everyone has the luxury of being able to dip in and out of these heightened states. For some it's a gift, a natural inclination that allows them to effortlessly slip into the theta state whenever inspiration strikes. But for others it can be a double-edged sword—too much daydreaming, too much wandering in la-la land, and suddenly you're lost in a fog of distraction and absentmindedness.

Take this fifty-year-old engineer's brain, for example (pictured)—a brilliant mind trapped in a perpetual dream state, unable to focus or achieve his full potential. His brain learned to live in theta as a result of a single childhood trauma where a babysitter was mean to him. It wasn't gross abuse or anything, but it put his brain in the theta state, where it got stuck . . . until he came to 40 Years of Zen.

This image shows the process unfolding during the Reset Process, where the brain shifts gears. It transitions from a daydream-dominant state back to a relaxed, alert state.

THETA

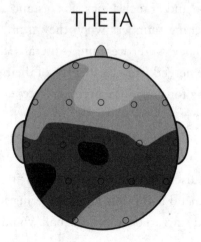

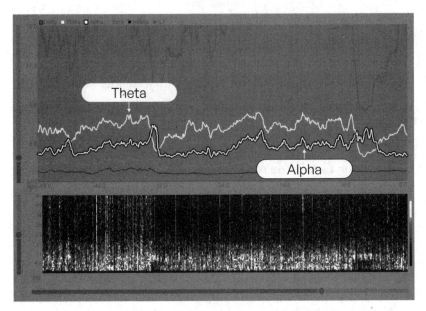

Being in any of these states isn't inherently good or bad. Each state has its function and role to play in shaping your experience of the world. We've uncovered from our deep dives into these advanced states that you can learn to dial in each state like a pro with practice and familiarity.

When you venture into the realm of interconnectivity and intuition and tap into that deep inner knowing, you open yourself up to a world of possibilities. Many clients at 40 Years of Zen have shared that when they're in these states, it's like gaining access to a higher plane of existence where angels, ancestors, and deities roam freely. The boundaries between the physical and spiritual worlds blur into nothingness. For some it's not uncommon to experience out-of-body sensations, journey beyond the physical body's confines, and explore the vast expanse of consciousness itself. Think about when you dream. It's similar. That's because this is exactly what's happening when you're sleeping, but now it's trainable and can be accessed while awake. There are a variety of brain-tuning techniques to get you there.

It's important to note that context is key. Instead of just turning the knobs on the control panel of your mind to adjust your brain wave frequencies, you want to understand the broader landscape of consciousness and how each state fits into your life. When we talk about transcending the dream state, we're talking about moving into the **alpha** state.

Alpha frequency (8–12 Hz) is your brain's way of saying, "Hey, let's chill for a sec." You're not all caught up in the hustle and grind; you know how to relax and observe. You're aware of what's happening around you but not fixated on reacting to it. That's because you're more internally focused, which can feel challenging in our modern world.

Alpha is where those choppy, out-of-control waves get upgraded. As you navigate the waves of your mind, suddenly they're smoother and more majestic. You're riding a wave of clarity, and it feels incredible. Then, suddenly, you realize you're not just riding an epic wave but tapping into something bigger. You feel like you're part of the whole universe. Maybe those brain waves are the secret to unlocking the mystical experiences you've been chasing. Your brain is the surfboard, riding the waves of consciousness toward your healing and evolution. Pretty mind-blowing.

Meditation can also put you in a relaxing and restorative state. But achieving those deep alpha brain waves can take years, even decades, of daily practice. This state helps support being present and "in the moment." Just before athletes hit that zone where everything flows, they experience a burst of alpha.

But it's not all rainbows and butterflies. Sometimes diving into alpha can stir up some deep stuff hiding behind the scenes. You know, the memories you think you've "gotten over," or maybe you've hidden them so well you assume they've vanished for good? Unfortunately, stuffing things deep down won't heal the wound. That's why people say, "Healing is in the feeling." For example, you can't suppress your way out of a horrible childhood. You must feel the emotions and move them out of your body if you want to be free.

Above the calm and collected alpha state, we've got the relatively low amplitude of the **beta** state (12–38 Hz)—the zone where executive function and decision-making take center stage. Think of it like preparing for a big game or feeling the pressure of an important presentation.

Beta waves are like a caffeine fix for your brain—they're great for getting stuff done but can also hijack your experience. Ever felt stuck on a never-ending hamster wheel, constantly hustling without a moment to catch your breath? That's beta in action. Or have you ever tried to go to sleep, but your mind won't shut up when your head hits the pillow? That's also beta. So, unless you're gearing up to crush a game of Ping-Pong, Bruce Lee–style, you may want to dial down beta and give yourself a break.

Finally, we hit the secret of the Zen masters, the holy grail of meditation—**gamma** (38+ Hz, though 40 Hz is typical). This is a newer brain state that many believe is difficult, if not impossible, to train.

Gamma are the speed demons of your brain, zooming around and making connections. They're multitaskers and help you simultaneously process information from different brain areas at lightning speed. Gamma waves might be subtle, but they pack a serious punch. Think of gamma as having your own cheer squad promoting compassion, positivity, and open awareness. Plus, they're crucial for memory encoding and recall. Given that they're above the frequency of neuronal firing, how gamma waves are generated is still a bit of a mystery. We know they have a hand in shaping your perception and consciousness—and they feel incredible.

Experiments on Tibetan Buddhist monks have shown a correlation between transcendental mental states and gamma waves. In 2004, researchers hooked up electrodes to eight seasoned monks and monitored their brain waves as they went deep into meditation. When these monks focused on feelings of compassion, their brains lit up like a fireworks show, flickering in perfect harmony at a frequency of 25–42 Hz—the rhythm of gamma waves.[2] We're talking about neuronal structures dancing in sync, creating an off-the-chart symphony of brain activity.

The gamma-band vibrations lighting up the monks' brains were unlike anything seen in humans before. And get this: while beginner meditators showed little to no gamma activity, the signals started to strengthen in those who stuck with the practice, hinting that the ability to produce gamma waves is trainable despite previous beliefs.

But why does this matter? Gamma waves are vital to unlocking a heightened state of consciousness, bliss, and razor-sharp intellect. It's like switching gears in your brain, unleashing a flood of feel-good vibes and mental clarity. And the benefits continue beyond that. You can link meditation to everything from stress reduction and mood elevation to boosting cognitive function and extending lifespan.

At 40 Years of Zen, we've taken this discovery to the next level. For over a decade, we've been pioneering neurofeedback to supercharge gamma waves, helping people unlock their brain's full potential like never before with our Reset Process, outlined later in the book.

But something to keep in mind: gamma rarely goes it alone. You can create the perfect mind-expanding cocktail for consciousness with a dash of delta, a sprinkle of alpha, a pinch of theta, a touch of beta, and just the right amount of gamma. With the right combination, mystical experiences, spiritual awakenings, and life-changing moments become your reality, reshaping the story of your existence. These moments are like software updates for your soul, giving you the power to rewrite the code of your operating system.

Things that constantly drag your brain waves in the wrong direction—worry, fear, loneliness, stress, anxiety—make them more chaotic, less rhythmic, and less powerful. These heightened negative emotions (ego) also waste energy. But through our extensive research on over 1,500 brains, we've uncovered that you can realign these brain waves. And the best part? They will continue to evolve for months after training—and stay that way.

So, let's bring it back to gratitude for a minute because its impact on your brainwaves is massive. When truly immersed in gratitude, your brain waves shift; your relaxed, alert brain waves soar along-side your gamma waves for a euphoric experience. But most of us don't know how to flip that gamma switch without extensive training.

At 40 Years of Zen, we've cracked the code on inducing profound states of gratitude using specific sounds, targeted electrodes, or even pharmaceutical assistance. And just one experience of pure grati-tude can be life-changing. If you've ever wished you could hit the reset button on your worries, fear, and self-judgments and focus on gratitude—like, really focus on gratitude as a felt experience—now you can. Gratitude is the first step to unlocking those Zen-like brain waves, paving the way for a life of clarity, peace, and unlimited potential. We teach this during the Reset Process, and I'm sharing it with you in this book.

| BIOHACK YOUR BRAIN WAVES |

In biohacking, we're all about helping you fine-tune your brain wave orchestra. It's not necessarily about having more or less of one type of brain wave; it's about knowing how to handle them like a maestro. It's about understanding which brainwaves, at what volume, and how rhythmic they need to be to create that perfect harmony.

In Western medicine, we're often obsessed with finding the single root cause of everything. But let's face it: life is more complex (that would be helpful, though). As no single root cause exists for happiness or joy, there's no one-size-fits-all solution for creating the perfect balance of your unique brain waves. That's where the real art of biohacking comes in.

So, what are we doing with the tools and technologies used at 40 Years of Zen? We're teaching your brain and body how to fine-tune each note, making it louder or quieter and creating the perfect rhythm for your unique symphony of consciousness. It's about unlocking your brain's full potential and composing a masterpiece of well-being, one clean note at a time.

Just as learning to sing in perfect pitch is a practicable skill, so is teaching your brain how to perform "just right." So instead of muddy alpha, you have clean alpha, where everyone's simultaneously marching in the same direction. This is the hallmark of high performance, and it's the hallmark of a well-ordered, well-organized brain. It's also the hallmark of mystical states, depending on what song you're playing at the time.

So, if gamma is gratitude, alpha is where you can experience heightened states of forgiveness—they each have their own songs you can play within these ranges. Alpha isn't just about forgiveness. For instance, if you want to increase your alpha state, all you have to do is close your eyes and focus on the middle of your forehead, where your third eye would be. Just like that, your alpha triples. Simple, right? You didn't have to work to forgive anyone. You didn't do anything other than quiet the distractions and focus inward. This inner exploration is what's been missing.

Your neurons, equipped with hundreds to millions of mitochondria that move around, are the powerhouses of your brain.[3, 4] Imagine a big concert at a stadium, and you see a row of generators out back making extra power for the lights and sound. Well, that's your mitochondria. They will move their power resources around when needed and form new networks to do it more efficiently. That's why meditating regularly doesn't just calm your mind; you create new neural connections and power them better. Each mitochondria within a neuron is like a fish in a school, deciding where to go. And when you multiply that by billions of neurons, you have a complex network, just like a school of fish, all working together and deciding which direction to swim. The powerhouses within your cells guide this dance of consciousness.

"Peace is not the absence of chaos or conflict, but rather finding yourself in the midst of that chaos and remaining calm in your heart."
—*John Mroz*

When you learn to manage and use these altered states to your advantage, your brain shifts from chaos to orderliness. An orderly brain can do lots of different things. It can focus and get an A on a test, a combination of alpha and beta. It can be relaxed and peaceful and connected to everything on a walk in the forest, or it can feel one with the music at a concert—this happens because of a combination of different states working together to create a felt experience.

So, you're learning how to play the brain like an instrument and play different types of music. Each of the brain states is just a different genre of music. But you're playing it to a school of fish swimming inside your head, which could be chaotic or beautiful. This is what brain states are all about.

UNDER THE COVERS: BREATHWORK AND SEXUAL ENERGY

21,600—that's the average number of breaths you take each day. This number can vary based on activity level, health status, and environmental conditions. But think about that. Every day, your MeatOS keeps you alive by taking in and letting out air. Let's break this down in nerd-speak because it's actually not a simple process, and yet here you are, reading this book and breathing without thinking about it.

When you take a deep breath, your diaphragm and intercostal muscles (muscles within your rib cage) expand your chest cavity. This expansion creates a slight vacuum in your lungs, drawing air in from the world around you, whether it's through your nose or mouth. This air travels down your windpipe, or trachea, and settles into your lungs, eventually reaching those little air sacs called alveoli. As the air makes itself at home in your alveoli, oxygen starts its journey. It effortlessly seeps through the thin walls of these sacs and into the surrounding capillaries—your tiny blood vessels are like the bustling streets of a busy city. From there, oxygen-rich blood takes a ride on the pulmonary veins, heading straight to the left side of your heart. Once on board, your heart wastes no time sending this precious cargo out through the aorta and into the world of systemic circulation. It's like FedEx for oxygen, delivering it to every nook and cranny of your body, ensuring that all your cells get their fair share.

But wait, there's more. As your cells happily gobble up oxygen for energy, they produce something called carbon dioxide—a waste product to deal with. So, back to the lungs it goes, hitching a ride in your bloodstream. When it arrives, your body switches gears, and it's time for a breather, literally.

Exhalation is like a sigh of relief after a long day. Your diaphragm and intercostal muscles take a well-deserved break to allow your chest cavity to shrink. As it does, the now carbon dioxide–laden air is gently ushered out of your lungs, ready to be released back into the world. The dance of gas exchange continues with each breath, keeping your cells happy and your body humming along smoothly.

Okay, can we take a moment of silence and awe for your miraculous body and breath? Seriously. Imagine if you had to think about that process 21,600+ times every day just to stay alive—you'd get nothing else done. Pretty impressive, isn't it?

| JUST BREATHE |

On a permanent basis, breathwork is more effective than meditation to quickly get your brain into altered states. When I first dove into breathwork two decades back, it was like a roller-coaster ride for my brain. Within a few seconds, that panic alarm starts blaring—"You're gonna run out of oxygen! You're gonna die!" But here's the thing: Science shows we can hold our breath for way longer than we think. Like, two to three minutes, easily. Some people can even push it to five or seven with the right techniques. So, that panicked voice? It's like your car's check-engine light flashing—a heads-up, not a red alert.

See, the thing about breath is it's like food. You need it, but missing a meal won't kill you (though you might not be too thrilled about it). It's the same with breath. Your body might freak out when the tank's empty, but trust me, the air always returns. It's like a reminder to your system: "Chill out, we got this." I've seen people go from full-on panic to chill mode in thirty seconds flat with breathwork. You're training your brain to trust that everything will be all right, even when it's doing its best impression of a new puppy being left alone for the first time—massive meltdown mode on steroids.

There's an almost endless variety of breathwork techniques, each set to steer you in a different direction. We'll start with the calming breaths. These are the ones that slide you into that peaceful, intuitive zone, sparking creativity and nudging your brain waves into that smooth alpha state. These are the Zen masters of breath, calming down that busy, buzzing beta energy. Then we'll move into different types of altered states breathwork, ending with other dimension breathing techniques.

| CALMING: BOX BREATH |

This is one of the most famous types of calming breath. I almost hesitate to write about it because it's often repeated on the podcast and during speaking events. But it's so good that it would be a huge disservice not to share it with anyone unfamiliar. So, if you've heard me talk about this, let this be another reminder to give it a shot.

Besides bringing you back to reality when life throws you curveballs, this simple breathing technique is like a mental reset for your brain. It calms your nervous system, boosts your focus, and quiets the stress hormones so you can relax. Plus, it's backed by science[1] and loved by badass special forces operators to get out of fight-or-flight mode. Sure, it won't shoot you into a whole new galaxy of consciousness, but if it can turn the chaos swirling in your head into a peaceful state, that's a win, right? Here's how you do it:

Step 1: Find a quiet spot to get comfy, sit up straight, and take a deep breath through your nose for a count of 4 seconds. Feel your chest and belly fill up with air. If you tend to have a monkey mind like most people, close your eyes and let all the inner noise go.

Step 2: Hold that breath in for another 4 seconds. Feel the tension build, focusing on remaining calm and present. It's only 4 seconds, you can do it.

Step 3: Now, slowly exhale through your mouth for 4 seconds, letting all the trapped air out. Imagine you're releasing all the stress and chaos from your mind with each exhale.

Step 4: Hold that empty breath for another 4 seconds. Embrace the moment of stillness, and let your body fully surrender.

If it helps to have a mantra to stay present, you can silently repeat to yourself "let" on your inhale and "go" on your exhale. Repeat this cycle for a few rounds, however long it takes for you to find that Zen-like state of tranquility. If you're feeling adventurous, increase your time as you get more comfortable. Ramp it up to a 10-second box breath, or even 20 if you feel like a pro.

So, what's happening to your brainwaves during this practice? Picture your brain as a superhighway buzzing with activity. Well, depending on what you're up to, your brain waves are cruising at different speeds, like cars on that highway.

First up, we've got beta waves. These are the speed demons, zooming around when you're in the zone. But sometimes they can get out of control and make you feel stressed or jittery, like you just drank a gallon of Red Bull.

But your brain waves shift gears as you start doing those slow, rhythmic box breaths. Beta takes a back seat, and alpha waves move into the driver's seat. Remember, alpha are those chill waves. They're the Sunday drivers on the highway, cruising below the speed limit, maybe triggering the heck out of you—until you've learned to tame your triggers and find your Zen state. They're alert, but they're not rushing to get anywhere. They're the perfect travel companions when you want to tap into your intuition and creativity.

If you sink into the box breath, you might even catch some theta waves. These are the dreamers of the brain wave world, popping up when you reach that deep, meditative state. These are the ones responsible for those aha moments and flashes of insight.

| CALMING: UJJAYI BREATH |

All right, let's break down this calming technique, often referred to as "ocean breath." Coming straight from the playbook of ancient traditions like yoga, specifically hatha yoga and pranayama practices, this technique originated in India thousands of years ago, where it was developed as a way to enhance spiritual growth, mental clarity, and physical well-being. *Uj* means "to expand" or "to extend," and *Jayi* means "victorious" or "uplifting." Together, Ujjayi breath creates a sense of expansion and victory for anyone using it.

If you've ever been to a yoga class, you know about Ujjayi breath. It's also popular in mindfulness and meditation practices, martial arts, and traditional Chinese medicine (TCM).

Visualize yourself taking slow, deep breaths through the nose, but you're constricting the back of your throat while you're doing it. Maybe that doesn't sound relaxing, but once you get the hang of it, it will send you into another realm of relaxation. Think of it like you're gearing up to snore, but you're not quite there yet.

This breath sounds like waves crashing on the shore or wind whispering through the trees. It's calming, peaceful, and therapeutic. If you want to fall asleep easily, do ten rounds of Ujjayi breath and watch how quickly you drift off. It's a secret weapon for those sleepless nights. Here's a little tip. As you dive into these breathwork techniques, you might face a challenge: holding your breath empty—this is that pause after you let all the air out. But trust me, it's all part of the process, and the rewards are worth it. Here's how you do it:

Step 1: Sit upright or lie on your back, close your eyes, and take a deep breath through your nose.

Step 2: Now, as you breathe out through your nose, constrict the back of your throat a bit, like you're fogging up a mirror. You should hear this soft, oceanlike sound as you exhale.

Step 3: Keep that oceanic sound going as you breathe in and out, slow and steady.

Now let's talk about your brainwaves during Ujjayi breathwork. You hit your mat, ready to move your body, and settle into your Ujjayi breathing. As you start that slow, controlled inhale-exhale action, your brain waves take notice. First come alpha, ready to chill out while still dialed into your surroundings. As you sink deeper into your practice, you might start tapping into theta waves—the dreamers of the brain wave world that show up when you're in that blissed-out, borderline-sleepy state. These are the helpers to get you to unwind, let go, and possibly tap further into your creative juices.

ALTERED STATES: NADI SHODHANA PRANAYAMA

This isn't your average calming breath—Nadi Shodhana Pranayama crosses the border as you move into altered states. You might know it better as "alternate nostril breathing," which has been around for ages. This traditional breathing technique is about harmonizing your left and right brain hemispheres, balancing the energy channels, and dialing up mental clarity and physical vitality.

This is a supercommon thing you'll find in yoga or meditation circles. It's like the warm-up to the main event, helping you calm your mind and get in the zone. It is important to keep your breath easy and natural—no need to force it. Just focus on the rhythm of your breath, and you're golden. Here's how you do it:

Step 1: Get comfy, sit tall, and close your eyes.

Step 2: Place your left hand on your left knee, palm open to the sky or in Chin Mudra (where your thumb and index finger gently touch like the "okay" sign).

Step 3: Use your right hand to place the tips of your index and middle fingers between your eyebrows. Your ring and little fingers are on your left nostril, and your thumb blocks the right.

Step 4: Close your eyes and take a deep breath in and out through your nose.

Step 5: Close your right nostril with your thumb and slowly inhale through your left nostril.

Step 6: When you reach the top of your inhale, switch—close your left nostril with your ring and little fingers, release your thumb, and exhale slowly through the right nostril.

Step 7: Repeat the process, inhaling through the right nostril and then switching to and exhaling through the left.

Keep going for a few minutes, alternating sides with each breath. Research[2] suggests that practices like alternate nostril breathing can shake things up in your brain in all the right ways. They can tweak your brain waves, nudge your mental state, and even boost your cognitive processing. It's like a mini spa day for your brain.[3] You feel refreshed and ready to do life again, only with a calm mind and body.

When you dive into Nadi Shodhana Pranayama, the alpha waves kick into high gear to signal you're in a super-relaxed mental state. You'll also get some theta waves, the creative geniuses of your brain. As you continue with your alternate nostril breaths, you might notice your inner artist unlocking and an enhanced mental clarity. Beta takes a step back during this exercise so you can keep your stress levels down and forget about your to-do lists. Even though Nadi Shodhana Pranayama is more of a beginner's move, with time and practice it can amp up gamma—the heightened perception, problem-solving, and consciousness brain wave.

While studies have shown some pretty cool effects, it's worth mentioning that everyone's brain is a little different. So, what works like magic for one person might not have the same effect for another. It depends on factors like your familiarity with the practice, your environment, and your body's unique quirks.

Controlled breathing, like Nadi Shodhana Pranayama, can be powerful. But there's a lot to understand about the very complex interplay between your breath and brainwaves. So, pay attention to how you feel and how your brain and body respond after each session. Then choose the one that works best for you and stick with it.

| ALTERED STATES: YOGA NIDRA |

If your brain feels like it could use a long nap, try yoga nidra. The word *nidra* actually means "sleep," and *yoga* means "union."

So, this idea of yoga nidra is a practice of conscious surrender where the body goes into a state of deep relaxation or sleep but remains awake and aware. It can help reduce stress,[4] improve sleep, boost creativity, and even enhance your mood. Plus, it's a great way to give your brain a little TLC, helping you feel more focused and alert. Here's how you do it:

Step 1: Find a cozy lie-down spot like your yoga mat or bed.

Step 2: Close your eyes and take a few deep breaths, releasing any pent-up tension or stress.

Step 3: Tune in to your body, noticing any areas of tightness or discomfort, and do your best to relax them consciously.

Step 4: Set an intention for your practice—quieting the mind, letting go of the to-do list, being present, or whatever you'd like.

Step 5: Follow a guided yoga nidra meditation or create your own by focusing on different parts of your body, your breath, or visualizations. Tracee Stanley has some available on YouTube[5] if you want to check those out.

Step 6: Allow yourself to drift into deep relaxation, noticing and letting go of thoughts and distractions as they pop up.

Step 7: Stay in this state for as long as you like, soaking up the relaxation and rejuvenation.

Step 8: When ready to return to reality, slowly bring your awareness back to your body and surroundings, gently wiggle your fingers and toes, and open your eyes.

Step 9: Take a moment to notice how you feel after the practice. Carry that sense of peace and relaxation throughout your day.

So, where are your brainwaves? As you read this, you're probably in a mid-high beta state (alertness, focused attention, cognitive processing). Let's shift gears a bit and tune in to your breath. Feel it flowing in and out, bringing you into a serene, inward-focused state. Now you're moving into the alpha state. Yoga nidra takes us even further, slipping us into the calming territory of delta brain waves. Think of it like stepping into the space between waking and sleeping. It's that liminal space. You might have heard of the hypnagogic state—that fuzzy, calm zone right before you doze off. You're teetering on the edge of dreamland, still aware but drifting.

There was a study where participants did yoga nidra for two weeks. Before and during practice, they kept track of their sleep habits in a diary. Then the researchers hooked the participants to all these fancy machines to measure their brain waves while doing yoga nidra.[6] They looked at EEG, EMG, and EOG to see what was happening in their brains. **EEG** (electroencephalogram) is a test used to evaluate the electrical activity in the brain. **EMG** (electromyography) measures the electrical activity of muscles. **EOG** (electrooculography) measures the electrical activity of the eyes. Even though the participants were doing yoga nidra, they were still technically awake the whole time. But get this: their brain waves showed signs of slow waves in certain areas, like the ones you'd experience during sleep.

After two weeks of yoga nidra practice, the participants slept better than ever. They logged more sleep hours, slept more efficiently, and woke up feeling refreshed. Yoga nidra is a restorative and simple solution that you can incorporate at any time of the day to improve your sleep quality at night.

I interviewed Tracee Stanley about yoga nidra on *The Human Upgrade* podcast.[7] Tracee is a renowned teacher and author who unveils the transformative power of rest in her book *Radiant Rest*. She explains yoga nidra as "falling asleep to the ego and awakening to the soul; when we're in that liminal space, we have so much connection to the unconscious, to the dream world. Thanks to people like Dr. Richard Miller from iRest and the research that they've done at Walter Reed Hospital, we know that it works." She goes on to say, "Yoga is not a competition. It's a practice of meeting yourself over and over and over again. And that's one of the most beautiful things that we can do. We fall in love with life. We want to devote ourselves to life. And when we do that, we want to take care of this body and help other people take care of their bodies, their creative selves, their spiritual selves, their physical selves. It becomes way more expansive." I couldn't agree more.

OTHER DIMENSIONS: SUDARSHAN KRIYA, THE "ART OF LIVING BREATHING TECHNIQUE"

I had the incredible opportunity to sit down with Gurudev Sri Sri Ravi Shankar, the powerhouse behind an international movement energizing over 50 million people daily with transformative breathwork. We met at the Art of Living Center in Los Angeles, which he founded in 1981. Around then, he started spreading the word about Sudarshan Kriya, often called the "Art of Living breathing technique," along with other life-altering breathing practices. These techniques are both simple and powerful. They're all about cutting through the stress, amping up your energy, and boosting your daily dose of joy and peace. You can listen to the conversation on *The Human Upgrade* podcast.[8]

Here's the truth: most of us breathe shallowly, skimming the surface of the breath's potential. But when you learn to harness the power of deep, intentional breathing, you upgrade your body's software—you increase your energy, lower stress, and sharpen your focus by changing how you breathe.

The core of the practice involves a specific rhythmic and cyclical breathing pattern. There are three distinct phases: slow, medium, and fast-paced breaths, each followed by a holding period. It ends with meditation as a way to get into a heightened state of awareness and inner peace. Here's how you do it:

Step 1: Find a quiet, comfy spot free of distractions. You can sit on a chair with your feet flat or cross-legged on the floor. Keep your back straight but not stiff.

Step 2: Close your eyes, clear your mind, and relax your body— start at the top of your head and work your way down to the tips of your toes.

Step 3: Notice your natural breathing pattern. Feel the air moving through your nostrils, filling your lungs, and leaving your body.

Step 4: Begin Ujjayi breathing, inhaling deeply through your nostrils and exhaling out your nostrils with a closed mouth, creating a soft hissing in your throat. Focus on the rhythmic sound and sensation of your breath. This helps calm the mind and prepares it for the subsequent phases of the kriya.

Step 5: Continue Ujjayi breathing for a few minutes. Transition to Bhastrika (Bellows Breath)—rapid, forceful breaths in and out through the nose, with your mouth closed. Maintain a steady rhythm of about 20–30 breaths per minute for a few minutes. This helps to energize the body, clear the respiratory system, and release accumulated tension.

Step 6: Return to Ujjayi for a brief period to restore calmness.

Step 7: The final phase involves chanting "Om," "So Hum," or another chosen mantra three times, focusing on the vibrations and resonance of the sound. Finish with a few moments of deep, mindful breathing. This is a powerful way to harmonize the body and the mind.

Step 8: Repeat this sequence with a trained instructor or a soundtrack guiding you to make it easier when journeying into hourlong sessions.

So, back to your brain. As you dive into this practice, alpha waves start humming, dialing down the stress, and pumping up the relaxation—imagine your brain kicking back in a relaxing recliner. Next, your theta waves get a turbo boost, launching your mind into a vivid world of dreams and creativity. Meanwhile, the frantic beta waves that can make you feel like you're juggling flaming torches get dialed back. You're still alert but without feeling jittery or anxious. Then your gamma waves kick into high gear, sharpening your brain to a razor's edge and enhancing your processing power and memory. It's like upgrading your brain's CPU to handle complex tasks with incredible precision.

By guiding your breath in this way, you're doing so much more than just breathing; you're training your brain to enter a state of profound clarity and tranquility. It's a full-blown brain upgrade powered by nothing more than your breath.

This practice can take you into profoundly altered states. It certainly does for me—and fast. You just lie there breathing and chanting, and it might seem like utter nonsense. But the thing is, your unconscious is not supposed to make sense. It's about the experience. Your brain tries to make sense of everything, believing many things that aren't even real because they're useful. But what if I told you some of the best stuff in life doesn't make sense? And that's okay.

A warning to anyone reading this far: doing this kind of intense, altered-state breathwork is like microdosing on psychedelics. Just remember, as with anything, more is not always better. You can microdose every day and have an increase in neuroplasticity (great). But do two grams of mushrooms every day and watch your relationships and career fall apart (not great). Respect the power of the practice, and it might just change your life.

OTHER DIMENSIONS: TUMMO BREATH

The tummo breathing technique, also called g-tummo, is the ultimate breathwork power-up. It's straight from the heart of Tibetan Buddhist tradition, mentioned in sacred texts dating back to the eighth century. This technique is one of the Six Dharmas of Naropa, a set of advanced Tibetan Buddhist tantric practices used to reach enlightenment at an accelerated rate. It combines visualization, breathing, and muscle contractions to enter a meditative state.

In Tibetan Buddhism, tummo is the fierce goddess of heat and passion. Think of this practice like your body's inner furnace, cranking up your energy levels and sharpening your focus. The ancient monks used tummo breath to elevate their body temperature because, due to the altitude in the Tibetan mountains, temps often drop below zero. Yet, despite the frigid weather, the monks would sleep outside peacefully on cold rocks, warm like babies.

In an MRI study, researchers got a peek inside the brains of meditating monks. They found that these monks had a unique blood flow pattern that gave their brains superpowers for bodily functions like temperature and metabolism.[9] The commonality between the monks? Tummo breathing. But its benefits stretch even further than that. It can kick insomnia to the curb, give anxiety and depression a run for their money, and squash stress. Here's how you do it:

Step 1: Find a quiet spot to relax, close your eyes, and place your hands on your belly.

Step 2: Clear out any mental clutter, and let your body soften as your mind relaxes.

Step 3: Picture a fire burning hot in your belly, like you're a hollow balloon with a wild flame inside. Keep this visual during the entire practice.

Step 4: Inhale deep and slow through your nose, leaning back and puffing out your chest. Picture oxygen fueling the flames, making them grow bigger and hotter with each breath.

Step 5: Exhale forcefully through your mouth, like you're blowing through a straw. Curl your spine forward and imagine the heat spreading throughout your entire body.

Step 6: Do this five times, focusing on the heat cranking up with each round. When you hit the fifth round, gently swallow and feel your breath settle below your belly button. Squeeze your pelvic floor muscles tight, holding your breath like it's your last one left.

Step 7: Hold that last breath for as long as possible. Then, let it all out and give your muscles a well-deserved break.

Step 8: Repeat this fiery practice a few more times, and feel the heat build inside you with each breath.

During tummo breathing, your brainwaves move from alpha into theta. Delta and gamma are not typically associated with this type of breathwork. However, it's possible that with continued practice and mastery, people might experience subtle enhancements of delta and gamma wave activity.

OTHER DIMENSIONS: THE WIM HOF METHOD

Wim Hof, also known as "The Iceman," developed a method that's like upgrading your smartphone to the latest OS—the hardware is your body, and the breathwork is the software upgrade. His method is similar to tummo breathing but with a twist. The Wim Hof Method fine-tunes every function, boosting efficiency and performance, making you feel like a new person, all powered by breath. I use this method as one of my tools to make it to 180 years old and maybe even beyond. Only time will tell, but I always feel fantastic afterward. Here's how you do it:

Step 1: Start with 30 quick, deep breaths—inhale like you're filling up a balloon to the max, and exhale without force.

Step 2: After your last breath out, hold it. Stop breathing for as long as you comfortably can.

Step 3: When you can't hold it any longer, take a deep breath, hold it for about 15 seconds, and then let it go.

Step 4: Do this whole cycle three to four times. Each round builds on the previous one, sort of like stacking upgrades on your body's MeatOS, making you more resilient and energized.

Now, that's just the breathing part of his method. If you want to dive into the other pillars—cold exposure and mindset—that's another level of biohacking. You can catch Wim Hof on *The Human Upgrade* podcast.[10] Regardless, you start with the breath first. From there you can shift to cold exposure. Then, while engaging your breath and cold exposure, focus on controlling your mindset with mental resilience training. We won't go into those details here, though—this is all about moving into altered states with your breath.

So, what happens in your brain? First, your gamma waves ramp up, accelerating your brain's processing power—think high-speed problem-solving and heightened awareness. Next, alpha waves get a boost during those breath-holding moments, perfect for Zen-like focus. Occasionally you'll see theta waves peek through, especially if you sink into the practice, which can feel like you're rebooting your brain's meditation and creativity circuits. If you're still wondering if your breath is a superpower, you're a lost cause. Just kidding. It can be confusing, overwhelming, and downright wild to imagine the enormous impact our breath can have. But it's all backed by well-researched science. And speaking from experience, it works.

There's more to discover with the Wim Hof Method. You're rewiring your brain and tweaking your nervous system, among other things. Here's what else is happening, based on neuroscience:

1. **Hack your autonomic nervous system:** This is what controls the things you don't think about, like your heartbeat and breathing. The Wim Hof breathing technique calms your fight-or-flight response and boosts relaxation.

2. **Experience altered states:** Want euphoria without psychedelics? This is the place to go. The intense hyperventilation and breath hold can shift your blood gasses, leading to experiences from deep euphoria to visual trips. It's a totally natural high brought to you by the real star: your breath.

3. **Turn down the pain dial:** Whether through endorphins (your body's natural painkillers) or shifting your consciousness, this method can change how you perceive pain. It's kind of like applying an Icy Hot patch to aches and pains. Only it's the "Iceman" patch helping you handle discomfort in a whole new way.

4. **Squash inflammation:** When you dampen inflammation, you can alleviate "sickness behavior"—the fatigue and exhaustion accompanying illness. This method signals your immune system to stop overreacting so it can peacefully do its job to help you heal.

5. **Boost stress resilience:** Wim Hof breathwork may rewire brain activity patterns linked to stress, like turning down the volume on your amygdala, the brain's alarm center. Instead of being a stressed-out mess, you become a stress-fighting machine.

6. **Supercharge your brain's flexibility:** Consistent practice boosts your brain's plasticity, building a more resilient and adaptable brain.

OTHER DIMENSIONS: HOLOTROPIC BREATHING

Think of this like Navy SEALs training for your mind and emotions, crafted to unlock deeper levels of self-awareness and healing—using only your breath. Holotropic ("moving toward wholeness") Breathwork was developed in 1974 by Dr. Stanislav

"Stan" Grof and his late wife, Christina Grof, as a replacement for LSD after the psychedelic era hit a legal snag. After treating thousands of patients with LSD in Czechoslovakia (it was not the Czech Republic back then) and seeing unbelievable breakthroughs, Stan knew he needed to find a way to continue diving deep into the psyche, and he pivoted. He embraced yoga and crafted his breathwork that mimicked the LSD state without any substances based on scientifically analyzing what people saw in therapy while on LSD. As giants in the field of psychedelic research, he and his wife single-handedly created the field of transpersonal psychology. It was revolutionary.

It was a time of mind expansion and exploration, but now psychedelics were off the table (legally speaking). Stan didn't let that stop him, though. Using Holotropic Breathwork as a radical way to continue exploring the human mind, he combined rapid breathing techniques, evocative music, and a bit of existential curiosity to unlock a new level of understanding and healing. You can find out more about it on *The Human Upgrade* podcast.[11] Here's how you do it:

Step 1: Find a breathing buddy. One person breathes deeply and rapidly, transcending ordinary consciousness, while the other observes. Safety first, enlightenment second.

Step 2: Settle into a quiet and comfortable space—this will be the launchpad for your mental expedition.

Step 3: Select music that feeds your soul—from pounding drums to soothing symphonies and everything in between. Each track guides your journey, so be intentional about what you choose. For inspiration, do an internet search for "Holotropic Breathwork soundtracks."

Step 4: This is where the breath cranks up. We're talking fast, deep, transformative breaths that change the body's chemistry just enough to send your mind into new states.

Step 5: Release—laugh, cry, shout, dance—whatever wants to come up, let it pour out of you. This is all about releasing anything bottled up inside.

Step 6: Afterward, relax and chat with your partner (or a group) about your experience. This debrief is crucial to make sense of what just happened.

The first time I paid any attention to Holotropic Breathwork, I was a thirty-year-old engineer, newly single, and feeling pretty lost. Sure, I knew about meditation, but I wasn't actively seeking it. Nobody talked about it back then. But then a friend reached out: "Dave, you have to try this." "What is it?" I asked. "Trust me, if I tell you, you won't go." This piqued my curiosity. I was desperate enough to bite.

So, without any details other than the time and place, I found myself at this personal development retreat, clueless about what I had just gotten myself into but open-minded. After mingling in a room for a while, the facilitator asked everyone to get comfortable on their yoga mat. As soon as everyone was in position, an epic movie soundtrack of sorts played, and we began this intense, rapid breathing.

It felt like tripping balls—my mind was on a hyperdrive tour of the universe. But there were no drugs involved. You're basically hyperventilating, oxygen levels all over the place, but combined with the music and the environment, it dug up stuff deeper than anything I've experienced, even more profound than my trips with ayahuasca. And I did this with none other than Stan Grof himself, the godfather of transpersonal psychology.

According to Stan, we've all got these birth stages we go through, from hanging out in the womb to the panic of being born. His work suggests our major hang-ups trace back to these moments, and this breathwork lets you confront and clear those hang-ups, no drugs required.

So, there I was, doing Holotropic Breathwork with the master himself. I'm breathing intensely, the room is vibrating with energy, and I'm diving into the emotional roller coaster of my birth, my past lives, and my psyche. I remembered having the cord wrapped around my neck during childbirth, and some other things later confirmed with my mom that I couldn't have consciously recalled otherwise. It was a mind-blowing realization: the world is infinitely more complex and interconnected than I ever imagined. It's a deep system cleanse for your soul, done safely by pros who know how to navigate these waters carefully and compassionately.

A quick important note about psychedelics. These substances can be profound tools, taking your mind to places you've never dreamed possible. We'll get into those in detail later. But if your intuition is telling you that psychedelics aren't for you, listen to that. You don't need them to reach these deep, transformative states; your breath can get you there. I'm not dismissing the value of a good psychedelic journey—they can be incredibly helpful, amplifying your experiences and breakthroughs. Remember, it's all about finding what works for you to unlock new levels of awareness. Who cares what everyone else is doing—you do you. For anyone wondering about whether or not they "should" use psychedelics, that's your call. Make sure you're fully supported and in a safe environment if you decide to go that route.

So, during all this, what's happening in your brain? Check this out:

Your session might start with you feeling alert, maybe even a bit anxious about what to expect. Beta waves rule your mind here, but as you start breathing rapidly, these begin to shift. As you get deeper into the breathing, your brain relaxes, moving you into an alpha state. Think of this as your brain's "idle mode," as it starts to loosen up, letting go of the stress and noise. This is about the time things get a little trippy. The deep, continuous, and intense breathing can put you into a theta state, typically seen during deep meditation and light sleep. This is where the magic happens during this practice. Imagine accessing the back-end code of your subconscious, uncovering insights and memories hidden beneath the surface. Sometimes you might dip into delta, but that's less common. Delta is more of a dreamless sleep state associated with healing and regeneration. If you hit this level during breathwork, it can be a powerful reset for the brain. But it takes work to get there.

During Holotropic Breathwork, your brain essentially downshifts from its usual high-speed, problem-solving beta state into the more expansive, surreal alpha and theta realms. This shift lets you process and release emotional baggage and stimulates new insights and ideas, making it a super-supportive tool for personal development.

OTHER DIMENSIONS: DR. JOE DISPENZA

Dr. Joe Dispenza leads one of the most transformative breathwork experiences I've encountered. Joe was a keynote speaker at my 2024 Biohacking Conference, bringing the hard science to breathwork and meditation, grounding his spiritual practice in solid research.

When you attend one of Joe's advanced retreats, prepare for over eight hours a day of intense breathwork and meditation. It's not for the fainthearted, but the rewards? They're monumental. People come out of these retreats reporting some of their most profound spiritual experiences. I've had the privilege to dive into one of these advanced sessions. Despite my extensive background in exploring altered states, Joe's methods opened up new pathways for me. I reached states of consciousness, particularly during healing sessions, that offered what felt like direct access to the Divine—something not found elsewhere, despite my spiritual journeys through Nepal, Tibet, China, and South America.

Joe doesn't just talk a big game—he walks it. He straps EEG caps on participants to track brain waves and doesn't stop there. He analyzes saliva, tears, blood, and even urine. Under the scrutiny of scientific instruments, Joe's practices have shown effects that surpass those of pharmaceuticals. These aren't small-scale experiments, either. These studies involve thousands of participants and generate billions of data points, conducted with the precision of the University of California, San Diego's Dr. Hemal Patel, a top mitochondrial biologist. They're not just impressive; they're groundbreaking, showing real, measurable changes in mitochondria after breathwork and meditation sessions.

Dr. Dispenza and Dr. Patel did something pretty cool—they tested people's blood at meditation workshops before and after the sessions. After meditating, they found that everyone had more natural virus-fighting elements in their blood. Meditation might do more than just clear your head—it could also amp up your body's defense against viruses like SARS-CoV-2.[12] If that's not reason enough to quiet your mind and focus on your breath for a bit, I don't know what is.

Dr. Dispenza and his team are on a quest to uncover how meditation can literally rewire our biology. Their massive QUANTUM study[13] (short for "QUest to ANalyze a Thousand hUmans Meditating") found some seriously hopeful news for anyone battling cancer. Just seven days of meditation cranked up levels of chorismate mutase, a critical enzyme that boosts the body's anticancer and antibacterial defenses. Plus they found that the levels of HAD hydrolase, an enzyme that creates resistance to cancer treatments, decreased during these seven days. This is big news for how meditation can impact our health at a cellular level.

This is biohacking at its finest, pushing the boundaries of what we understand about the mind, body, and spirit. Dr. Joe Dispenza is doing more than just enhancing the spiritual experience. He's revolutionizing it with undeniable scientific evidence. That's the kind of stuff we logical-minded people love—even those of us who have come to embrace the woo-woo stuff now, too.

| SACRED SEXUALITY |

You might be surprised to find a book on Zen states and high-performance altered states talking about tantra, sex, and, yes, even something called conscious kink. But there's a method to the madness. These aren't just topics to raise eyebrows or make you uncomfortable. However, if you are uncomfortable, that might be something to consider, and you might ask yourself, why? We all have a body with parts, desires, and needs. There's no shame in owning and honoring it. Like every other "state" discussed in this book, these "taboo" topics are also deeply felt states that occur both in the body and the mind. We might measure these states in the brain, but they're profoundly rooted in the physical.

When people come to 40 Years of Zen and go through the Reset Process, it's essentially about tuning in to the body's most primal signals—what you feel in your heart, your gut, and yes, even in your first chakra (or root chakra, located at the base of the spine at the perineum). For those not fluent in yoga-speak, we're talking about your reproductive system. These taboo topics aren't just about sexuality or biology, but about grounding yourself in reality. Your first chakra is a critical node in your body's energetic sensing network, profoundly influencing your brain's processing center.

Get this: If you've ever walked into a room and something felt off, that sensation didn't start in your head. It likely started in what tantra refers to as your yoni or lingam—or what's more commonly referred to as your vagina (pussy) or penis (cock). If that makes you blush, cool. Laugh it off and keep reading. It's about time we remove the stigma around the very natural, primal hunger we all have to experience pleasure. The aim is to access and understand the energy of your most basic yet powerful physical senses to achieve higher states of awareness and performance. And it just so happens your first chakra holds a lot of power.

Tantra is about more than spirituality or connection; it's a practice of longevity and accessing sacred altered states through the powerful channel of creation energy—essentially the same as sexual energy. The point is to harness and purify this potent force that originates in your body and then elevate it to enrich your mind.

There's some fascinating research out there on the link between religious experiences and orgasms. Studies suggest that the intense, profound feelings you get during orgasm can sometimes feel spiritual or transcendent, similar to religious experiences.[14, 15] It's like your brain is tapping into the same neural pathways during these peak moments, whether in the bedroom or a place of worship. On the outside, it might look like someone's just having a great time in bed. But internally, pleasure can be a transformative and profound experience.

At 40 Years of Zen, clients sometimes hit a wall when they strive to break through new heights, whether it's a state of heightened awareness, forgiveness, or expansiveness. Often they're stuck on a looping thought or a deep-seated worry about past criticisms. When conventional techniques stall, we suggest a shift: imagine a sexual fantasy. Did you just squirm? Perfect. Again, laugh it off and keep reading.

The crucial piece of this shift is to move out of the mind and into the body and feel it coursing through your entire being. This technique has reliably increased and organized alpha brain waves in our clients, facilitating a breakthrough to more apparent, more focused states of consciousness. They might have some gamma, but their beta drops. Because who's going to think about making love if you're in a fight-or-flight state? This technique helps to shift yourself out of anxiety and into connectedness consciously.

One of tantra's most incredible gifts is transforming something society deems shameful and taboo into something sacred. Carrying shame is like dragging a heavy anchor—it zaps your energy and muddles your alpha brainwaves. And we like these creative, relaxed, alert brain waves. You can't bask in a state of profound grace if shame has its shackles around you. Tantra helps lift these burdens.

There's a related practice emerging, conscious kink, pioneered by somatic therapist Kimi Inch,[16] who presented at my biohacking conference. Yes, the term *kink* might make you think of getting a spanking—and according to surveys, this desire is more common than you might think. I can't help but wonder: Could this be traced back to those childhood moments when you got caught sneaking out and ended up facing the wrath of a wooden spoon? Maybe that's when you mastered escaping to more pleasurable realms in your mind during less-than-ideal physical circumstances.

But this isn't something most people talk about at dinner parties unless maybe you're at Kimi's dinner party. Conscious kink—indeed, kink in general—isn't about abuse. (If abuse is occurring, it's not kink.) Conscious kink is about exploring physical sensations to induce profound altered states—states that aren't necessarily orgasmic or Kundalini.

If you're unfamiliar with Kundalini, it's the ultimate biohack hidden in your body, waiting to unleash your untapped potential. Deep within you, at the base of your spine, lies a primal force or energy. In Sanskrit, *kundal* means coiled, and *ini* means power.

So, think of Kundalini as this dormant superpower, coiled up and ready to act. This is the essence of all consciousness, the very life force that pulses through every part of the universe and sits quietly within each of us. When awakened, Kundalini Shakti has the potential to elevate your mind and spirit, pushing the boundaries of what you think is possible and catapulting you into enlightenment. If you've ever heard the term "kundalini awakening," this is what it means.

Awakening this energy involves a combination of practices designed to cleanse and activate the chakras, ultimately leading to spiritual enlightenment. Start by setting an intention and creating a quiet, sacred space. Focus on deep breaths, moving into "breath of fire"—a powerful breathing technique involving rapid, forceful, and passive exhales—to cleanse your energy channels. Chant mantras like "Sat Nam" ("truth is my identity") to focus your mind. Move through specific yoga poses and kriyas designed to awaken your Kundalini energy. Visualize a coiled serpent at your spine's base, slowly rising through your chakras (there are seven main chakras that run along your spine). Finish with deep relaxation in savasana to integrate the energies.

These states can offer deep healing and a sense of connectedness, arising from sensations that aren't inherently painful—they could be as gentle as a feather's touch (quite literally if you're practicing conscious kink). It's about being present with a partner and exploring how mild to intense physical sensations can transport you physically, emotionally, mentally, and spiritually. It's a practice that aligns with Tantra but stands out because you can engage in conscious kink fully clothed. In contrast, Tantra typically involves getting down to business at some point, although Tantra doesn't have to do that.

I bring up these practices because, over the years, after giving a keynote speech on this, people consistently come up and share their experiences with creation energy, orgasmic energy, and even the effects of ejaculation on mental performance in men. We have science to back these discussions; there's no reason to feel ashamed. They are profound, scientifically supported ways that many people achieve healing altered states.

In fact, according to Jaiya,[17] a leader in somatic sexology and the creator of the Erotic Blueprint Breakthrough™, people vary in their sexual expressions. She's identified five Erotic Blueprint Types™ that you can think of as love languages for the bedroom. These blueprints help us understand and navigate our and our partners' unique sexual desires and needs to enrich our intimate connections and overall well-being. I interviewed Miss Jaiya on the podcast,[18] so if this topic interests you, check it out. It's juicy!

People are diverse, and what resonates with one might not work for another. Some people are all energetic (one of the blueprint types) and might respond well to Tantra and its deep sensual practices. Others might find that conscious kink pushes their buttons. It doesn't matter. Whatever your thing is—soulful eye-gazing, synchronized breathing, heart-to-heart connection visualizing mystical Tantra, or maybe it's getting a spanking—embrace it. Life is way more pleasurable when you put outside approval and fear aside and lean into your curiosity.

What's important is recognizing how these experiences can transform the chaos in your brain into focused energy, guiding you toward a specific mental space. This is why, at 40 Years of Zen, when a client is stuck, we often explore unconventional paths to meditation. And yes, it's perfectly okay to entertain a fantasy about your partner or whatever else frees your mind. All you're doing is telling your brain, "Hey, let's get out of this state and into something that feels better." Just a note of caution: for the purpose of the practices outlined here, steer clear of porn; it doesn't create the genuine personal connection of self-awareness these practices aim to cultivate. Using *ethical* porn as a tool for healing—to provide those with sexual/intimacy trauma a sense of empowerment and control—is a discussion for another time.

Practices like conscious kink, Tantra, meditation, and even psychedelics can all come with a dark side if they're misused. But when handled with care, these powerful tools can elevate consciousness without harm.

Tantra and conscious kink, which often begin with breathwork, imagery, and settling into your body, suspiciously resembles mindfulness during a yoga class. This is because, at their core, they aim to guide you into similar transformative states. Holding an intense yoga pose might awaken your mind and leave you feeling amazing. Or, maybe while doing that position, someone spanks you, and it puts you in an altered state. That's awesome, too, as long as they're not spanking you with kale. Rude. The point is, how you get there doesn't matter. The goal is to find practices that align best with your wiring and help you access these life-altering states safely, easily, and quickly.

So, let's take a look at your brain waves during these transcendent practices.

Your Brain on Conscious Kink

Initially, as the anticipation builds, your brain's beta waves might rev up. These waves are associated with active, engaged thinking and problem-solving. But they're also linked to stress and anxiety. As the kink session builds and you start to find your flow, these waves can decrease, making room for more relaxing brainwave states. As you relax deeper into the experience, alpha waves increase. This state is important as you transition into a state of physical and mental relaxation while maintaining a clear mind with a sense of awareness.

Your Brain on Tantra

Tantra often begins with a conscious decision to engage deeply with the practice. This activation of beta waves signals waking consciousness and logical thinking, helping you focus your intentions and actions. As your breath becomes more rhythmic and you settle into the tantric experience, your brain relaxes while your alpha waves increase. This is great for mind-body integration and deep emotional and physical connection.

As the tantra practice deepens, usually during longer, more meditative, or intensely connected moments, theta waves swoop in and make themselves known. This is typically where profound insights, emotional releases, and a sense of unity with oneself and your partner can occur. Gamma waves might ramp up if you enter advanced meditative states, like the ones where you feel an increased sense of consciousness or compassion. This can also feel like unity or oneness, much like you hear about in spiritual practices.

It's possible to tap into delta waves in the most profound tantric practices, but it's not as common. These waves are predominant during deep, dreamless sleep, so reaching delta during a tantra session might feel like a deep sense of interconnectedness with all things, deep peace, and spiritual awakening.

| CREATION ENERGY |

This isn't a book on the neuroscience of breathwork—it's a toolbox loaded with accessible, highly effective tools and techniques to radically transform and enhance your life. These methods can help you evolve as a human and experience more peace, happiness, freedom, compassion, and joy. And they're much cheaper than pharmaceuticals and even your daily high-quality meals.

You might have opened this chapter and rolled your eyes at the thought of using breathwork to improve your reality. If so, you'd be among plenty of others who dismiss breathwork as trivial. Hopefully, the information you've just read changed your mind or at least made you curious. When used with intention, these are some of the most profound practices I know of to radically transform your life. Whether it's the electric surge you feel during a Joe Dispenza workshop, the deep shifts of Holotropic Breathwork, or the intense energy of Tantra and conscious kink, these practices are about channeling life force in massive ways.

Imagine being at a hotel during a conference and walking by to see two thousand people in a room. They're breathing deeply, and Dr. Dispenza's voice is booming over the loudspeaker with instructions, "Breathe deeper, now squeeze," followed by a collective moaning. It sounds like they're filming porn or having an orgy, but they're not. What's actually happening is a massive release of Kundalini, that vital creation energy, through intentional breathwork and meditation that feels like you're shooting electrical energy up your spine and out the top of your head—and it often sounds and feels like an orgasm. Why do erotic-related practices hit so hard? Because they tap into the very energy we use to create life, making them incredibly potent for accessing altered states.

You'll often hear breathwork instructors emphasize posture: "Sit up with your back straight." When I first started practicing yoga with the Art of Living breathwork and even during meditations in a Tibetan monastery over twenty years ago, hearing this annoyed me. Why does this matter? Joe Dispenza broke it down scientifically: Sitting up straight helps create a wave in your cerebral spinal fluid, impacting your brain structures, including your pineal gland. The wiggle of your pineal gland can release Kundalini energy and, according to Joe, even help manifest your desires in the physical world. And it probably does.

Whether or not you buy into all aspects of these teachings, the physical effects are undeniable. Ordinary people can appear as if they're experiencing the peak of ecstasy when it's really just the powerful release of this dormant energy—which, by the way, most people only tap into during exceptional moments or, well, really good sex. But guess what? You can use this same energy to build companies, create new life, and inspire global movements.

How do I know? Because I've leveraged creation energy for decades. Over the last twenty-five years, traveling the world to learn from different masters, I've used every technique in this book numerous times. All of them, at some point or another, have helped manage the school of fish swimming in my brain. They invite the experience of heightened states of consciousness, grace, gratitude, and forgiveness—and there are more tools to discover every day. These kinds of heightened experiences are possible for you, too. Unless you think you're already fully enlightened. But let's face it, you're probably not—that's not a judgment, it's just the truth.

If this information piqued your curiosity then get ready, because we're just getting started. You can achieve altered states through so many different modalities. As you move through this next part of the book, I will guide you through some of the most profound ones I've personally used and those we've seen the most impact with at 40 Years of Zen, all according to science.

GO SPANK YOURSELF

A few years back, at one of our biohacking conferences, we set up this three-story platform on a rooftop and had people jump off into a massive stunt cushion below—don't worry, we have insurance. Even the hotel owner joined in. But when he reached the edge and peeked over, you could sense his fear moving upward, turning his face white like a ghost. "No way, I can't do this," he said with a shaky voice. Jumping off buildings isn't everyone's idea of a good time. But after a little pep talk, he calmly shut his eyes, sprinted toward the dreadful drop-off, and leaped into the air. This literal leap of faith is a moment where you're pretty sure you won't die, but it feels like you might. Your MeatOS kicks in—in the form of fear—to keep you safe. The trick to hacking your impressive MeatOS is to push through something scary and come out okay on the other side. Your success signals your brain that you're more resilient than you thought. Do this enough times and you build your mental resilience, making you dangerous in the best way possible.

It's the same with cold therapy. Nobody in their right mind thinks, *Yay, let's freeze in icy water and call it relaxation.* It sounds miserable and not that cool (no pun intended), but that's not true. When you've trained your brain and body to survive and *thrive* in discomfort, your limits expand, and you grow. And once you step out of that icy cold box, you're not only alive—you're invigorated. There's beauty in pushing your limits. It turns out that pleasure can follow pain.

Throughout history, cultures worldwide have danced with pain, embracing brief moments of discomfort for profound reasons. This is because it resets your dopamine sensitivity.

Imagine your brain as a mega control center that decides how much you like something, like your favorite song or your fancy morning latte. Dopamine is what makes you feel that surge of thrill when something positive happens. Sometimes, if you do a lot of stuff that consistently gives you these dopamine hits, your brain gets lazy. It stops getting as enthusiastic about the little things that used to bring it pleasure because it's getting them all the time, and they lose their allure.

This is where the idea of intentional (and consensual) pain can be beneficial. I know it sounds weird. Why would you want to feel pain? But here's the interesting part: When you do something challenging, like jumping into an unheated outdoor pool in the winter, your brain sends out a rush of dopamine to help you feel better quickly. Your brain says, "Hey, you're doing something hard, but I've got your back!" It's a mental test, for sure. But you can totally ace it with practice.

Doing this kind of tough stuff every once in a while improves your brain's ability to embrace, even enjoy, pain without harming yourself. Mixing in a few challenges helps your brain get excited about the small, everyday things again. It starts to appreciate simple joys, like how amazing your bed feels after a really long day or how delicious the perfect steak tastes when you're super hungry. It helps you stop taking things for granted and amplifies your gratitude.

| PAIN, PLEASURE, AND PURPOSE |

When you hear the term *masochist*, what comes to mind? Someone enthralled in the world of BDSM? A marathoner who chooses to run a crazy amount of miles while their knees scream in pain? Maybe you think of someone with piercings all over their face and body—or ice bath aficionados. Whatever comes to mind, the truth remains: every single one of these people *chooses* to feel pain on purpose—all in search of something pleasurable later. And while masochism can be about sex, it doesn't have to be. These tendencies are natural. How they manifest in each person may differ, but the underlying desire is the same: feel pain now to feel pleasure later.

Some of the most intriguing practices mix a pinch of pain with a dose of purpose. Some you know of, while others you may question their reasoning (we'll get into that). You may even find some extremely odd, but you're curious to know more (we'll get into that, too). Masochism is human; intentional and consensual pain is not new. Think about competitive food eaters who sweat and pant through eating their hundredth water-soaked hot dog, all before they vomit. Or lithe ballerinas dancing in pointe shoes without toenails because "the show must go on." Workaholics are another prime example of the masochist role at play. Sure, it feels bad while you're doing it. But pleasure often follows, and that's what these pain-seekers are running toward, sometimes in a somewhat bizarre way.

Take tattoos, for instance. Some people get them to look edgy, but it's a rite of passage for many, where enduring the needle's sting can symbolize various personal or cultural transformations or milestones. Then there are those who revel in the fiery thrill of eating extremely spicy peppers as a sport or diving into vats of wasabi while their face melts and they gasp for air. These challenges test our limits, endurance, and sometimes our ability to not immediately reach for a gallon of organic raw milk. Some call it crazy, while others stand by their decisions as opportunities for growth. I guess you could say it's a matter of perspective.

Another fascinating example comes from certain monastic traditions, where monks engage in self-flagellation. I used to be horrified by the thought of this. Like why would you do something that hurts yourself? But they aren't inflicting harm or causing irreparable damage. Yes, the practice of whipping yourself first thing in the morning might sound extreme and probably not as relaxing as waking peacefully with the sun. But there's a purpose. The sensation allows the monks to lightly stimulate their pain receptors and heighten their senses, making the rest of their day's experiences feel more profound by contrast. Initially, this practice might seem shocking, but it sets a sensory baseline that transforms their perception of everyday experiences. It kind of makes you think of conscious kink—it's just another form of flagellation with the help of a friend. You could do self-flagellation like monks, but partnering seems like it might be more accessible. Give it a try, or don't. That's entirely up to you.

Back in ancient Greece, the original Olympic athletes were hardcore. Imagine sprinting long distances in full armor—sounds really hard, doesn't it? These guys weren't just training to win laurel wreaths; they were building grit and resilience, qualities as essential on the battlefield as in the sports arena. The Greeks believed that enduring physical pain could fortify the mind, preparing an athlete to compete and conquer. So many popular movies showcase and celebrate this ritual—*Troy, 300, Spartacus, Hercules, Wonder Woman*, to name a few. It's incredible what they put their bodies through in preparation to fight.

Then you've got the Native American tribes that still perform a variation of the Sun Dance today without the element of self-torture. This isn't your average eighties dance-off with epic guitar solos, embarrassing style, and even worse hair. No. Back in the day, participants pierced their chests, tethered themselves to a central pole with ropes, and danced around it, pulling against their piercings in a grueling test of physical and spiritual endurance. Why? As a sacrifice for the greater good, a prayer for the community's prosperity, and a profound demonstration of personal commitment and bravery.

In various hot spots around the globe, from Greece to India and Japan, fire-walking is a big thing. Yes, literally walking over hot coals. I do not recommend trying this at home as a party trick during your next barbecue. Don't do it on a first date. Or, actually, maybe you should. You can see how they handle challenges right out of the gate. Let me know how that goes.

People fire-walk to test their courage, purify their spirits, or even attract good luck and health. You step into the flames of fear to walk out stronger—maybe with slightly sore feet. Speaking of modern fire-walking, Tony Robbins incorporates this practice into his events like Unleash the Power Within, which I had the pleasure of speaking at in 2017. Participants often leave feeling invigorated, empowered, and ready to tackle their challenges head-on, much like the ancient practitioners hoped. It's wild to experience it firsthand. But also, to see others who are terrified to do it and come out on the other side ecstatic at what they just did, tears streaming down their cheeks, faces plastered with joy, that's pretty awesome, too.

Then there's fasting, which I have been recommending for years. Fasting isn't just about skipping meals to lose a few pounds—it's about upgrading your entire body and brain. When you fast, you flip a metabolic switch that shifts your body from burning sugar to burning fat. It's like hitting a reset button on your body's energy systems. We're not just talking about keeping your body lean but about extending your life, preventing disease, and seriously ramping up your brain power. And it's a universal favorite that transcends borders and religions. Whether it's Ramadan, Yom Kippur, or Lent, ditching food and drink from dawn to dusk isn't just about following rules—it's a deep dive into self-discipline. It purifies the body and mind and is a spiritual reboot that millions find mentally clarifying, stripping back to the essentials and finding strength in simplicity.

People talk a lot about how hard or depriving fasting is, like they're always starving and cranky. Well, like any new challenge, it might suck at first. That's true. But if you do it right, your body will learn to adapt, and it won't suck forever. Fasting the right way feels good, not bad. But it might take practice to get there. I wrote all about it in *Fast This Way*, so you can check that out for details on different ways to fast if you're curious.

Let's talk about something pretty intense and understandably controversial—sati. Back in the day in India, this practice involved burning a widow alive alongside her deceased husband to ensure all the sins of them and their family were clean. Pretty extreme. It was all about devotion—their way of showing loyalty and love. And, through this pain, ensuring pleasure in the afterlife.[1] I don't know about you, but I'd prefer to show that while my partner is alive and skip death altogether—that's kind of the point of biohacking: living as long as possible in a healthy body and mind. Thankfully, we don't see this cultural practice today; it was banned in 1829 by the first governor-general of British-ruled India. But it shows how deep, ancient cultural beliefs can drive people to take some pretty dramatic actions.

These practices show us that across cultures and ages, pain isn't just an obstacle; it's often a vehicle, transporting the enduring and the brave to higher realms of spiritual and personal fulfillment. This is just another way of saying "altered states." A little pain for a whole lot of gain. It makes you wonder if it's time to upgrade how you test your limits—done safely and consensually, of course.

| HURTS SO GOOD |

The idea of "hurts so good" is partly about seeking pain but even more so about the *value* of doing something painful. There's an entire book about it by that name. Written by a science writer and researcher—and a self-proclaimed high-sensation-seeking masochist—the book opens with a pretty spicy masochistic scene that might make the average person squirm, possibly even cringe or have their jaw hit the floor. Warning: the personal experience they share is graphic and may trigger people with a history of sexual trauma; read at your discretion. But that's not what this is about.

In their book *Hurts So Good: The Science and Culture of Pain on Purpose*,[2] Leigh Cowart dives deep into this wild world where pain meets pleasure. They start by exploring how everyone feels pain differently and why some of us even like it, thanks to the chemicals in our brains. When you push yourself through a rigorous workout or dare to handle those spicy foods, your brain releases feel-good chemicals like endorphins and dopamine, which we already covered. It's your brain's way of giving you a mental high five for pushing through a challenge.

But it doesn't start and stop with sports and food. Have you ever wondered why you can't stop watching true-crime documentaries or why scary movies keep you hooked? It's because seeing others in pain can make us feel a rush of relief and pleasure when it's over. It's science. Neuroimaging and neurophysiological studies show that feeling others' pain involves the same neural structures as those involved in the first-person experience of pain.[3]

BDSM is an umbrella term for a variety of sexual practices; the acronym stands for bondage, discipline, dominance, submission, sadism, and masochism. As an overall practice, BDSM utilizes pain as a clear path to pleasure. The trust and thrill of pushing boundaries *with consent* in a safe environment (SSC, or Safe, Sane, and Consensual, is the number one rule above all) can be exhilarating. It might sound intense, but it's just another way for people to explore and express their deepest desires and find a unique kind of freedom through kink.

What we're talking about here is something called BPET—Brief Pain Exposure Therapy. But we're going to modify the acronym and definition slightly to BICEP: Brief Intentional Conscious Exposure to Pain. Think of this like hitting the gym for your neurotransmitters—those tiny chemical messengers in your brain that control everything from your mood to how much energy you feel. BICEP can be beneficial as long as you're not harming yourself or others in the process. This is an area of research that shows surprising and counterintuitive results, especially for people with ADHD or depression and anxiety.

A 2014 study showed that cryotherapy sessions significantly reduce symptoms of depression.[4] There is also scientific evidence that a single session of exercise can lead to immediate improvements in ADHD symptoms.[5] So, while it may not feel great while doing either of these, some might argue that the benefits far outweigh the pain.

When you do something strenuous, like an all-out sprint or an intense sauna session, you challenge yourself physically, mentally, and sometimes emotionally. Here's what happens: Your brain goes, "Okay, we need to figure out how to deal with this so we don't die," and starts pumping out some powerful stuff. The first is dopamine, a feel-good chemical usually released when something feels good or pleasurable. But during pain, it's more about getting you through the challenge, helping you focus, and pushing you to overcome it.

Then there are endorphins—these are your body's natural painkillers. They jump into action during these difficult moments to help manage the pain and make you feel downright euphoric afterward. Have you ever heard of a runner's high? That's your endorphins at work. But that's not all. There's also serotonin and norepinephrine. Serotonin helps keep your mood balanced, but during a pain challenge, it dips and strengthens, helping you feel even better afterward. Norepinephrine signals alertness and energy, keeping you sharp, especially in stressful situations.

What's cool is that by doing these tough things on purpose, you train your brain to handle stress better, be more resilient, and improve your mental health. You're upgrading your brain's ability to cope with life's challenges using pain as a catalyst for self-growth.

So next time you wonder why someone would choose to run an extra mile (or 26.2), eat that scorching pepper, sit through a gruesome horror movie, or be tied up and smacked around with floggers, consider this: seeking pain can lead to discovering more profound pleasure and purpose, becoming a stronger version of ourselves.

| MASTERING THE CHILL |

You were probably wondering when we would dive into this. We saved one of the best for last. It's an OG pain-to-pleasure practice that I've personally engaged in for years. But in the beginning, it totally sucked. But remember, not everything pleasurable feels that way when you start—do it anyway and see what happens. Now, you can dive into this intensely frigid adventure in several ways. You've got your standard cold plunge at around 45 degrees Fahrenheit, which gives you a nice kick of physiological perks like activating your brown fat—your body's built-in-calorie-burning furnace. You might even snag a rush of endorphins (remember, those are your body's natural happy pills).

But then, there's the hard-core version—the 37-degree cold plunge. This one might take some encouraging self-talk, but you will feel amazing when you finish. It's like the ghost pepper of cold plunges. It demands more grit and willpower, and trust me, it's a less comfortable experience. But the payoff? Huge. You're not just getting the physical benefits; you're tapping into profound pain-relieving perks, and willpower wins. Most of this magic happens because it cranks up your dopamine—the chemical in your brain that helps you feel more alert and alive. After a plunge like that, your body is ready to welcome dopamine more efficiently throughout the day, making everything else more enjoyable. The chillier plunge will be more arduous, but you reap greater rewards. Here's a tip: Whether you're braving the 45 or the 37 degrees, dip your hands in the water. It's the most difficult part but amplifies the benefits, making the pain even more worth it.

Warning: You might just start to like your job, kids, spouse, neighbors, and entire life even more. Sounds horrible, right? Kidding. These are great things to look forward to! All because you took time to yourself to push your limits and trust your body to do its job while breathing your way through a frosty ice bath. Good for you.

There's a spectrum of how we can engage with discomfort to unlock joy. According to the insights from Jaiya's work on erotic blueprints, about 20 percent of people find distinct happiness in these practices that shock the body and exacerbate pleasure. Whether getting that metaphorical spanking from a cold plunge or more literal experiences, it's all about the same neurobiology. Whatever floats your boat; I'm not here to judge. It's all about finding what makes you tick and using it to boost your happiness and resilience while improving your brain.

| PAIN HACKING |

Let's tie this all back to your wildly beautiful brain. Initially, when you first feel pain, your brain lights up with fast-moving beta waves—to recap, these are your brain's red-alert signals. But then your brain starts to pump out endorphins, which relieve pain. As the endorphins kick in, your brain relaxes and shifts from the hectic beta waves to the smoother alpha and theta waves. As the pain eases up or you simply get used to it, you suddenly feel blissful. How? This blissful state is thanks to a remarkable phenomenon called pain offset relief—the calm you feel once intense pain stops. You also have that dopamine we discussed in the mix, which rewards you with good vibes. It's not really all that bad, right? Not if something good comes from it, anyway.

Think of it this way: If life is a gym for your soul, these painful practices are a pair of heavy weights. By lifting them, you not only build muscle; you boost your brain's feel-good chemicals and toughen up your emotional resilience—you turn pain into your playground. You might not laugh when you first jump in or bite down, but when you feel the zing of energy pulse through your veins and the mental clarity that comes from these challenging experiences, it's all worth it. Who said feeling good was supposed to be easy? If it hurts so good today, imagine how great you will feel tomorrow. Take it from a seasoned biohacker: the best gains often come wrapped in a bit of pain.

TRIP LIKE I DO

A lot of people have wild stories from college about tripping out at raves or music festivals with psychedelics. Me? I was a bit of a late bloomer in that department and didn't light up a joint until age twenty-six, while in Amsterdam, where it was legal. And when it came to shrooms, I had zero knowledge of how to use psychedelics, but still had an amusing first experience.

My curiosity sparked after diving into a book called *DMT: The Spirit Molecule.* It's about this eye-opening research from the 1970s at the University of New Mexico, focusing on DMT—one of the two active ingredients in the well-known psychedelic ayahuasca. But back in 1999, ayahuasca might as well have been a typo on the computer screen; nobody knew how to spell it, let alone what it was or how to use it properly. Reading about all the incredible spiritual experiences people had on this very hard-to-find, at the time, psychedelic, the undeniable fascination led me to Peru.

After settling into a guesthouse, I stumbled through some comical attempts at high school–level Spanish to convince the receptionist to help me find ayahuasca. Reluctantly, she finally connected me with a local shaman. It went something like, "Dondé ayahuasca?" "You're white," she replied. "Yeah, I know. But I've done my research," I said. "You'll throw up. It's only for locals." "Could you please ask? I'm prepared for this," I pleaded.

Two days later, a shaman showed up with his dog and took me to the little mud house where he lived. We went shopping for herbs before climbing up a mountain, where we stopped to set up camp. Without explanation, he surrounded us with a circle of stones. During preparations, he gave ayahuasca to his dog, which seemed strange. "Why do you give that to your dog?" I asked. "He goes on the journey with me and helps me," he replied. Then he laughed. "Plus, it keeps the farmers from shooting him." Which made us both laugh.

The shaman guided us through a traditional ceremony, serving the bitter, earthy-tasting liquid until I fell into a dreamy, magical state. I came out relatively early feeling good and wanted to integrate. "I'm going for a walk," I said. The shaman shot out of his seat. "No!" Confused by his exaggerated response, I stood on one leg and touched my nose to prove everything was fine. "I'm within my faculties," I assured him. "You're still open," he replied. "Who cares? Really, I'm okay." He just shook his head and looked at me like I was an idiot. "Do you see the circle of stones?" "Yes," I said. "Those are not there to keep you in. Those are there to keep everything else out while you are open. If you cross that line, I will have to spend time cleaning up the things that will stick to you. Don't cross that line until it's time. Got it?" *Ohhhhh.* Now the stones made sense. Out of respect for his process and "Grandmother Aya," I waited.

That was my first time adventuring with ayahuasca. While the journey wasn't as profound as I anticipated, it was undeniably eye-opening—enough to make the other participants switch religions (seriously).

I didn't feel called to ayahuasca again until I turned fifty. But that first experience made a lasting impression. After receiving shamanic training years later and befriending gurus from multiple different traditions around the globe, it's clear that ayahuasca is a bit of a wild card. It's not your run-of-the-mill psychedelic; it can install malware in your brain, your consciousness, your soul—anywhere in your MeatOS. It's a uniquely dangerous psychedelic that requires a skilled shaman, ideally from the Shipibo people, to guide you. To become a legit shaman takes eight years of training in the jungle while consuming ayahuasca on a very regular basis. It's like having a master's degree or PhD in protecting someone spiritually—it's a big deal. Respect the medicine, the journey, and your guide. Ayahuasca is not a psychedelic to play around with "just for fun." It's a confounding plant to work with, but it can also birth beautiful insights and growth from the darkness.

| NOT ALL PATHS LEAD TO PARADISE |

As we explore psychedelics, remember that they're not all cut from the same cloth. They can unlock your brain in ways you can't imagine, enhancing learning and flexibility with increased BDNF (brain-derived neurotrophic factor) and NGF (nerve growth factor). So, not only do you access altered, valuable mystical states that allow you to understand what's going on in a way that you wouldn't see in everyday reality, but the benefits of those states or anything else you do afterward, like meditation or integration work, will stick better because the brain is more flexible.

But there's a catch—some of these experiences can leave marks that aren't easy to shake off. That's why environment, mindset, and having an experienced guide are crucial if you choose to journey with any of them, especially if you're inexperienced.

Let this book be your road map or a way to approach these different altered states to find the things that work for you, with or without psychedelics. Psychedelics are usually not addictive or not highly addictive, but you should still use them with caution. Some people with a substance use disorder will use psychedelics to escape reality, but not because they're addicting (that's a misconception). LSD and ayahuasca are generally not known to cause physiological withdrawal symptoms like those associated with substances like alcohol, opioids, or benzodiazepines—or even caffeine and nicotine. Some users might experience a craving or desire to repeat the experience, especially if the trip was transformative. But it would be tough to take those every day unless you're training to be a shaman, where it might be required, at least for a short period. Experienced guides do not recommend regular use. And it's probably not the right way to enhance your longevity or spiritual state, either.

I feel compassion for some of the influencers in the space who openly brag, "I've done eighty-seven ayahuasca ceremonies, and now, I am a god in the bedroom." When are they going to get the message that it's not working? You've got to know when to say "enough is enough" and focus on integration. The idea is not to do it repeatedly but to learn the lessons and upgrade your life accordingly. If you feel like you have to keep going back because you are still dealing with the same crap and things aren't changing, there might be something deeper to look into, potentially without substances. Otherwise, you will continue chasing the feeling you get while under the influence instead of working on truly healing and integrating what you learned. Whatever you decide, have a guide to help you see and navigate your blind spots with compassion and clarity—no need to dive in alone. In fact, for your safety, please don't attempt a solo trip with these mind-altering substances.

| WARNING: INTENTIONAL USE ONLY |

People use psychedelics for many different reasons. Maybe you'd like more access to your altered states and to get there more quickly. Or you know you've got some stuck energy or traumas to work through, and you can't seem to go deep enough on your own. It could simply be to experience what it feels like to fully be in your body and drop out of your mind for a bit, especially if you tend to be an overthinker. Whatever your reason for embarking on such a journey, the proper use of psychedelics is to show you the door and to open it, leading to a greater understanding of yourself and the world around you. It's up to you to integrate your vision with everyday life.

When it comes to using any technique for spiritual awakening—whether it's yoga, psychedelics, or whatever—it helps to think of it like the Buddhist symbol of the raft. Buddha described his teachings as a raft that takes you from the shore of birth and death to the other shore of nirvana. But here's the thing: when you reach that shore, you leave the raft behind. The same idea pops up in Zen Buddhism with meditation problems. They say it's like knocking on a door with a brick. Once the door opens, you don't bring the brick inside. You leave it behind.

The feeling of ecstasy isn't the end goal with any of these altered states; it's just a step along the way. In Zen, when you have that awakening moment—known as satori—you'll feel that rush of ecstasy. But remember, that feeling is just a side effect, not the destination itself. Even some well-known psychedelic pioneers, like Alan Watts, only used LSD a handful of times before writing major works on psychedelics. He used psychedelics to expand his vision, and then he took action to integrate. The idea is expansion and continuous positive change, not unhealthy reliance.

I want to be doubly clear here. You can access the same altered states with other methods outside of these substances, like Holotropic Breathwork. Remember, Holotropic Breathwork became a replacement for LSD after its ban for therapeutic use. So, you don't have to take psychedelics. Like with many things, there are potential risks—and some of the risks are not small. Even with things that people think are healthy, like mushrooms or, in particular, ayahuasca, a meaningful number of people have mental breaks afterward. It can take months to heal psychologically if you have a bad reaction or if you choose to try it alone without the support of an expert to guide your experience and hold space for any darkness or reactions that arise.

It can be pretty uncomfortable when you uncover things buried for years, stuff you didn't even know existed in your MeatOS. That's why setting yourself up for the best experience is invaluable. Discomfort doesn't feel good, that's true. But it doesn't have to feel absolutely awful or downright debilitating, either.

While it's pretty rare, some small percentage of people, particularly those with Eastern European genetics, can get something called "serotonin syndrome"[1] from psychedelic use. It's like a serotonin overload in your brain, and if you have that genetic predisposition for this, then you can have serious complications. Your blood pressure goes exceptionally high, your whole body shakes, and you can stroke out unless you have access to, ideally, intravenous benzodiazepines. But even taking it in oral form can make a difference. What that means is that if you've never used psychedelics before and you don't know how you're going to respond, maybe doing it by yourself in the jungle isn't the best idea.

This chapter is not a call to use psychedelics. It's a call that if you decide to use them as a part of your spiritual path, part of your healing path, you do it in an environment with the least harm and the most benefits.

The first and most accessible psychedelic is the one that was all the rage in high school: cannabis. It's everywhere. But here's the scoop from Dr. Daniel Amen, who runs the Amen Clinics and has more than 600,000 brain scans of people, including lots of people who use cannabis and those who don't: regular use slows down your brain. It's not exactly what you want when you're aiming for high performance.

While occasional use may be anti-inflammatory and may benefit some brains, like those with autism or autoimmunity, regular use is not healthy for you or your brain. Dr. Amen is particularly well-known for working with Justin Bieber and Miley Cyrus to show them what regular use was doing to their brains and encourage them to do something different.

If you're looking to go into deep, altered states, cannabis probably isn't going to take you where you want to go. It can be a gateway to further psychedelic exploration, though. Just be aware of the risks, and be intentional with your use.

I understand that some people are devout supporters of cannabis. That's fine. There's no judgment here. This information is just a mix of science, experience, and over twenty-five years of curiosity and awareness from a neuroscience perspective. Take what resonates, and throw out the rest. This book aims to illuminate how to enter altered states to elevate your reality and live an exceptional life. Psychedelics are just one profoundly effective way to get there.

| ROAD TRIPPIN' |

Okay, we're going to nerd out a bit here. There is a ton of information to cover. So, to keep it concise and keep you interested, just know that we're only scratching the surface of psychedelic potential. I will give you all sorts of brain wave science, making it as straightforward as possible. Even if you don't think this is your thing, be curious. You never know. It might spark something you didn't know or hadn't thought of that could make all the difference.

Much like the Robert Frost poem, *The Road Not Taken*, there are two roads to choose from when deciding how to use psychedelics. One path is microdosing. Microdosing means taking a tiny dose, about 5 percent of what would typically send you on a cosmic journey. It's like giving your brain a gentle nudge instead of a full-on shove, enhancing your creativity and focus while keeping your feet planted on the ground. If you use it in chocolate bar form or similar, the seller might say it has half a gram in it or something. But it's really hard to measure how much is in each square this way, so just be cautious (and smart). If you want to be sure to know how much you're getting, go for the purest form, not mixed with candy, cookies, or any of the other snack options available.

It's a little-known secret amongst ultra-endurance athletes—these are the hard-core people who run 100-mile races—that a considerable number of them microdose LSD; it increases their endurance and does something beneficial for their brains. Again, that's only 5 percent of a full dose. So, years ago, I decided to microdose LSD during a business trip to Los Angeles. *Trip* being the operative word.

I didn't want to travel with a little vial of water, so I cut a tiny little piece of LSD on paper into twenty equal-sized pieces. These are little microdots, making them easy to carry while traveling. Well, so much for equal-sized. Not moments after stepping onto the stage in front of one hundred influential people, I started talking about something business-related while making jokes that only I laughed at. And the realization hit, *Oh, crap, I'm mildly high*, because one of those little tiny dots was bigger than the others. It was probably more like a quarter dose, or 15 percent of a dose, instead of 5 percent of the dose. Live and learn, right? It could have been a lot worse! Thankfully, it was still a fun experience—maybe even more so because of the fits of laughter, but we'll never know.

If you're going to microdose, don't wing it. Follow a protocol. And not just a random one from the internet. Find an expert, a guide, to show you how to have a safe experience. A typical protocol is using just 5 percent of a full dose three times a week. This is most common with LSD and mushrooms to get the cognitive-enhancing benefits without going on a galactic journey. That might be worth exploring if that's what you're after. But don't take it from me; do your research.

After that somewhat embarrassing experience onstage, I had the honor of chatting with Rick Doblin on *The Human Upgrade* podcast.[2] He's the visionary behind MAPS, the nonprofit that has been crucial in bringing psychedelic research back to the forefront. After that conversation, I decided to put microdosing to the test by using 5 percent of a typical LSD dose every day for a whole month. I experienced a mild brain enhancement, a gentle mental upgrade with a hint of creative sparkle. It was nothing drastic or life-altering, but it was interesting.

What we're talking about in the rest of this chapter, though, is the second road you can travel down: using full-dose psychedelics. I'm not going to recommend the exact full doses for each of these because this isn't a book on psychedelics, and I'm certainly not a psychedelic expert. Also, because the strength and strain you use may differ from what someone else uses. This information is just part of exploring some methods to achieve altered states; it's merely to inform, not promote.

Another important reason to work with an expert is to understand what a full dose means for your brain and body. The health of your detox pathways plays a big role in dosing. Nobody really talks about that. Some people can handle more without losing their minds, while others need much less to reach the same altered state. So, if psychedelics are your chosen path, get a solid plan in place, including integration work (this is crucial), so your transformational trip doesn't turn into a terrible tragedy.

If you're considering psilocybin (magic mushrooms), they can be profound, but the experience varies by strain. And if you're into brain science, listen up. Paul Stamets, a legendary micologist, has shown that pairing a low dose of psilocybin with another mushroom strain and niacin can lead to unprecedented whole-brain regrowth. All the other uses show potential growth in the hippocampus but not in the rest of the brain. Paul has a pharmaceutical company that is exploring this, and I'm an investor because I genuinely believe it could change the game for stroke, brain injury, and PTSD recovery.

As someone who's had a brain injury and has had brain issues in the past, anything that is going to help cultivate a healthier, stronger, younger brain is very high on the list of collaborative ventures. Science is truly incredible.

| YOUR BRAIN ON PSYCHEDELICS |

We're about to explore how different psychedelics impact your brain when you take a full dose; we will not be discussing microdoses of any of these. So, get comfortable because you're in for a real trip.

Think of your brain waves like a bunch of radio stations, each psychedelic tuning into its own channel. From the mind-bending effects of LSD to the intense visuals of psilocybin, each substance creates a distinct experience for your brain.

But before we dive into the deep end, there are some things you need to know. Just like you'd want the perfect playlist for a party, you need the right environment and mindset for a safe trip. So, as we explore the effects of different psychedelics, keep in mind that it's all about understanding how these substances can expand your mind while you remain safe and grounded.

Again, to avoid confusion, I'm not saying you should go out and get high as a kite and run from your problems. The aim is to provide you with optional tools to use responsibly if the psychedelic path resonates. And if not, cool. You can tap into altered states in plenty of other ways. That's what this book is about. Take the info, choose your preferred method, and embark on a journey toward enlightenment however you see fit.

| PSILOCYBIN |

Psilocybin is the magic behind "magic" mushrooms. It enhances BDNF, a crucial protein that helps your brain learn and adapt, like a brain fertilizer for learning, memory, and cognitive function. Various neurodegenerative and psychiatric disorders, like Alzheimer's disease, depression, and schizophrenia, show low levels of BDNF.[3]

A psilocybin journey can offer profound healing and vivid visuals, but as mentioned, the effects vary widely based on the strain. Different types of mushrooms deliver different experiences—some might send you on a visual ride, while others get you more in tune with your body. So, choose your adventure wisely.

Exploring Full-Dose Brain Waves and States

Let's break down what happens to your brain when you take a full dose of psilocybin. Psilocybin takes your brain waves on a wild ride, shaking up how your neurons chat and changing how you perceive the world. With some fancy brain-scanning tools, researchers are digging into how this stuff tweaks your mind, especially at higher doses that send you on a full-blown trip.

Changes in Brain Wave Patterns

- Alpha waves, typically seen in relaxed states, tend to drop when psilocybin is in the mix.
- On the other hand, beta waves—your go-to for problem-solving—take a back seat with psilocybin. It's likely why logical thinking fades away, and introspection takes the lead.

- Meanwhile, theta waves ramp up, bringing deep emotions to the surface and firing up creativity and spontaneity, contributing to introspective and spiritual vibes.
- Finally, gamma waves are enhanced, linked to heightened perception and mental clarity. They power up your cognitive functions, helping you connect the dots between your senses and memories.

Impact on Functional Brain Connectivity

The big one here is how psilocybin disrupts your default mode network (DMN)—the part of your brain that keeps your sense of self in check. When psilocybin rolls in, blood flow and connectivity in the DMN take a nosedive, leading to that classic ego-melting experience.

On the flip side, psilocybin cranks up your brain's global connectivity, turning your mind into a supercharged communication hub. It's like mental speed dating, where different parts of your brain start mingling like never before. This explains those wild, mind-bending sensations where you hear colors and see sounds—like you have synesthesia, only temporarily.

These changes in brain waves and connectivity give us a peek into the brain's insane ability to adapt. Psilocybin puts your brain into a superflexible state, which studies show has the potential to positively impact treating conditions like depression[4, 5] and PTSD, where rigid brain patterns are part of the problem.

If we're considering the use of psilocybin in therapy, nailing down how it affects the brain at different doses is imperative. Its ability to disrupt fixed brain patterns suggests it could help shake things up in a good way. However, because everyone's brain is unique, careful administration and more research are necessary.

At full doses, psilocybin rewires your brain waves and connections, leading to significant shifts in how you see the world. These
changes could unlock new ways to understand consciousness and
create innovative treatments. All from a dirty piece of fungi grown
in nature.

| MDMA |

This party starter has been turning dance floors into lovefests
for decades. But beyond the glow sticks and good vibes, there's a lot
more to MDMA than meets the eye. This compound, also known
as "ecstasy" or "Molly"—or 3,4-methylenedioxymethamphetamine
if you like a good tongue-twister—shows solemn promise in therapeutic settings, particularly in helping people face their deepest fears
and traumas.[6]

MDMA is a huge heart-opener and acts like a processing lubri-
cant for your brain, turning down the dial on fear and ramping up
the volume on empathy. It creates a space where people feel safe,
connected, and more willing to open up about the tough stuff. So,
while it's often linked to rave culture, MDMA is making waves in
clinical research, offering new hope for those grappling with PTSD
and other mental health challenges.[7]

Exploring Full-Dose Brain Waves and States

MDMA is a psychoactive powerhouse that primarily affects your
serotonin system, but it doesn't stop there. It also interferes with
your dopamine and norepinephrine circuits, shaking up your mood,
emotions, and how you connect with others.

A friend of mine took a wild ride with MDMA, journeying for a whopping eight hours with a therapist skilled in psychedelic therapy. The session started with the therapist smudging her body outside to clear the negative energies around her. Once inside, they set intentions in a quiet room before she took the initial dose. The first forty-five minutes were about waiting for it to kick in while lying on a mattress pad on the floor with blankets, pillows, candles, and soothing music. Then, like magic, her body melted into the floor, her limbs seemed to vanish, and she felt her chest open up as if revealing her heart to the world.

Dry mouth? Check. But also, an overwhelming sense of love and euphoria, bringing up old traumas without the usual emotional charge. Each memory floated back with compassion and curiosity as she shared them aloud with the therapist, who held a safe space for her journey to unfold. Abandonment, sexual abuse, harassment, injustice, deeply rooted generational wounds—years of pain that had weighed her down despite a lifetime of inner work, suddenly felt weightless.

She trusted her intuition and declined the therapist's offer of a second dose—she was confident she was getting what she needed from that first dose. (The body knows its limits—listen to it.)

After the session, she returned to her body and gently sat up. The therapist brought her some fruit and water, and they debriefed. "How long do you think you were under?" asked the therapist. "Two or three hours, maybe?" Her jaw dropped when she learned she'd been deep in it for eight hours. It felt like a blip, but she had unpacked decades of pain in that time, all without feeling retraumatized.

She left that private session feeling lighter, more connected, and deeply in tune with herself and the world around her. It was a profound experience because she had the right environment, an experienced guide, and clear intentions for the journey she wanted. This kind of healing is possible. Just remember, everyone's journey is unique.

Changes in Brain Wave Patterns

- First, MDMA cranks up alpha waves, bringing that calm, meditative vibe that dials down anxiety. That's why people often feel so relaxed and open after taking it.
- Next, there's an increase in beta waves, which means you're super focused and alert. This heightened awareness makes you feel more in tune with your emotions and senses.
- Then come theta waves, which MDMA amps up, unlocking more profound emotional responses and introspection. It likely helps facilitate those emotional breakthroughs in therapy, like my friend experienced.
- Finally, it enhances gamma waves (high-level thinking and perception). That's partly why the sensory and emotional experiences of MDMA are so intense.

Impact on Functional Brain Connectivity

MDMA shakes up the brain beyond just brainwaves—it changes how different parts of your brain interact. First, it gets the left and right hemispheres talking more, which might be why it cranks up emotions and tears down those usual social barriers. These changes suggest that MDMA enhances emotional sensitivity and empathy while improving communication between the hemispheres, even after your trip is over. It doesn't just affect your immediate experience; it might help with long-term emotional growth, especially when used in therapy.

Unlike psilocybin, which can mess with your default mode network (DMN), MDMA gives it a little nudge that enhances positive vibes and your sense of self, potentially helping people feel less isolated.

Researchers at Johns Hopkins University found that MDMA can reopen a "critical period" in the brain, making it more receptive to learning social behavior rewards, similar to how our brains perform in adolescence.[8] This breakthrough explains why MDMA is so effective in treating PTSD—by enhancing social reward learning and strengthening patient-therapist bonds. With the Food and Drug Administration (FDA) fast-tracking MDMA as a breakthrough therapy, it's clear this psychedelic is a powerful tool for reprogramming the brain and tackling trauma.

The idea of "critical periods" isn't new; researchers first saw this in snow geese in the 1930s. Imagine a baby goose just hatched. If Mama Goose isn't around within twenty-four hours, the little guy will bond with whatever's available, even if it's just a random object. But if Mama Goose disappears after forty-eight hours, the hatchling's window of opportunity has closed, and it won't bond with anything else. As a parent, this is heartbreaking to think about.

| KETAMINE |

Ketamine is well-known as a surgical anesthetic and a party drug. In the last few years, it has emerged as a powerful tool for mental health and personal development when used with medical supervision.

In 2017, before ketamine clinics were common, I traveled to San Diego to experience it for myself in a psychiatrist's office. I wanted to share about this type of psychedelic therapy on *The Human Upgrade* podcast.[9] Seven years later, there are hundreds of ketamine clinics treating anxiety and depression. Ketamine has a profound effect on helping your brain change rapidly, making this a potent nootropic when used occasionally or as a cognitive-enhancing substance. As a note, studies show that using it frequently for recreational purposes causes catastrophic bladder damage,[10] so don't do that.

Its potent therapeutic effects are why we launched KAN (Ketamine Assisted Neurofeedback™) at 40 Years of Zen. For the last eleven years, we have manufactured our own EEG equipment for monitoring and improving your brain function and leading you to states very similar to psychedelic therapy without ketamine. But now ketamine is an optional addition to the program because of its healing potential. Combining ketamine with over a decade of experience in neuro-feedback is a revolutionary leap forward. We're taking cognitive enhancement and personal development to the next level, blending cutting-edge science with proven brain-training techniques. It's not just an upgrade; it's the future of mental and emotional transformation.

I'm working closely with a medical director who has nearly thirty years of experience using psychedelics to create best practices for a safe and highly effective ketamine program. Ketamine has many positive effects on the brain linked to longevity, a biohacker's dream. Its ability to enhance neuroplasticity—the brain's capacity to reorganize itself by forming new neural connections—is at the core of ketamine's transformative effects.

This section about ketamine will be a little more robust because I am so excited to share the science and hours of research we've dedicated to understanding it to bring it to the world at 40 Years of Zen. If you're ready to dive in and get science-y, let's talk about turning your adult brain into a teenage brain again, minus the poor decisions and mood swings. We'll explore how ketamine is helping people reshape their mental landscapes and why adding it to the world's premier brain upgrade program makes so much sense.

Reason #1: Enhances Brain-Derived Neurotrophic Factor (BDNF)
After receiving the appropriate dose of ketamine, you get a significant increase in BDNF levels. In my book *Head Strong*, I wrote extensively about this vital protein that supports neuron

survival and growth. Biohacking practices I have recommended for years, like intermittent fasting and high-intensity interval training, will increase levels, but not as much as ketamine does. BDNF plays a crucial role in long-term potentiation (LTP)—when the connections between neurons strengthen. LTP is essential for learning, memory, and overall cognitive enhancement. When you activate BDNF with ketamine, you get more robust neural connections. Because of this, ketamine can support a personal development process all by itself. But you'll see an even more dramatic improvement when you stack it with the neurofeedback tools at 40 Years of Zen.

Reason #2: Activating mTOR Pathways

If you've read my *New York Times*–bestselling longevity book, *Super Human*, then you're probably familiar with the mammalian target of the rapamycin (mTOR) pathway. Biohackers like me manipulate it for longevity. As I write this, my extrinsic age lab test shows that I'm nineteen and a half years younger than my biological age, so I think it's working!

mTOR is one of those Goldilocks molecules—you don't want too much or too little. One of its primary functions is to support tissue growth. It's essential to have high levels of tissue regeneration occasionally so your body can repair itself. However, excessive amounts over time could theoretically increase cancer risk, so it's probably best to keep levels low on average, with a few spikes here and there. Ketamine stimulates mTOR in the brain,[11] which is crucial for synthesizing proteins necessary for new synaptic connections. mTOR activation is one of the reasons why ketamine rapidly promotes the formation of new pathways in the brain, significantly enhancing neuroplasticity and aiding in recovery from conditions like depression or just helping your brain learn new advanced meditation neurofeedback states in less time.

Reason #3: Targeting NMDA Receptors

Ketamine's primary action is as an antagonist of NMDA (N-methyl-D-aspartate) receptors, which are critical for synaptic transmission and plasticity. By blocking these receptors, ketamine causes a beneficial increase in the activity of glutamate, the brain's most abundant excitatory neurotransmitter. This shift enhances synaptic activity and encourages the brain's neural networks to rewire themselves. When you do personal development work to be less anxious and triggered or to develop a feeling of inner peace, your ability to rewire your brain quickly matters.

Reason #4: Inhibiting GSK-3

Ketamine provides neuroprotective effects because it inhibits glycogen synthase kinase-3 (GSK-3), which impedes neuronal survival and plasticity. Ketamine hinders something that inhibits neuron plasticity. Basically, it cancels out a negative. That supports the creation and maintenance of healthy neural circuits. You need healthy neural circuits to live a functional life, and you need them even more if you are doing deep work like we do at 40 Years of Zen every week.

Ketamine offers a unique opportunity. The drug's rapid effect on neuroplasticity can help overcome ingrained patterns of thought and behavior, facilitating profound personal insights and emotional healing.[12] Ketamine can catalyze change, providing the neurological support your brain needs to accelerate personal growth.

Ketamine's potential is vast, so treatments under strict medical supervision are essential. Proper dosing, monitoring, and supportive therapeutic environments are necessary to harness ketamine's benefits safely and effectively. As with any medical treatment, individual experiences vary, making professional guidance crucial to enhancing outcomes.

Exploring Full-Dose Brain Waves and States

In ketamine's past life, it was more commonly known as an anesthetic. Now it's the cool kid on the block thanks to its fast-acting antidepressant powers and ability to create trippy, dissociative states. At therapeutic or full doses, this stuff alters your brainwaves and connectivity patterns in ways that give it its signature psychological effects.

Changes in Brain Wave Patterns

- Ketamine ramps up theta waves, which is why it sends users into dreamlike, dissociative states.
- Gamma wave activity increases, which is associated with high-level cognitive functions like perception and consciousness. This surge in gamma activity could explain the hallucinatory effects and dissociation that ketamine brings, as well as its antidepressant magic, by enhancing brain flexibility.
- Ketamine's effect on alpha and beta waves is all over the place. Some studies show a drop in these waves, which might correlate with reduced awareness of the outside world and more focus on what's happening inside your head.

Impact on Functional Brain Connectivity

This stuff can dramatically shuffle your brain wave activity, leading to those wild, altered states and shifts in mood. Think of it as a hard reset for your brain, helping to break the cycle of those dysfunctional thought patterns that can come with mood disorders. Ketamine has gained a reputation for its potential to treat depression, especially when it's stubborn and resistant to other treatments. It acts fast, which is crucial when time is of the essence. But, because it can also cause dissociation and has a risk of abuse, using it in a clinical setting requires careful handling and close monitoring. We have a seasoned practitioner to support this addition at 40 Years of Zen to ensure client safety.

| LSD |

LSD: the psychedelic that's been blowing minds since the 1960s. Often hailed as the poster child of the counterculture era, LSD (acid) isn't just about tie-dyed shirts and peace signs. It's a powerhouse when it comes to altering perception and expanding consciousness, making it one of the most researched psychedelics out there. It rewires your brain waves and cranks up the cross talk between brain regions, leading to those vibrant visuals, intense emotions, and a sense of interconnectedness that people rave about.

Exploring Full-Dose Brain Waves and States

LSD, or lysergic acid diethylamide (say that five times fast), is a potent psychedelic known for completely flipping your perception, mood, and sense of reality upside down. This mind-bending magic happens thanks to serious rewiring of your brain's neural activity and connectivity. As with all psychedelics, use with caution and expert guidance.

Changes in Brain Wave Patterns

- First off, LSD slashes alpha wave activity, especially in the part of the brain that handles a lot of high-level thinking. Think ego dissolution, where your sense of self quiets down.

- Next up, LSD turns up the dial on the deep emotions and dreamy states of theta waves. This could be why you get those intense, introspective insights and emotional highs during an LSD trip.

- LSD also ramps up gamma wave activity, meaning more attention and better memory. This surge in gamma waves might explain those vivid visuals and heightened senses.

- Last but not least, LSD increases beta wave activity, which usually means your brain is in high gear, thinking, and alert. This increase might cause a rush of intense, sometimes overwhelming thoughts like you've got a circus of monkeys in your head.

Impact on Functional Brain Connectivity

LSD rewires your brain's connectivity in a major way, leading to some interesting effects. These can include mind-bending experiences like synesthesia—where you might see sounds or hear colors—and unexpected thoughts from nowhere.

It also shakes up the default mode network (DMN), which generally keeps your sense of self in check. When LSD disrupts this network, that classic ego dissolution[13] kicks in, which might lead to long-term positive shifts in mindset. And let's not forget how it amplifies connectivity in the frontal cortex, linking it more closely with other brain regions. This could explain the bursts of creativity and problem-solving skills reported by people who've used LSD in a controlled environment.

These changes in brainwaves and connectivity suggest that LSD temporarily reorganizes your brain's inner workings, allowing for experiences that are way beyond what you'd feel in everyday consciousness. This could give us a peek into the very roots of how consciousness works. For clinical use, LSD's profound effects offer a lot of promise for therapy, particularly in treating depression, PTSD, and addiction.[14] It can break up rigid thought patterns while increasing emotional and mental flexibility. But because its effects can be powerful and unpredictable, I always recommend using it in a safe environment, under professional guidance.

| DMT AND 5-MEO-DMT |

These two psychedelics are the "crown jewels of altered states." DMT, the "spirit molecule," is known for its intense, vivid visual experiences that transport you to otherworldly realms. At the same time, 5-MeO-DMT, derived from the *Bufo alvarius* toad, delivers a different kind of trip—more about dissolving the ego and merging into a state of pure consciousness.

These compounds work their magic fast, providing an intense yet brief peek behind the curtain of ordinary perception. If LSD is a deep-dive exploration, DMT and 5-MeO-DMT are more like an express elevator to the outer edges of consciousness.

Exploring Full-Dose Brain Waves and States

DMT, or N, N-dimethyltryptamine, is a powerful psychedelic that can transport you to otherworldly realms in minutes. You can find it in certain plants and animals, but guess what? Your own body makes it, too. At full throttle, DMT rewires your perception, mood, and thinking by stimulating brain activity and connectivity in unbelievable ways.

5-MeO-DMT, the sibling to regular DMT, is like strapping yourself into a rocket headed straight to the heart of pure consciousness. It can shift your entire reality in just a few minutes, delivering an experience that combines cosmic unity and ego dissolution. Since it's so good at rewiring your brain's activity and connectivity, it sends you on a journey that's less about vivid visuals and more about melting into a state of transcendence.

Changes in Brain Wave Patterns

• When DMT or 5-MeO-DMT kicks in, alpha waves drop, just like with LSD and psilocybin. This reduction might weaken your brain's usual filtering, leading to that intense sensory overload that makes this trip trippy.

• They ramp up theta waves, which could explain the vivid, dreamlike visuals and that out-of-this-world feeling users often talk about.

• They also crank up gamma waves, which could be why DMT trips come with such complex visual hallucinations and mind-bending thought patterns.

• Some research shows that DMT alters beta waves,[15] which are important for focused thinking, but scientists are still determining what this means for the DMT experience.

Impact on Functional Brain Connectivity

DMT isn't just a psychedelic that alters your brainwaves; it also changes how different parts of your brain connect and communicate. Similar to other psychedelics, DMT enhances global connectivity, creating a state of hyperconnectivity that allows brain regions that don't usually communicate to start mingling. This could explain the intense synesthetic effects and the hallucinatory sensation of encountering "entities" or alternate dimensions.

DMT also disrupts the default mode network (DMN)—your sense of self. This disruption leads to the classic ego dissolution that can make you feel like you've blurred into the world around you. There's also evidence that DMT enhances activity in the temporal lobes,[16] which is crucial for processing sensory input and memories. This leads to profound emotional and mystical experiences that users often report.

Theoretically, DMT's effects suggest that the brain undergoes a temporary yet dramatic reorganization of its inner workings, enabling experiences beyond ordinary consciousness. This could offer insights into the nature of consciousness itself and open up new ways to explore the therapeutic potential of psychedelics.

People have reported feeling much less anxious and depressed after using 5-MeO-DMT.[17] A study shows that it sparks structural changes in brain cells that might help keep neurons from breaking down[18]—like you have a Benjamin Button effect happening in your brain.

| IBOGAINE |

Straight from the heart of West Africa and pulled from the *Tabernanthe iboga* shrub, this compound has a reputation for sending you on a long, intense journey that's more like a marathon than a sprint. Consider it a personal life review with a dash of cosmic insight.

Ibogaine stands out for its potential to help people kick addiction.[19] It's no silver bullet, but many who have tried it claim it slashes cravings and withdrawal symptoms like nothing else. Straddling the line between ancient shamanic wisdom and cutting-edge addiction research, ibogaine is forging a unique path in the world of psychedelics.

Exploring Full-Dose Brain Waves and States

Traditionally, it's been a key player in West African spiritual ceremonies. Now it's turning heads in the Western world for its potential to tackle opioid addiction and other substance dependencies.[20] Ibogaine offers a blend of mind-bending experiences alongside unique physiological effects.

Changes in Brain Wave Patterns

- It ramps up delta wave activity, leading to the dreamlike states people report while on ibogaine. This could explain the "waking dream" vibe that characterizes its intense visions.
- Ibogaine also cranks up theta waves, which might be why users experience vivid memories and deep introspection during their journeys.
- It dials down alpha wave activity, which usually filters out unnecessary sensory input. With less filtering, more sensory information reaches your conscious awareness, potentially explaining the intense sensory and perceptual changes during an ibogaine trip.
- Ibogaine also affects beta waves. These changes might be responsible for the altered state of alertness and deep introspection that characterize the ibogaine experience.

Impact on Functional Brain Connectivity

Ibogaine has a profound impact on brain connectivity, which contributes to its potential therapeutic effects. Like other psychedelics, ibogaine alters the default mode network (DMN), a network responsible for maintaining ego and self-referential thoughts. Changes in the DMN may help explain the personal insights and reduction in egocentric thinking that ibogaine users often report.

Ibogaine also seems to modulate the brain circuits linked to addiction.[21] It affects the mesolimbic dopamine pathway, a crucial part of the neurobiology of addiction. This modulation may help reset addictive behaviors and ease withdrawal symptoms. There's also evidence that ibogaine enhances connectivity between different parts of the cortex. This increased connectivity might help users integrate the emotional and cognitive aspects of their experience, possibly leading to insights and resolving past traumas. The way it changes brain wave patterns and connectivity suggests a temporary reorganization of brain function, disrupting addictive patterns and allowing for deep psychological introspection that could be crucial in breaking the cycle of addiction.

Its psychoactive and physiological effects, especially its ability to reduce withdrawal symptoms and cravings, make ibogaine a strong candidate for addiction therapy. However, its use is not without risks, including potential heart-related side effects, which means careful medical supervision is essential. We need more research to fully understand how it works, optimize its dosage, and ensure its safe use in therapy.

| AYAHUASCA |

Amazonian shamanic practices have used this legendary brew for centuries. Made from a mix of the ayahuasca vine and *Psychotria viridis* (chacruna leaf), this potent tea offers a blend of DMT and other compounds that take you on a journey unlike any other. It's known for its intense, introspective experiences that often involve vivid visions and deep emotional insights.

In recent years, ayahuasca has caught the attention of people beyond the jungle for its potential therapeutic effects, particularly in treating trauma, depression, and addiction.[22] With its rich history and fascinating blend of mind-altering ingredients, ayahuasca stands out as a unique and powerful tool for self-exploration and healing.

Exploring Full-Dose Brain Waves and States

The Amazon's secret brew is not your average cup of tea; this potent combination makes "aya" one of the most powerful psychedelics out there. One of its components, the caapi vine, contains harmala alkaloids, which act as MAOIs and let that DMT hit you fully when you drink it. Ayahuasca isn't just an ancient elixir; it's a gateway to a whole new level of consciousness and self-discovery, to be used with caution.

Changes in Brain Wave Patterns

- Ayahuasca reduces alpha wave activity, similar to what happens with DMT alone. This drop in alpha waves might break down the usual barriers of waking consciousness, opening you up to introspection and external stimuli.
- During an ayahuasca experience, theta waves increase, which aligns with the vivid visions and deep emotional introspection often shared by ceremony participants.
- Ayahuasca enhances gamma wave activity, indicating heightened perception and cognitive integration. This could be why users experience intense visual hallucinations and report feeling like they've gained new insights.
- Some studies suggest that ayahuasca might increase delta wave activity,[23] which might explain the trancelike states often described by people who use ayahuasca.

Impact on Functional Brain Connectivity

Ayahuasca acts like a wild card in the brain's deck, rewiring neural connections like installing the latest software in a computer. When you sip this psychedelic brew, your neurons sing, suddenly harmonizing with regions they've never met. This hyperconnectivity leads to synesthetic adventures where your senses meld together, creating a symphony. During this mental concert, the default mode network (DMN), which usually keeps that inner voice reminding you of who you are, gets switched to silent mode. As a result, your sense of self dissolves, leaving you feeling at one with the universe. That "me versus the world" mindset? Gone.

Ayahuasca also plays maestro with your temporal lobes, increasing emotional and memory volumes. It's like unlocking a vault where your most profound memories and emotions are stored, helping you process any past traumas lurking. By reconfiguring those neural networks, it can offer fresh perspectives on everything from past pain to present predicaments, making it a potential ally in treating conditions like depression, PTSD, and addiction.

There's a buzz around ayahuasca's therapeutic potential because of the mental insights and emotional catharsis it provides. However, its intense effects require a safe and controlled environment to ensure that its therapeutic power doesn't overwhelm the mind. So, this isn't your casual cup of tea; it's a journey that needs careful preparation and guidance. This one is a trip and requires an experienced shaman, not just some random psychedelic user off the internet.

As we wrap up our adventure into the world of psychedelics, let's give a nod to the incredible potential these substances pack. They can unlock your brain's hidden superpowers and open up dimensions of thought you didn't even know existed, offering insights that can shake things up. But remember, with great power comes great responsibility. Psychedelics aren't your weekend joyride. They require intention, preparation, and a safe space to unleash their healing powers.

As a reminder, you don't need to rely on psychedelics to access altered states of consciousness. You can dive deep into your mind's potential without these substances, whether through meditation, breathwork, a float tank session, or an ice-cold plunge. When used wisely and with respect, psychedelics can provide a profound inner journey that opens doors to uncharted territories of your mind, taking you on a ride that's both exhilarating and transformative. They are just one of the ways to reach these altered states; they're certainly not the only method.

I can't close this chapter without giving a shout-out to Ken Jordan, the cofounder of the Crystal Method musical act and one of the primary pioneers of electronic dance music (EDM). These guys are legendary. If you've ever found yourself hooked by the catchy beat in the trailer for the movie *The Matrix*, it's thanks to them (sampled from a track found on the *Spawn* soundtrack). After talking consciousness with Ken, I realized that their iconic track, "Trip Like I Do," felt like the perfect title for this chapter.

BETTER LIVING THROUGH CIRCUITRY

Are you training to be average? You probably are without even realizing it. But you're not average. So, all the work you're unconsciously putting into being "more average" is sucking up precious energy and dimming your power. You know what's cool, though? Now we can measure your unique baseline using cutting-edge brain science. With the help of these brain-measuring tools—EEG, Q-EEG, and neurofeedback—we can see your strengths and weaknesses and amplify them so you can achieve your full potential with less energy in less time. Let's start from the beginning, though, because there's a guy worth mentioning who made all this possible.

In 1893, a curious man named Hans Berger experienced a fall that nearly ended his life. His sister, miles away, sensed something was off and had their father send a telegram to check on Hans. This cosmic incident sparked something in Hans, and he became borderline obsessed with the mind. He wanted to know how thoughts could travel between people miles apart. He dove into psychiatry, determined to unravel the mysteries of the brain, and his curiosity paid off bigtime with his invention of the first-ever EEG machine.[1] EEG, or the electroencephalogram, is basically a brain activity checkup. Tiny electrodes are placed on your scalp to measure the brain's electrical impulses, which never stop, even when asleep. The result? Wavy lines that map out your brain's activity.

Fast-forward to 1924, when the EEG machine made its official debut, revealing alpha brain waves for the first time. However, Hans published his groundbreaking work in 1929. Imagine being on the cutting edge of brain science and waiting to share that knowledge with the world. If only he could see everything that has transpired since his incredible achievement, all because he followed his deep curiosity and created something worthwhile.

Sadly, despite his monumental contributions to science, Hans Berger's story took a tragic turn. Plagued by the belief that he was facing a fatal illness and battling depression, he took his own life in 1941. And to think, just a year earlier, he was nominated for the Nobel Prize in Physiology or Medicine. Thankfully, he left a legacy that continues to evolve and impact the lives of so many. Today the vast majority of EEGs are used to diagnose malfunctioning brains. Only in recent years have we started using them to create or find and enhance superbrains, or unusual abilities in humans.

BRAIN TECH: NEUROFEEDBACK, EEG, AND Q-EEG

When this brain science first emerged, accessing EEG machines was quite expensive. But thanks to advances in signal processing— almost free now—and AI, we can look at brain signals in new ways. Think of signal processing as taking the mess of information your sensors pick up and turning them into clear signals to improve systems or enhance your health and performance. The kind of EEG cap I've been using for two years costs under $10,000 to make, not including software. Twenty years ago, you'd shell out over $100,000 for the same capabilities. Technology has made these tools way more accessible, driving the evolution of human consciousness.

Even though all three are very important, there are distinct differences between EEG, Q-EEG, and neurofeedback.

EEG (electroencephalography) is the primary tool for listening to your brain's chatter. Think of it like putting a microphone in a crowd, capturing the noise of your neurons as they communicate. This tool shows us the raw data and is foundational for understanding what's happening moment to moment, displayed as those classic wavy lines on a monitor.

Q-EEG (quantitative electroencephalography) analyzes the raw EEG data, quantifies it, and maps it out visually. It tells us that your brain is active and *how* it's active. Is there too much anxiety? Is your operating system exhausted? Q-EEG breaks down the frequencies and locations of the brain activity, giving us a detailed chart of your neural patterns and showing us areas that might need a tune-up.

Neurofeedback is more interactive and guided by the feedback from both EEG and Q-EEG. It's like a personal trainer for your brain, using sensors that pick up your brain's electrical chatter. Your neurons fire away as you think, feel, and go about your life. The sensors then feed that information to a computer that acts like a mirror, showing your brain its real-time activity. Whenever your brain hits a sweet spot—the ideal state for whatever you're aiming for, like better concentration or calmer responses—the system gives you a thumbs-up. This cohesion could be through sound, a visual reward on the screen, or even vibrational. In some neurofeedback systems, a teddy bear vibrates when you get into the "state" you're training—alpha, gamma, etc. I find a combination of primarily auditory and sometimes visual works best, which we use at 40 Years of Zen.

Your brain loves scoring points, so it starts figuring out how to stay in this Goldilocks zone. Over time, and with enough practice, this training helps you naturally keep your brain waves in check, enhancing your mental capabilities. It's part science, part mental fitness, all designed to amplify your brain toward efficiency to achieve your highest potential.

When you show up at 40 Years of Zen, we attach some nodes on your head to scan your brain waves with an EEG. Our neuroscientists then analyze your brain activity and craft a personalized "brain map" using the Q-EEG data to support your goals. Throughout the week, we dive into neurofeedback sessions that let you flex your brain's power and do some really impressive stuff. But the best part? The rewiring of your brain continues for months after you've completed the program, and the results are long-lasting.

THE SILENT EPIDEMIC WREAKING HAVOC ON YOUR BRAIN

In a podcast interview, I sat down with Dr. Aditi Nerurkar, the author of the book *The 5 Resets*, and we talked at length about stress and resilience. She made an important link between stress and heart health, specifically, how emotional stress can lead to heart attacks, even in people who seem perfectly healthy otherwise. During our conversation, I couldn't help but think about the power of EEG and neurofeedback and how these incredible tools are challenging us to push the limits of simple diagnosis, using them to enhance and heal our brains. Possibly even teaching us how to build resilience against stress.

Coincidentally, a friend visited between that interview and writing this book, and she shared something vulnerable. During a nasty divorce in 2018, she had a heart attack. The cause? Emotional stress. She is an otherwise healthy and vibrant woman who leads a conscious, active lifestyle, but stress got the best of her—and it could have cost her her life. Now, years later, she's still dealing with symptoms. You can't see stress, but you can feel it—if you're paying attention.

According to the American Institute of Stress, around 83 percent of people deal with work-related stress, and for 25 percent of them, work is their number one stressor.[2] Additionally, a survey from Indeed found that approximately 52 percent of employees feel burned-out.[3] Deloitte's research shows that 77 percent of workers have hit burnout at their current job.[4] The main culprit? A lack of support and recognition from leadership. Another source mentioned that stress in the workplace affects the mental health of 76 percent of workers.[5] It's unsurprising given the hustle mentality in the U.S., or what Dr. Nerurkar calls "toxic resilience"—productivity at any cost.

If you are among these statistics, you're not alone. The good news is you don't have to stay there. Stress resilience depends on many factors, like biology, upbringing, and environment. Our brains can change thanks to neuroplasticity, so you can train yourself to handle stress better.

Think of how your brain and body adapt to handle stress. Short bursts? No problem, like Navy SEALs training or ER doctors handling emergencies. But for most people, it's not just short bursts. Chronic stress has become the norm, and it's seriously messing with our HPA axis (hypothalamic-pituitary-adrenal axis), the body's built-in alarm system. It connects your brain and adrenal glands—the small triangular-shaped glands that sit on top of your kidneys and produce hormones that regulate your immune system—metabolism, blood pressure, and stress response.

Imagine the HPA axis as the communication network that links your brain to your body's response team, releasing stress hormones like cortisol. It's responsible for the fight-or-flight response that helps you react to immediate threats. This was great when our ancestors were fending off saber-toothed tigers, but we're not running from wild animals today. Instead, more people face modern-day stressors like financial obligations, global unrest, isolation, and relationship troubles. When stress is chronic, your fight-or-flight system stays on at a low hum, causing burnout, which often looks like apathy, low motivation, and sleep troubles. Sound familiar? When ignored, this chronic state of stress contributes to even more severe and often silent consequences.[6]

Lucky for us, you don't need a near-death experience to figure out what's happening in your brain. These days, EEG tech is accessible and affordable enough to use on a large scale to understand and enhance the human mind. Instead of just diagnosing brain death, comas, sleep disorders, or epilepsy, we can explore how to improve the human condition.

| DATA DRIVES A WELL-BEHAVED BRAIN |

Growing up in a home where brain health was a big focus, my curiosity was piqued early. From the time I was in the womb, my mom dealt with epilepsy and had to be on various antiseizure meds. Growing up, it was just part of life, knowing her brain could suddenly short-circuit into seizures without warning. Eventually, she underwent surgery to sever part of her corpus callosum—the brain's superhighway connecting the left and right hemispheres—so the healthy part of her brain wouldn't get taken over by the damaged section that caused the epilepsy.

Nowadays, EEG is very well researched, and we know that neurofeedback can train your brain to do incredible things. But in the 1990s, hardly any neurosurgeons knew this was even possible. Watching my mom recover for a year after her surgery and being told she might not move well again was hard. Sure, she woke up from surgery answering the phone with her stomach, but at least she was alive. This experience had a profound impact on our family.

This personal backdrop set the stage for my battles with ASD and crippling brain fog in my twenties. Frustrated by these hurdles, I had to find solutions. So I loaded up on twelve different smart drugs (nootropics) and dove headfirst into brain-hacking, exploring EEG and neurofeedback as tools not just for understanding but actively improving brain function.

When I began doing neurofeedback, I started recognizing my brain challenges, especially under bright fluorescent or LED lights. Like my mom, my brain would just shut off; only my shutdowns came with brain fog. Even in meetings, biting my cheek until it bled or chugging coffee didn't help. It felt like I'd been given Valium and was wading through mud. During neurofeedback sessions in a dark room with just the glow of the computer screen, I observed my brain waves slipping into a disordered theta state, similar to the severe episodes my mom faced but without the physical twitching. It felt like a psychological echo of her seizures, a mushy brain state where I was mentally paralyzed.

This personal connection to brain dysfunction, from my mother's experience to my struggles, deepened my commitment to understanding and improving brain function. Knowing how much control we can have over our brain's behavior through biohacking, I'm dedicated to pushing the boundaries of what's possible, transforming my health, and helping others biohack theirs.

Understanding that a lack of effort wasn't the reason my brain wasn't working right was important. Despite the brain fog, there was a clear catalyst for my career taking off in my twenties: speaking up. It stopped the mental shutdown when I talked and engaged my auditory cortex. In every meeting since my first job, my brain would switch off after ten minutes of enduring buzzing fluorescent lights, stale air, and boring topics. So, I'd say something. And it turns out that you tend to get promoted if you're the guy who always speaks up in meetings and you're not entirely clueless.

Seeing my brain waves hit that theta state on the EEG machine for the first time was a relief. Things made a lot more sense. But I hit a snag as I got deeper into my neurofeedback practice and started consciously entering those dreamlike states where all the creativity and intuition live. My brain had learned to shut down automatically whenever it drifted toward that state, a survival tactic. If I didn't figure out how to manage it so it would stop controlling me, I was afraid I'd get fired or lose my driver's license. That's how disorienting it got.

It took about two weeks of intense daily work to smoothly transition into those dream states without my brain slamming on the brakes. But eventually, it got easier, and I got better. So, if you're like me, just know it's possible to shift into a magical, esoteric state of consciousness on purpose, even if your default is a bit more chaotic.

How could I have figured any of this out if I couldn't measure my brain waves? How would I know it wasn't just a lack of effort or thinking I was stupid? Which, trust me, crossed my mind more than once. I know my IQ; it's above average. Looking at what I've accomplished, I'm not dumb. But sometimes I felt like an idiot because my brain wasn't behaving.

This book and the Reset Process are all about teaching your brain to behave. Many tools and techniques are available—some are free, and others can be pricey. However, we can prove they work with EEG because it's quantitative. You don't just have to believe it works; you can measure it. That's the beauty of biohacking.

| TACKLING TRAUMA WITH BRAIN SCIENCE |

Many people who come to 40 Years of Zen have faced trauma. Around 70 percent of adults in the U.S.—that's 223.4 million people— have faced some kind of traumatic event at least once in their lives.[7] That's a lot of people walking around with hidden battle scars. Trauma hits when something so intense happens that it completely overwhelms you, leaving you scared, shocked, and helpless. It's like your brain hits a wall because the stress is too much.

It might feel easier to stuff those memories deep inside or try to forget they ever happened. But trauma, even the things you tuck away, can linger and cause all sorts of symptoms you think are unrelated. Your intense emotions toward something, like the example of the guy cutting you off in traffic and your impulse to give him the finger, likely stem from something that happened in your past. These emotions are probably unrelated to your intensity toward this stranger with bad driving etiquette. But because the two experiences happened at different times in your life, you don't even think about the car accident you were in as a kid, where your mom was hurt, and you were really scared. And unconsciously, this experience sends you into fear mode, wanting to do whatever you can to retaliate and protect yourself.

When these scary events trigger feelings you aren't prepared to deal with, your brain might default to fight-or-flight mode—your body's response to threat or danger. One of the things we work on with the Reset Process is managing that fight-or-flight response so your body and brain don't go into massive overwhelm or shutdown, and you can return to a peaceful state more quickly.

If you find yourself going into fight-or-flight mode, this is your brain ramping up its beta waves. These waves crank up when preparing to confront whatever threat you're facing. Your amygdala—the emotion processor of your brain—also kicks into high gear, getting your body ready to either take on the threat head-on or get the hell out of there. This little part of your brain is essential for figuring out how to handle the scary stuff.

Kids who face scary situations tend to disassociate—the brain's version of hitting the eject button when things get too intense. Adults do this, too. If you recall a frightening childhood memory and it feels like you're watching it from a video camera in the corner of the room, that's a sign you left your body during the event. You're viewing the scene from outside yourself because you have disassociated. If you remember it as an active participant, you stayed present during the experience. Disassociation is a survival tactic—useful for stressful situations but not great if it happens often or becomes your default when things are tough or scary. It's hard to navigate and resolve these traumas if you aren't willing to face them. Have you ever heard the saying in personal development, "The only way out is through," which stems from Robert Frost's famous quote on human suffering? It's the same with trauma. You can't wish, hope, or pray it away; it will follow you until you feel it, acknowledge it, and heal the wound around it.

People disassociate for all sorts of reasons. Maybe you were bullied, or you grew up in a toxic home environment, or you were in a horrible accident—any strong, negative memory (conscious or not) can trigger this response. And if it happens enough, or just really intensely, even once, you might find yourself daydreaming more than engaging with the world. But the good news? You can train your brain to snap out of it. The Reset Process is perfect for this. I will lay out the entire step-by-step process for you later so you can experience it yourself.

EVOLUTION'S EDGE: FROM CAVEMEN TO BIOHACKERS

Thinking about our evolutionary past on the savanna, it's clear that humans have always had specialized roles to thrive. These roles—your chronotype—are why about 15 percent of people are night owls—our tribe's "night watch." Another 15 percent are early risers or morning larks, the "morning watch," keeping an eye out at dawn. Most of us are active during typical daylight hours, while a few who never sleep well act as our "backup alarms." These patterns still exist in our population today, showing that some of us are naturally inclined to be farmers or gatherers, maintaining the steady pace of daily life. In contrast, others are the hunters, primed for quick, decisive action.

Lieutenant Colonel Dave Grossman, whom I've interviewed on the podcast,[8] spent his career in the military studying the brain states and physiological responses of first responders and combatants. His research highlights how these ancient roles manifest under modern stress. His findings show that first responders experience intense physiological reactions automatically—these are not conscious decisions but survival mechanisms. This insight has brought significant relief to many who previously couldn't explain why their bodies reacted so intensely in emergencies. It's not just training; it's evolutionary biology at work, driving them to act fast when faced with a crisis.

When I spoke to Dave on the show, he shed light on our biology and societal roles. He pointed out that while most people (about 95 percent) will instinctively run from a fire or explosion, a small percentage (5 percent) will run toward it. These people, driven by their biology to protect and help others in emergencies, are what we might call the "hunters" rather than the "farmers." If you're a hunter and you do traditional brain training or meditation techniques, they'll bore you and possibly put you to sleep.

This reaction is why guys like Dr. Doug Brackmann—a psychologist, author, and performance coach known for his work in helping people with high drive and innate intensity harness their potential (think Navy SEALs, pro athletes, and executives)—have identified types of meditation that work best for the military. He teaches sniper meditation and says traditional, calm-inducing meditation techniques that might benefit a farmer do not suit a hunter. Instead he teaches forms of meditation like zazen, a Japanese practice tailored to warrior minds. This type of meditation involves sitting with a straight back, head slightly bowed, focusing intently on a single spot on the floor. Unlike the farmer's approach of letting thoughts flow and go, this sharpens and focuses the mind, setting a warrior's brain free.

At 40 Years of Zen, we use neurofeedback to explore and harness these ancient brain-wiring patterns. We start with a quantitative EEG (Q-EEG) brain scan. Gathering this data isn't to push you toward being average; it's to unlock your superpowers and understand your weaknesses. We use this data to diagnose and tailor neurofeedback sessions that align with your unique brain type. This approach ensures you're not just spending hours meditating or doing deep personal development work and hoping you're in the right state. Instead, based on feedback, we're actively guiding your one-of-a-kind brain into its ideal state.

Consider the implications of using an at-home EEG device without this tailored approach. Many devices aim to normalize brain function, potentially pushing a unique brain toward average or even into a less productive "zombie zone." However, with the proper knowledge and the right technology, you can harness your brain's true potential, whether for profound meditation or heightened operational readiness. These outcomes show the power of understanding and applying neuroscience in a way that respects and enhances individual differences.

Most people are familiar with Transcendental Meditation, or TM, a practice that's been transformative for millions since the 1970s. However, not all experiences with TM are the same. While some practitioners enter profound, well-ordered states with expansive brain waves, others might just be dialing down their brain activity to a near halt. They sit there for hours, thinking they're deep in meditation, but their brain waves are flat, and they're not reaching those transformative states.

Both groups might look identical from the outside as they sit in meditation. Some reap the benefits, while others are none the wiser, believing they achieve the same results because the process looks the same. Merging hard data with personal experience isn't just smart. It's essential. With tools like Q-EEG scans, we can see what's happening inside your brain. Then every minute you invest in meditation becomes a step toward pushing your mental and emotional limits sky-high, maximizing the payoff of every session. This technology is your secret weapon for fine-tuning your meditation practice and supercharging your brain's potential.

From an EEG perspective, we identify the parts of your brain that aren't communicating well. Maybe a section isn't syncing up with another, and we need to turn that connection up. When you enhance these connections, suddenly you find you can focus better, remember more clearly, and regulate your emotions more effectively. As biohackers and brain nerds, we're not in the business of being average, right? Using EEG, we can see where your circuits are weak and strengthen those circuits with neurofeedback.

At 40 Years of Zen, the first 70 percent of our program is all about intentional neurofeedback. Think of it as having a high-tech copilot who nudges you the moment you start to drift off the mental highway. This beats old-school feedback, which is about as timely as snail mail. Imagine getting instant feedback whenever something's off. Not next Friday, but right now. You would tweak and adjust in real time, making every minute count. By the end of the week, you'd look back on a streak of supercharged performance, like you've been sipping on rocket fuel (or Danger Coffee).

This rapid feedback slots into what we call "evoked potential"— that tiny 350-millisecond window where feedback doesn't just tickle your consciousness but integrates directly into your brain's operating system. This kind of ninja-fast integration lets pros like martial artists, dancers, or even professional Ping-Pong players excel at their crafts. They don't overthink; their bodies just get the memo instantly and act.

As Bruce Lee said, "Stop thinking and get out of your mind." That's the secret to mastering pretty much anything. Neurofeedback trains your brain to know what to do next, cranking up your learning speed. It's about sharpening your mental skills and upgrading your physical prowess and overall performance.

| NIRVANA WITH NEUROFEEDBACK |

Yes, if you live in the jungle—knocking back ayahuasca like it's your day job the way traditional shamans do—after a decade, you straddle two worlds: your everyday life and a psychedelic-induced altered reality. You learn a lot by going this route, but it takes forever. Now, imagine if you could tap into feelings you've never felt before, not because you thought hard about them but because a computer nudged your brain and body into *feeling* them before your conscious mind even got the memo. Then, suddenly, you get it and realize you can bring on these states with your thoughts whenever you choose. That's next-level transformation.

As we've peeled back the layers on how the brain works and what it can do when the neural signaling is on point, even the Dalai Lama got in on the action. In the late 1980s, he launched the Mind and Life Dialogues—way before I plugged into my first neurofeedback session in 1996. This isn't about neurofeedback per se but about fusing neuroscience with meditation to turbocharge the practice. The Dalai Lama brought together top-notch leaders and brain scientists to unpack how meditation changes the brain. It had nothing to do with diving deep into Buddhist scripture; it was pure, unadulterated curiosity about the inner workings of meditation, stripped of any religious context.

They hooked up Tibetan monks to brain scanners and struck gold. They found that meditation wasn't just something to do to relax;

it reshaped attention, emotional control, and self-awareness. This data kicked off what we now call "contemplative neuroscience," a new field where geeks with brain scanners meet ancient meditation pros to figure out the best ways to meditate. It's genius.

Instead of mindlessly meditating and assuming something's happening, why not take control of your experience? Imagine meditating under the watchful eye of the Dalai Lama himself—sure, he wouldn't be adjusting you a thousand times a second (though I'd totally sign up for that!), but the idea is the same. It's about making those micro-adjustments to perfect your meditation on the fly, using science to amplify your spiritual practice and your brain's efficiency. That's the kind of edge neurofeedback gives you.

I'm not knocking the power of sitting with a spiritually powerful person—it can be profoundly impactful. But if we're talking efficiency, nothing beats neurofeedback when you dial it in just right. The Dalai Lama might be an incredible teacher, but let's face it: there's only one of him. But there are millions of us. If neuroscience can give us the Zen monk brain without the monk lifestyle, think about how that could change the world.

Consider this: the hallmark of Buddhist meditation is compassion. Genuine compassion is automatic, like wishing well to others without thinking about it. Imagine if our default setting wasn't fear or desire but genuine, unhesitating goodwill. We could create our own nirvana. How do you reach that state? How do you wish well to the guy who just cut you off in traffic or the mother-in-law who's on your case for the hundredth time? These aren't just minor annoyances; they're the kind of everyday challenges that steal your energy and eat at your well-being.

Neurofeedback is the answer to reaching this state of automatic compassion. The beauty of this type of training is that it teaches you to shift these responses time-efficiently. It reduces the mental and physical costs of negativity, which means less wasted energy, less stress on your system, slower aging, and a happier existence. It's about transforming your brain and your whole approach to life.

The most direct feedback we can harness today comes from our brain waves. If you invest time in learning something, why not learn to master your brain's responses? With neurofeedback, meditation becomes an active process of reprogramming, not just a passive experience. Sure, there's a place for passive recalibration of brain networks, but the real magic happens when you actively engage with the feedback. Observe what's happening, then change it on the spot.

What if we could push that even further? Now that we understand the electrical activity in the brain, could we introduce specific signals to prompt or enhance certain states? That's the frontier we're exploring, and it's as exciting as it sounds.

| KNOW YOUR LIMITS |

Even in the cutting-edge realm of neuroscience, we've got blind spots. Humans operate within a perceptual window shaped by our response times and the span of our lives, around eighty-five years. But hey, if you're a biohacker aiming for extreme longevity, maybe you're like me, optimistically adding a hundred years to that figure.

Now imagine we're trying to detect forms of life different from our own, say, something as mundane as rocks, but these aren't your garden-variety rocks. Imagine they lived for 10 million years, and their idea of a quick decision took about 10,000 years. We'd likely never detect them because they operate outside our time perception.

I've had some interesting chats with folks from SETI, the Search for Extraterrestrial Intelligence. They're constantly scanning the cosmos for signals that align with humanlike timelines. But what if other life-forms are living just a quarter of a second or zipping through existence in a millionth of a second? Unless they leave behind some convenient corpses, we'd probably never know they existed.

What about the activities in our brains that might slip past EEG because they're not on the typical wavelength? There's a whole underground scene in neuroscience focusing on this. Beyond the familiar delta waves, there's something called **slow cortical potential**. These are the brain's underlying rhythms, incredibly slow, occurring maybe once every twenty seconds, forming the bedrock of our brain activity. At 40 Years of Zen, we've pioneered methods to train these slow cortical frequencies to intensify the brain's voltage, enhancing overall electrical activity, and it's highly personalized. Just like we can't prescribe a one-size-fits-all diet, we can't set a universal brain Reset Mode. Each brain has its natural peak settings, and finding that is more art than science, tuned to individual sensation and feeling.

Could there be brain waves even slower than these, ticking by just once a day? It's entirely possible; we might not yet know how to detect them. Like much of life, our brain waves likely play out in harmonics, resonating with rhythms we've barely begun to explore. Who knows what secrets are waiting in those uncharted frequencies?

Also, we've run into a real challenge measuring brain waves above about 50 Hz—50 cycles a second. It relates to a historic clash between Nikola Tesla and Thomas Edison and one of Tesla's peers, Royal Rife. The debate was intense: Should we power the world with direct current, like what you get from a 9-volt battery, or with alternating current, which pulses on and off? Edison championed alternating current (AC), and well, he won. Most of the world now runs on AC, which unfortunately emits powerful electromagnetic noise around 50 or 60 Hz. This makes capturing brain waves in this range a nightmare unless you cozy up in a well-shielded Faraday cage—basically, a container made of conductive materials, like metal mesh or sheets, that blocks out external electrical fields and electro-magnetic radiation.

We've observed that advanced Zen meditators are not just your average brain wave producers. They're hitting spikes at these high frequencies and sometimes even higher. At 40 Years of Zen, we don't just stick to the slow and steady states; we train in these superfast brain waves using technology. It's entirely plausible that our brains hit 100 Hz, or even 1,000 Hz during peak experiences—like those mystical moments, major life transitions, or under the influence of substances like DMT. These aren't the things Big Pharma or even most med-tech firms will bother with. They're too busy selling pills and gadgets. But for those passionate about pushing the boundaries of human consciousness, these high-frequency brain waves are un-charted gold mines.

It's not just about identifying these frequencies; it's about figuring out the best ways to use feedback. When your brain does something right, what's the best way to learn about it? Should you hear it, see it, feel it? We've discovered that immersive sound—a sound that envelops you rather than coming at you from one direction—dramatically enhances feedback effectiveness. This finding is just the tip of the iceberg in our ongoing exploration of sensory feedback, and it's one of the innovative approaches we've patented.

This technology is cutting-edge stuff, taking control of your brain state without relying on pills. Sure, pharmaceuticals might help in some cases, but they aren't the only answer. Depending on your chosen technology and techniques, our Reset Process can either be a slow burn or a rapid-fire transformation. And that's what this book offers you—the freedom to engage with these techniques at any level: for free, on the cheap, or through a deep dive with the high-end stuff.

ALL THE TOYS

Welcome to the future, where your brain is no longer just the command center of your body—it's the ultimate playground for cutting-edge technologies designed to amplify, enhance, and even transform your mental state.

The "future" is happening now. These incredible tools and technologies are pushing the boundaries and redrawing them. From the God Helmet that might just let you chat with the divine to TMS devices that zap away the blues better than a double espresso, technology is advancing faster than I can write this book. Just remember, everything has a dark side. So, while these tools have the potential to liberate your mind, understanding how to use them properly is vital.

An important note: some things you'll read might sound strange, impossible, or dumb. That's okay. When I started the biohacking movement, a science-based endeavor, I was concerned about credibility. If I pushed too soon, would anyone believe these things were possible? But now, biohacking is a $63 billion industry, with tens of millions identifying as biohackers. Biohacking isn't just about losing weight or getting fit—it's about fully activating your brain. That's where things get exciting. The methods in this book are some of the things that can transform how we think and feel, regardless of how unbelievable they might sound. So, of course, exploring them feels like a treasure hunt to a biohacker.

A word of advice: stay open-minded. Life is weird, and so are our brains. That includes the many methods available to access altered states and upgrade your brain for high performance.

| BRAIN-BUILDING BEATS |

One of the most timeless biohacks for fine-tuning your brain is good old-fashioned sound therapy. Chanting is like the original playlist for mind and mood management, melding breathwork with the rhythmic power of your voice to alter your mental state. The star player here? Om-ing. Rooted in ancient Hindu scriptures and resonating with theories like the Big Bang, Om is considered the primal sound of the universe, the cosmic vibration that kick-started everything. You've probably experienced this during yoga when the whole room vibrates with that powerful, collective "Om." It's more than just sound. It's an acoustic bridge to higher consciousness, syncing your brain, breath, and spirit in profound harmony within and around you.

Another ancient form of sound therapy is Tibetan singing bowls, those ethereal instruments that turn sound into an almost tangible experience. These bowls emit a sound so pure and resonant that you can practically see it with the naked eye. If you've never experienced the profound effects of these magical bowls, do yourself a favor and do an internet search for classes near you. To take it a step further, pair this sound and vibration with something like yin yoga or yoga nidra to experience pure, out-of-body bliss. It's incredible how the combination of all your senses kicks in and takes you to another dimension.

Then, there are the solfeggio frequencies, specific musical tones deeply interwoven with the fabric of the cosmos. Each frequency corresponds to different spiritual and physical aspects, offering everything from emotional release to enhanced creativity. While they might sound like they belong in a new-age music shop, the science is undeniable. These frequencies induce distinct changes in brain wave patterns, offering a scientific footnote to their mystical reputation. They enhance alpha (chill mode) and theta (deep meditation and creativity), and some solfeggio frequencies can even help you hit those low and slow delta waves (deep sleep and healing). While they focus more on alpha and theta states, they can still help balance your beta by reducing stress and anxiety.

Finally, there's binaural entrainment. This technique involves playing one tone in one ear and a slightly different tone in the other. For example, if you want to tune your brain to a relaxed alpha state, typically around 10 Hz, you might play a 500 Hz tone in one ear and a 510 Hz tone in the other. While these are just steady, continuous tones, your brain doesn't treat them as separate inputs. Instead it becomes a master DJ, blending and mixing these tones to reconcile the 10 Hz difference. These two tones together create a perceptible mental "wobble" as your brain juggles the sounds to find harmony. The result? Your brain locks on to that 10 Hz frequency, sliding smoothly into an alpha state. This classic method usually involves tuning forks or crystal bowls, using a different tone in each ear. Imagine striking different notes; suddenly you're not just hearing music. You're shifting into a whole new state of consciousness. Depending on your chosen frequencies, this is a powerful way to guide your brain into deep meditation, laser-sharp focus, or relaxation. It's like hacking your auditory system to rewire your brain's state. This method has laid the groundwork for several brain-enhancement technologies developed by pioneering companies over the years.

Bill Harris's company, Centerpointe Research Institute, stood out in this arena. Bill, an incredibly generous philanthropist, made a considerable impact by selling over $100 million worth of brain-enhancing CDs. I had the privilege of using these CDs for about four years. I became good friends with Bill, and saw his brainwaves, before he passed away in 2018.

The core of Bill's technology, Holosync, involves playing slightly different sounds in each ear. His genius was knowing exactly which sounds to use and how to balance them just right. His approach is fascinating because it isn't about abruptly catapulting you into altered states. Instead, you listen to these CDs at bedtime or during meditation, and gradually, in about a month, you start noticing subtle shifts happening deep in your unconscious. This tool doesn't produce an overnight transformation; it's a softer, more gradual process. Think of it as the difference between sipping a fine wine and throwing back a shot of tequila. Sure, going all in and taking a heroic dose of LSD might blast you into new mental territories fast, but Bill's method is about easing you into it, making the journey as gentle as it was profound. It's a different kind of state change: subtle, enduring, and profoundly transformative. It's like your mind gently releases the baggage you didn't even know you were carrying. You feel lighter and more at peace.

| THE GOD . . . FEDORA? |

A guy named Stanley Koren, alongside neuroscientist Michael Persinger, developed what was initially called the Koren Helmet.[1] It soon earned a more celestial name, the "God Helmet."[2] These pioneers were on a quest to uncover the mysteries of creativity, religious experiences, and the effects of stimulating the brain's temporal lobes. Their invention? A funny-looking helmet equipped with very subtle, strategically placed electromagnets that could gently poke at your brain's spiritual buttons.

Now, get this: Persinger's studies revealed that while 80 percent of participants felt a presence in the room, around 6 percent of the people who used the God Helmet reported experiences so profound they felt like they had encountered a divine presence, meeting God, or whoever they believed God to be, during the session.[3] Imagine slapping on a helmet and having a meet-and-greet with your version of the Almighty! This incredible device captured the imagination of many, sparking a flurry of TV documentaries and a wave of publicity that, although somewhat forgotten now, was groundbreaking at the time.

Even the famed scientist and author Richard Dawkins gave the God Helmet a whirl. He didn't feel the presence of another entity. However, he did note some peculiar sensations, like changes in his limbs and altered breathing. He described the overall experience as being "enveloped in darkness," with just the helmet on his head and a sense of relaxation. Persinger theorized that Dawkins didn't have a more profound experience because his temporal lobes weren't particularly sensitive, at least according to a specific physiological scale. Regardless, he felt something that he could not explain.

Then there's experimental psychologist Susan Blackmore, who also tested the God Helmet in Persinger's lab. She said, "When I went to Persinger's lab and underwent his procedures, I had the most extraordinary experiences I've ever had. I'll be surprised if it turns out to be a placebo effect."[4] Same helmet, two different experiences.

Today, backed by more rigorous science, we understand that even subtle magnetic fields—the kind that are weaker than the magnet on your fridge—can have a meaningful impact on the brain, with results confirmed through double-blinded clinical trials.[5] Being a naturally curious biohacker, the God Helmet fascinated me. The problem? You couldn't just go out and buy one; you had to get all the pieces and build it yourself. So, that's what I did.

The kit didn't come with instructions, just several small parts and a clunky helmet that didn't fit well. I knew the "helmet" portion had to fit right to get a good reading, so I searched my closet, found an old fedora, and mounted all the tech to it. Yes, my God Helmet was a brown felt fedora. It wasn't sexy at all. It looked ridiculous—much like the helmet the kit came with. But as long as it worked, appearances didn't matter.

The small electromagnets wrapped around the fedora to connect via USB to a no-frills laptop I snagged from Best Buy running Windows; I'll explain why Windows matters in a minute. And because I'm a nerd, I reached out to a fascinating guy named Todd Murphy, who wrote a book about the God Helmet. He also wrote a book called *Sacred Pathways: The Brain's Role in Religious and Mystic Experiences*, with a foreword by the Dalai Lama, thanks to his compelling evolutionary theories on past lives.

My chats with Todd were nothing short of amazing. He walked me through the importance of how to assemble each piece. The components mimicked electrical signals from deep brain regions, typically monitored during neurosurgery on epilepsy patients. It's tough to see what's happening deep in the brain, but direct electrode measurements can reveal a lot. Todd was reassuring as I carefully placed each piece in the proper position. "Dave, it's not that complex. You're using weak magnets to induce an electrical field in the cells, that's it," he said. This is how magnets and cells work; this wasn't new information. It was about nailing the field's timing, location, and strength to target specific brain areas.

So, back to Windows. It turns out the original design's USB drivers were a bit sloppy. Call it lazy programming or whatever, but it sucked. So, in true hacker fashion, I rewrote the code to ensure precise control over the timing and signals, just as Todd explained. That tweak made a huge difference and unlocked the DIY God Helmet's true potential.

Then Todd dropped some serious knowledge. "If you really want to tap into the more exciting, esoteric places, you need to go to spaceweather.com and check the weather in space. I've found it very reliable that if the space weather is too calm or chaotic, you don't get nearly as good of a result." And yes, spaceweather.com is a real thing. It tracks the mood swings of space—solar flares, winds, and sunspots—and can affect your physiology in ways you wouldn't usually consider. Who knew? Todd did. And now you do, too.

If you read this and thought, *This all sounds absurd*, I get it. But when you talk to Todd or read one of his books, you realize this isn't some off-the-wall theorist. He's an insanely curious, intelligent person who wants to understand why our brains entertain ideas of past lives and deities—stuff we can't see but can feel. What's the mechanism behind these curiosities? How do we access these states on our own?

After that conversation with Todd and rejigging Windows, I successfully built a God Helmet and used it a dozen times. Now, I didn't meet God, but I definitely tapped into profound states similar to those I've reached with neurofeedback, breathwork, psychedelic experiences, deep meditation, chanting, and yes, even fasting in caves—all part of the biohackers' tool kit.

Since Todd's book on the God Helmet came out in 2019, more science has emerged. For a short time, we used clinical-grade, low-intensity electromagnets at 40 Years of Zen as part of the experience. But we realized they took more time than adding value, so we replaced them with better tech. They were a big part of the journey, though, and clinical-grade systems continue to explore brain stimulation today.

So, what happened to my God Helmet? Six months after the initial experiments, I went to fire it up again and forgot the Windows password. I still don't have it. But I do have the fedora, and I'm using the USB cable from the setup to connect the microphone I'm using to dictate this book. Maybe it's blessed; who knows?

THE FUTURE OF BRAIN UPGRADES

In July 2024, I hopped on a flight to Costa Rica, one of the few countries that embrace medical freedom enough to dive deep into your own biology. My goal? To experience the combined genius of Dr. Vince Giampapa and Dr. Sheldon Jordan at RMI, the Regenerative

Medicine Institute. Dr. Giampapa runs the show, based on Dr. Jordan's groundbreaking techniques.

Dr. Jordan is renowned for his work on resetting the central circadian clock in the brain using cutting-edge focused-ultrasound techniques. This innovation temporarily opens the blood-brain barrier, allowing stem cells to enter the hypothalamus—the brain's master clock and the control center for much of our inner life, including our perception of age. Dr. Daniel Amen, a preeminent brain scientist and psychiatrist, introduced me to this groundbreaking work in his decades-long quest to enhance brain health at all life stages.

For five days, I dedicated an hour each day to sitting still while wearing a peculiar-looking crown. This device sent a carefully focused beam of ultrasound into my brain. Afterward, I received an infusion of stem cells and growth factors, followed by two hours in a hyperbaric chamber to supercharge my brain's transformation. This protocol isn't just one of the most effective longevity therapies available today; it profoundly impacts your state of consciousness.

Emerging from the program, I found that my ability to enter altered states of consciousness had more than doubled. It felt like I had added a new power source inside my brain—a sense of youthful energy and meditative prowess reminiscent of my twenties. In this brave new world of brain upgrades, this therapy stands out as one of the most effective and profound hardware upgrades you can undergo. It pairs exceptionally well with neurofeedback and other personal development techniques.

Despite being only a three-hour flight from the U.S., such cutting-edge medical procedures remain out of reach for many, primarily due to cost. This weeklong program, which included stem cell treatments for all my joints, reproductive system, and face, cost less than half of a similar program from five years ago that didn't even touch my brain.

Direct brain upgrades like this will become more common in the coming years. Besides the time and energy I've invested in neurofeed-back, this is the highest return on investment I've experienced in my journey to enhance consciousness, mental clarity, and brain energy.

| IT'S ALL IN YOUR HEAD |

I used to advise a company called Hapbee. About a decade ago, a group of cancer researchers had this big idea. They wanted to dig deep into cancer drugs and explore the mysterious world of molecular resonance effects. With a hefty stash of funding—tens of millions of dollars—they built this insane helium-cooled, heavily shielded device. This device wasn't your average lab equipment; it completely isolated substances from interference: no space weather, no electromagnetic noise from earth, nothing.

They could then study any substance with a noncovalent bond (geek-speak for molecules that hang out together without forming supertight bonds) and capture the subtle electromagnetic signals they emitted. But they didn't just stop at recording these signals. They played them back on mice to see what would happen.

Here's the weird thing: placebo effects don't tempt mice. They don't know they're supposed to feel something. They just do. So, when these scientists decided to test THC, the active stuff in cannabis, the results were hilarious. The mice ended up on their backs, paws in the air, totally out of it, and then, predictably, they got the munchies. And it wasn't just THC. When they mimicked the resonance of espresso, the mice started zooming around like they'd been sipping caffeine-enriched mouse chow all day.

This groundbreaking research didn't just stay in the lab. It spun off into a commercial product, a headband you could wear that used subtle electrical fields to mimic these molecular vibes. Imagine slipping on a headband and getting the effects of a morning cup of coffee or a chill pill, all scientifically proven in double-blinded, placebo-controlled trials. Turning brain science into wearable tech that can change your mood or energy? That's biohacking at its most exciting, pushing the boundaries of what we thought possible and turning it into everyday reality.

If you think you're in full control of your brain, here's a thought: even forces as mild as the pull from fridge magnets might influence your mental state. Seriously. In the world of biohacking, we're all about fine-tuning both the external environment and our internal landscape to achieve complete mastery over our biology. Believe it or not, the magnetic fields surrounding you affect your brain's functions. Yes, even those subtle ones can have an impact. It's not just speculation. It's science.

But what about those cell phone towers or the magnetic fields humming through the walls of your home? What are they doing to your brain and your consciousness? Honestly, the industry might tell you it's nothing to worry about—backed by their own research, of course. But step outside that bubble and you'll find over 10,000 independent studies suggesting that these fields have real, tangible biological effects.[6] Some might be playing the caffeine signal directly into your brain, while others could be causing cellular disruption. And you'd never know any better.

The issue lies in something called the voltage-gated calcium channel. These are like little doors on your cells that open up when the proper voltage hits, letting calcium flood into a neuron. Electronically generated electromagnetic fields act on these voltage-gated channels and cause excess intracellular calcium. This calcium rush can cause inflammation and zap the neuron's ability to produce electricity.[7] It's one reason you won't catch me pressing a cell phone against my head. Except in those rare moments at conferences when I need to make a swift exit to see my kids without being stopped. I'll put my phone on airplane mode and pretend to talk to avoid being interrupted on the way out the door. I guess the secret's out. Nothing personal, but my family comes first. Other than that? Not a chance. Whether it's a signaling effect or a voltage-gated calcium effect, why take the risk?

By the time you finish this book, I don't want you to be worried about your cell phone. But know that keeping your phone pressed against your head or stashed in your pocket next to your reproductive organs isn't a great idea. Studies show it can decrease sperm motility[8] and affect fertility in both men and women.[9] That's why I steer clear of these practices. I like it when my brain works well and can access those mystical states without interference from voltage-gated calcium channel excitation. We can verify these EMF effects with good old-fashioned EEG. By measuring brain activity, we can see the changes these technologies induce. It perfectly blends ancient wisdom and cutting-edge science, revealing how dynamic and responsive our brains are.

Small changes are easy, no-brainers, like choosing wired earbuds or turning off the Wi-Fi at night. These swaps are not about living in fear but choosing smarter, simpler ways to protect and enhance your well-being. Because in biohacking, every little adjustment can upgrade your health and vitality.

| BRAIN SQUATS AND MINI VIOLINS |

There's a really cool technique called TMS—transcranial magnetic stimulation.[10] It's one of the few treatments, alongside ketamine, that's proven effective for those battling treatment-resistant depression. When we talk about TMS, we deal with magnetic fields that are a million times stronger than those used by the God Helmet (fridge-magnet strength). The difference is that TMS employs extremely powerful, repetitive pulses. The God Helmet and the clinical-grade equipment I've used at 40 Years of Zen utilize complex but gentle magnetic signals to mimic natural physiological processes. Think of it this way: TMS is like making a part of your brain do heavy lifting—essentially, brain squats. On the other hand, the softer approaches are more like having your brain perform a Mozart sonata on tiny, delicate brain violins. They're not in the same ballpark but profoundly impact brain function.

Given my past experiments with subtle electrical stimulation through my God Helmet and the cutting-edge tech from 40 Years of Zen, not to mention my early trials with Hapbee devices, I was eager to ramp things up with high-powered magnetic stimulation. This curiosity led me to a clinic in San Diego, where I experimented with ketamine therapy for a podcast episode. This was long before it hit the mainstream.

Post-ketamine, I entered a room that felt more like a high-tech lab from a sci-fi film. There I encountered an intimidating device that looked ready to probe the depths of my psyche. They secured my head in place, making sure I couldn't move. It was like being clamped under the world's most gigantic microscope. Then came the clicks of the electromagnet activating, each pulse sending a peculiar tingling deep inside my skull. It was an odd sensation, feeling a part of your brain you're not supposed to feel, as if the magnets were whispering directly to neurons tucked away in recesses I wasn't aware I could consciously access.

Was I depressed when I went in? No. Did I emerge feeling down? Not at all. But does TMS have measurable effects on the brain? Absolutely. So, if you're flipping through this book, maybe you're inspired to build your own God Helmet, or you'll think twice about pressing your phone against your head. Or perhaps, if you're wrestling with the kind of anxiety and depression that is more prevalent than ever, you might consider exploring ketamine therapy under professional guidance or pairing it with TMS. Because when it comes to the impact of magnets on our brains, we're way past the realm of tinfoil hats. These technologies hold profound implications for mental health and beyond.

You might laugh at Todd's groundbreaking exploits, though his research is rock-solid. And make no mistake, FDA-approved TMS machines are far from pseudoscience. They are powerful tools that transform lives by realigning the currents that animate our thoughts, backed by science. And you simply can't dismiss the research behind Hapbee's clinical trials. They've invested a decade and $40 million into researching the effects of magnetic fields inside molecules. To overlook this is to deny your biology. Your MeatOS tells you, "This information violates our reality, so it's unsafe." It's a natural response but not necessarily a helpful one.

Skepticism and outright rejection litter the path of scientific innovation. Michael Persinger, the mind behind the God Helmet, experienced this firsthand. His controversial theory suggested that paranormal experiences, from ghost sightings to past lives, might stem from unusual brain activity, such as cross-hemisphere communication. Although the validity of his claims remains a topic of debate, they certainly drew considerable skepticism.

Science, by its nature, resists change. When a disruptive, paradigm-shifting invention surfaces, the initial instinct is to shut it down. It's a pattern repeated throughout history. Think of Galileo or Ignaz Semmelweis, the Hungarian physician who advocated handwashing to prevent infections in maternity wards during the 1840s. Semmelweis ended up committed to an asylum in 1865, where he died fourteen days later, broke. Only after his death did doctors realize he had been right regarding his contributions to medical hygiene. He wasn't "crazy." He was curious and unafraid to follow that curiosity toward innovative solutions.

Is Persinger another Semmelweis? I can't say for sure. But, my discussions with Todd convinced me there's a logical, scientific, and medically oriented foundation explaining why this technology works. Whether we're talking about stimulating your temporal lobes with Persinger's original God Helmet or tickling other brain regions with the newer models like the Shiva and Shakti helmets, thanks to Todd's advancements in Persinger's work, we know these methods are impactful. Do these devices actually enable people to meet God, or do they simply create a convincing illusion? That's what ongoing scientific exploration is for.

The point is that facing criticism doesn't invalidate the brave minds and interesting findings behind this research. Instead, it highlights the challenging path of pioneering science. Keeping an open mind is crucial as you explore these intriguing possibilities. Be ready to question, test, and consider new ideas that might one day lead to profound breakthroughs in understanding the human mind. In other words, stay curious.

| CAGED |

Thinking about the magnetic fields' origins in these brain-stimulating devices is exciting. EEG traces taken from the limbic structures in the brain during open surgery modeled these patterns. This groundbreaking research happened inside a Faraday cage. As you'll recall, a Faraday cage is basically a metal box or mesh made of conductive, electrically grounded material. Have you ever seen those vintage photos of Nikola Tesla, where he's either juggling massive bolts of electricity or chilling inside a Faraday cage surrounded by electric arcs? A Faraday cage blocks all EMF emissions except for the earth's natural magnetic field.

Persinger's use of this kind of shielding was key. It allowed him to clearly distinguish the effects of external electromagnetic interference from those of geomagnetic disturbances on the brain. In other words, he was exploring whether earth's magnetic field fluctuations could impact us. His conclusion? It's more than likely.

The concept of blocking everything out hit home for me, especially after some revealing brain scans prompted me to focus on healing my brain. I knew that nonnatural electromagnetic frequencies weren't exactly beneficial for the human body, though they're not catastrophic, either. But dealing with a brain that wasn't running at peak power was frustrating. And I was determined to heal.

So, I got creative. I converted the garage of the house I was renting into an office, using metal-backed foam for the structure. I connected all the pieces with electrically conductive tape and grounded the setup. I had made my very own Faraday cage. Inside this sanctuary, my cell phone was useless (a great litmus test for EMF blocking). I would have total EMF blockage if I covered the windows with metallic foil. Uncover them, and I'd get a signal again.

I used this space primarily for meditation, with all electronic devices turned off. The isolation deepened and enhanced my meditative experiences significantly. It felt like meditating in a cocoon of silence, amplifying every breath and thought.

People flock to caves to meditate for a good reason. You can create a similar feeling of isolation by building your own Faraday cage. Some people take it to the next level, sleeping under a fine-metal-mesh Faraday cage to shield themselves from Wi-Fi. Many of the people who do this report much better sleep. It drives home the point that our environment profoundly influences our brain function. Everyone's sensitivity varies. You do you.

As I previously said, I'm not endorsing any notion of divinity linked to the God Helmet. But what I've experienced and what others have reported opens a fascinating window into how the brain interacts with magnetic fields. We are just scratching the surface of understanding how specific patterns, strengths, and locations of magnetic signals can deliberately alter our mental state. Yet, as with all powerful technologies, there's a dark side to consider. Just as fire can warm a home or burn it down, the technologies we develop to influence our brains hold immense potential to heal and harm. It's a thrilling and somewhat daunting frontier best approached with awe and caution.

| WELCOME TO THE DARK SIDE |

The first thing I ever sold over the internet came straight out of my dorm room at age twenty-three. I was scrambling to pay for my college tuition and stumbled upon what was essentially the precursor to Reddit. This was before web browsers were commonplace; the internet was all text-based. It was here I learned all about my favorite drug, caffeine. Inspired, I decided to create a caffeine-themed T-shirt for my friends. The shirt featured the bold declaration, "Caffeine: My Drug of Choice," accompanied by an image of the caffeine molecule. Today I have a tattoo of the caffeine molecule on my left bicep, the only tattoo I have, because I figured it was about time to say thanks. And yes, tattoos are probably bad for you.

This quirky venture caught the eye of *Entrepreneur* magazine and about eighty other publications. I was just a kid selling T-shirts over this "inter–something or another" when most people hadn't even heard of the internet yet. This was the era when Marc Andreessen was just starting to develop the first web browser. I was immersed in cyberpunk culture, captivated by the idea that "information wants to be free," and excited by the boundless possibilities technology seemed to promise. However, I also had concerns about the potential misuse of this new digital landscape. In an interview written about my entrepreneurial efforts, I cautioned that exploiting the internet for sheer profit could obliterate its culture. Something unique would be lost if it became just another medium to push random products.

Ironically, just two weeks after that article was published, the internet witnessed its first significant spam incident. A husband-and-wife lawyer team named Canter & Siegel, possibly inspired by the discussions around commercial opportunities I had unwittingly sparked, launched an infamous spam campaign that would mark the beginning of a less innocent era online.

So, I'm sorry for inadvertently contributing to the birth of spam. But it taught me something important: we can use every form of technology for tremendous good or significant harm. In my early career, I helped build some of the world's first data centers, laying the groundwork for the modern web. A platform that, while incredibly powerful, has also evolved into a tool for surveillance and control on a global scale.

Just like the dark side of the internet, if we sit back and allow others to wield power over us without our consent, using magnetic signals and sensory inputs to manipulate our brain states and even our perception of reality, we're in big trouble. By understanding the mechanisms behind these technologies, you empower yourself to remain in control. Ignoring or denying the existence of these influences only serves to relinquish your power to others. My overarching goal within the biohacking movement and this book is to equip you to take control of your biology so you are entirely unprogrammable.

These technologies—whether it's neurofeedback, magnetic brain stimulation, or even psychedelics—aren't just tools for self-improvement. They also have the potential to be used by others to shape your thoughts and behaviors without your knowledge. So don't let that happen. Beware of the dark side of these innovations through the lens of inquiry, not fear. Don't let hackers, governments, or media corporations dictate how you use these technologies. These are tools meant to enhance freedom and capability, not constrain humanity under the guise of control. As you venture deeper into what's possible with brain science and technology, do so with your eyes wide open. It's up to you to make sure these powerful tools enhance your life without compromising your autonomy.

PRESSING THE RESET BUTTON

You've made it. We have talked a lot about the Reset Process, and now it's time to discover what it is, why it's such a powerful tool, and how to use it to upgrade your life.

I named it the Reset Process because it resets your operating system's response, turns off alerts, and removes the wasted energy that goes into being continuously triggered by something terrible that happened to you, even if it's hidden so deeply that you don't know it's there. These are the invisible things that happen in that 350-millisecond window that you unconsciously store in your body. They follow you around and cause you to react, confusing you about why you feel so triggered.

I don't call it the "forgiveness process," because forgiveness is triggering for many people. Suppose someone did something awful to you. If you say, "I'm just going to forgive them," it might not feel safe or true. Your body holds on to that trigger because it doesn't want to feel that pain again—emotionally, spiritually, physically, or all of the above. So, of course, an automated system is in place to keep you from being exposed to scary things that could potentially harm you. It's for your benefit, but this safety system can sometimes lead to stuck emotions that create triggers and turn our lives upside down.

An avoidant part of you says, "I don't want to forgive them." We tend to double down here, like a child staging a protest, refusing to leave the playground when asked. Some of you prefer stubbornness because it keeps things as they are, which feels safer than forgiveness and the risk of possibly being hurt again.

How often has a well-meaning teacher, coach, or parent told you to forgive someone even though you didn't want to? You felt violated when they told you to forgive because it was wrong, and you're still mad—forced forgiveness wastes energy. So, yeah. Forgiveness is surrounded by all sorts of triggers.

| PREPARE TO BE FORGIVING |

It's time to dive further into the fifth F-word mentioned in Chapter 1, the newest addition to the stack: forgiveness. As you read this, check in with your physiological responses: your heart and root chakra. You might feel some unpleasant sensations when you think about forgiveness. That's okay. The Reset Process has nothing to do with telling someone you forgive them, so don't worry about that. I won't try to force you to do anything you don't want to do. This is your journey. Just know that if you're tired of carrying the baggage weighing you down, the Reset Process can help you let go if and when you're ready.

This process is a deep physiological release, different from sitting down with the person who wronged you and pretending to be at peace when you're not. You can choose to talk openly about this with the person who caused you pain, or you can simply run the process and never mention a word to anyone. It works either way. Frankly, telling a narcissist or sociopath you forgive them just gives them power. So, if you know you're dealing with a diagnosed narcissist or sociopath, don't speak to them at all. Just stop being reactive to them. It'll drive them nuts.

I've had some things happen throughout building the biohacking movement that I haven't publicly discussed. Situations that triggered two of the deepest emotions a person can feel: betrayal and injustice. When you do the right thing and get punished, or when you trust someone and they betray you, or when a lover breaks your heart, the important thing isn't what you say to the other person. It's that you find a way to let go of the pain so you can be at peace.

I've used this Reset Process on every single trigger—even kale. Just kidding; I haven't forgiven kale yet.

Jokes aside, this process is profound. It's changed my life and the many lives of those who have experienced it. It's so powerful that this entire chapter aims to help you understand it so you can use it and get the same incredible results as our clients who come through 40 Years of Zen. The Reset Process is the core of our program. I'm gifting it to you because I want you to experience the immense joy, liberation, and peace available in this lifetime.

The Reset Process is an amalgamation of different spiritual teachings about forgiveness. Forgiveness is a cornerstone of Christianity. You might have heard the famous quote: "Father, forgive them, for they do not know what they are doing" (Luke 23:34). Turns out, there's something to this.

Buddhism and Eastern religions focus on compassion—automatically wishing well for others. In the Middle East, it's about submission or surrender to the will of Allah. Each of these is a neurobiological skill you can develop. You don't have to be religious to embody these teachings and benefit greatly. Learning to forgive automatically or consciously reduces your burdens; it sets you free. Learning compassion reduces the long-term effects of trauma. Learning to surrender reduces struggles, allowing you to consciously choose when to let go instead of being forced to. And gratitude, well, it turns what you have into enough.

Some people hear *surrender* and think it equals weakness. But surrender isn't about giving up; it's about learning to be vulnerable, letting go of your ego, and finding freedom from the pain. I'm not endorsing any religious organization here, but spiritual teachings are valuable. They come from thousands of years of curiosity and exploration. The whole point of this book and the biohacking movement is to ensure that no one is in charge of you but you. By walking with forgiveness, compassion, the ability to let go, and feeling gratitude, you can achieve what is known as a state of grace. I'm not claiming to live in a constant state of grace. Have I felt it a few times? Probably. Maybe that's my ego talking. But what I do know is that the technologies and techniques in this book have taken me far from the angry, easily triggered person I used to be to a calmer, happier, healthier version of myself.

The Reset Process builds on the many principles I've learned, incorporating insights from various spiritual traditions and modern neuroscience. By resetting your triggers, you free yourself from the invisible chains of past traumas and emotions. You reclaim your energy and redirect it toward growth and creativity. This process allows you to approach life with a clear mind and an open heart, unburdened by the weight of unresolved feelings. And it's all based on extensive research on forgiveness.[1, 2]

| FINDING FREEDOM IN FORGIVENESS |

One of the most inspirational figures in forgiveness was the legendary South African archbishop and social rights activist Desmond Tutu. He was a master of forgiveness and reconciliation and wrote *The Book of Forgiving: The Fourfold Path for Healing Ourselves and Our World*. His wisdom in transforming deep pain into peace has inspired countless people around the world. He walked his talk as a true beacon of hope and compassion before passing away in 2021.

There's also Mohamedou Ould Slahi, a Mauritanian man who got caught up in the chaos after 9/11. Imagine being yanked out of your home, thrown into a prison camp in Guantánamo Bay, and accused of being a top terrorist without ever being charged. That was Slahi's life for almost fourteen years.

Guantánamo Bay isn't exactly Club Med. Slahi endured brutal treatment: sleep deprivation, beatings, and all sorts of psychological tricks to break him down. But the crazy part? He was innocent the whole time. It wasn't until 2010 that a U.S. judge finally said, "Hey, there's no solid evidence against this guy. Let him go." But it still took six more years to regain his freedom.

When Slahi was finally released in 2016, you'd expect him to be pretty angry, right? Who wouldn't be after all that? But this guy did something extraordinary. He forgave his captors. Can you believe that? He forgave the people who made his life a living hell. Slahi even met up with one of his former guards, Steve Wood. Steve read Slahi's memoir, *Guantánamo Diary* (a must-read), and felt awful about what Slahi had been through. So Steve reached out, and in 2018 they met face-to-face in Mauritania. Instead of holding a grudge, Slahi welcomed Steve with open arms. They had dinner together, talked things out, and became friends.

Think about that for a second. Here's a guy who went through unimaginable torture and came out the other side ready to forgive. It's a powerful reminder that our capacity for forgiveness is far more than we think, not just for us but for the whole world. If Mohamedou Ould Slahi can find it in his heart to forgive his torturer and break bread with him, imagine what you can do. It's not just about letting go of anger; it's about reclaiming your power and finding peace. That's the kind of biohack that changes lives.

Writing about these things creates a sense of profoundness in my biology. It's truly amazing how people choose these incredibly heroic acts of forgiveness and letting go. They make it seem so easy when it's usually not. But in the end, the temporary discomfort is always worth the freedom you feel afterward.

| WHERE TO START |

You might feel uncomfortable thinking about forgiving someone who's wronged you. That's normal. This reaction is your body trying to protect you. It believes that anger, or your reactivity, is keeping you safe. And frankly, that's bullshit. It's just your body filtering reality so you don't evolve because change is scary, and success is not guaranteed. But sitting in anger feels horrible, so why not do something different?

Think about the person you feel the most negativity toward, who always gets under your skin or has caused you pain. This is typically the person you want to run the reset with first because that's where you're losing the most energy every day. That automated negative response to them stops you from experiencing joy, happiness, and abundance. The Reset Process can change that, transforming negative charges or "triggers" into compassion, forgiveness, and love. You might think, *Dave, that's ridiculous. I will never forgive the guy who assaulted me.* And to that, I would say, "You don't have to. But what does carrying the weight of that cost you? Is it worth your peace, your happiness, your freedom?"

People who say there's nothing to forgive are either fully enlightened or, more likely, living in their heads and not tuning in to their hearts or other parts of their body. Usually you feel a lack of forgiveness in your root chakra, sacral chakra, or solar plexus, and primarily in your fourth chakra: your heart. Sometimes it can be higher up, like in your throat. Regardless of the location, you feel it somewhere in your body. The key is to learn to tune in and not disassociate from these feelings. Instead, feel them fully, acknowledge they exist, and be brave enough to let them go for your sake.

If you honestly think you have nothing to forgive, you might be reacting to the word *forgiveness*. If you genuinely believe nothing on earth triggers you, either you're lying to yourself, or you need to find the nearest spiritual academy and teach people how the heck you got there. I want to see your brain. The truth is, you just don't know what you have to forgive yet. And that's what this process helps you uncover.

So, how do you initiate the Reset Process if you feel there's nothing there? Ask yourself, *When's the last time something pushed my buttons?* Maybe it was your neighbor's comment about your garden or the grocery checker's attitude last week. Now you've got something. How did you feel? Where did you feel it? Try to remember the sensations in your body. Close your eyes if it helps you tap in deeper. These small things might feel insignificant. But these are the things holding you back from accessing deep inner peace. They burrow deep inside, like a tortoise squeezing itself into its shell, hiding reality from you so you don't change.

Once you've got something in mind, ask yourself, *When was the first time I ever felt that way?* Digging up the answer might feel challenging, but go for it. An unrelated memory might pop into your head. Maybe you suddenly think about falling off the swing. Instead of dismissing it, consider it a gift. Your body is showing you what it needs you to address. Run the Reset Process—which I'll walk you through in a minute—on that first memory that pops up. Maybe you're mad at the swing, your dad for pushing you too high, or the kid who laughed at you. As soon as you run the Reset Process, you might think, *I didn't even know that memory was in there.*

These triggers are invisible by design and built into your reality without conscious thought. Could you imagine if you were constantly sifting through every memory in your life, every day? It would be exhausting. When you uncover these memories, you'll find there's more to work through than you realized. This awareness is normal. It means you're human and flawed like the rest of us.

One of the most compelling cases from 40 Years of Zen was a woman we'll call Lydia. At around sixty, Lydia was always anxious and reactive, but she couldn't pinpoint who or what to forgive. During our sessions, she noticed tension in her throat when thinking about specific experiences, almost to the point of losing her voice. We dug deeper and uncovered that Lydia had been intubated as a premature baby, unable to understand or remove a tube stuck in her throat for months. No wonder her body held on to that trauma. As a baby, she was helpless. Her physiological reaction as an adult made perfect sense.

So Lydia ran the Reset Process on both the tube and the doctor who intubated her. When she finished, she shed massive tears and was shaking. She said she felt free for the first time in her life, experiencing joy without feeling triggered. She was taken back to the intubation and could remember it, but it no longer affected her. This woman had a great career, family, and kids, but she'd been unhappy and reactive most of her life. She had no idea that experience was at the root of her pain and triggers. She could have saved herself years of anguish if she'd known sooner.

| WHOLE-BRAIN, WHOLE-BODY |

Many people who attend 40 Years of Zen can get through about 75–80 percent of their big issues in five days using our enhanced, rapid Reset Process. Once you learn it, you can do it faster and faster, especially with neurofeedback to avoid mistakes. It's like learning to type quickly. The more you do it, the more it becomes second nature. When our clients come back for level 2, they often find more of the little stuff to clear. Typically, first, you clear the boulders, then the rubble. However, in the process I will take you through in this book, we will start small to get you used to how it feels in your body. Then, with continuous practice, whether you use our technology or not, you can keep clearing out the layers until you have a clean slate.

As you progress, you will feel safer in your body and environment.

The energy available for accessing deeper spiritual states increases, and you will start to feel the profound effect of this important work. Carrying hidden anger or resentment is costly. Removing the dead weight of the past opens you up to experience more of the beauty available. I've seen people forgive humanity for being stupid or even the Nazis for what they did to their families. This process of healing deep and visceral stuff deserves your undivided attention and compassion.

If you have a long history of doing personal development work, you might feel like you've done all this already. I felt the same way when I started exploring forgiveness. I thought I'd dealt with my birth trauma, being born with the cord around my neck and thinking someone was trying to kill me. I'd done rebirth processes and released my anger. I didn't think there was anything left to do. But I was wrong.

The biggest difference with the Reset Process is that it's a body process, not a mind process. You might say, "I've rationally forgiven this person, so I'm good." But if it still bothers you, if you grit your teeth, if thinking about them makes you exhausted, if you tune out in certain situations, avoid challenges, sabotage relationships, yell at your kids when you're tired—something's still in there wreaking havoc on your peace. Acknowledging your triggers and choosing to do something about them is admirable and takes work. The good news is that once you release the triggers, you get way more energy back. Temporary discomfort for long-term pleasure? Sounds great!

| PREPARING TO ENTER RESET MODE |

When we teach the Reset Process at 40 Years of Zen, it's usually to clients spending five days practicing it repeatedly with neurofeedback. There are nuances, so I'll explain each step here with the reasoning behind it. You'll find clear instructions, including a QR code, at the end of this chapter. Use the QR code to access and print the Quick

Reference Guide. Put it on your fridge or wherever you'll see it daily. You can also use the QR code to ask questions about the book.

The Reset Process is a specific type of meditation based on insights from psychology, psychiatry, and ancient practices about forgiveness. It aims to help you feel at peace as fast as possible. You don't need fancy equipment to do it, but technology can help you reach the desired states more easily, which is why people come to 40 Years of Zen to learn it. I'm sharing my Reset Process in this book so you learn how to control your nervous system (triggers and responses) without spending days, weeks, or years meditating in a cave or monastery.

Some steps might not make sense initially because this process interacts with felt states and parts of your MeatOS that your body usually hides. Suspend logic and follow the steps outlined for the best results.

To do the Reset Process, you're going to engage your imagination. Unlike typical visualization guides, this process involves more than just sight. It includes your sense of touch and interoception (your brain's ability to sense internal states). For example, interoception signals you to drink water when you're thirsty. It also includes your sense of smell, taste, and sound. When I talk about visualizing or imagining, you will engage every sense in your body, especially touch and interoception. For this technique to work, you must feel it in your body, not just think about it or visualize it. This is a whole-brain, whole-body process.

| THE RESET PROCESS |

When you use the Reset Process, you enter the Reset Mode. This is an eight-step process that puts you in charge of yourself in a way you likely haven't experienced before. You may uncover old memories that you thought you'd already overcome. Don't judge yourself.

Exercise compassion. Tell your brain and body how much you appreciate them for keeping you safe. Then get to work untangling the mess so you can get rid of the junk you no longer need.

If, as you go through this process, you find your mind floating off to your to-do list, pause. These thoughts are just distractions. You might feel frustrated, but remember, this is a *process*. You're not sprinting to the finish line. You're taking a leisurely walk. Come back to the present moment, focus on your breath and the sensations in your body, and continue. As memories surface, acknowledge them. You may come across your inner child asking for your attention. Remain curious. What do they need from you to feel safe to go into these memories? If you're not sure, ask them. Then get quiet long enough to hear what they say.

This process is deeply personal. I am giving you the framework to follow, but the work you do while in this process is yours. Give yourself space to feel, emote, and release. How this happens will look different for everyone. Trust that however your brain and body experience this process is perfect.

Before we begin, take a deep breath. Tell yourself how proud you are of yourself for choosing to embark on this deep self-discovery and healing journey. Maybe you're practicing this process independently instead of at 40 Years of Zen, and that's fine. I'm beside you. You can do this.

Step One: Choose Your Environment

The first step in the Reset Process is selecting your environment. Unlike many of the other transpersonal techniques, which can also be useful, the Reset Process involves creating a mental space where you can reset and turn off specific triggers. Your environment can be where you are now, a place you love to visit, your childhood bedroom, nature, a temple, or a church—anywhere you choose. The critical piece is being able to envision it with your eyes closed. Closing your eyes helps produce two to three times more alpha brain waves, providing a sense of calm, which is beneficial for this process.

While you can create a new environment each time you do the reset, many people prefer to use the same mental space consistently. Think of this place as your little sanctuary to do some really powerful work. Safety, comfort, and peace are great feelings to aim for when choosing your space. The key is envisioning it clearly with all the sights, smells, and sounds. Immerse yourself in your surroundings. Use your peripheral vision, even though your eyes are closed, to sense the light, the temperature, and any movement like wind through trees. This is your safe space.

Step Two: Select an Unimpeachable Spiritual Being as Your Guide

Choosing a spiritual guide might seem irrational to your logical brain, but it's a crucial part of the Reset Process. If you're feeling triggered by this step, just go with it. Choose your guide, someone or something symbolizing a spiritual, unimpeachable being.

Some options include religious figures like Jesus, Muhammad, Buddha, or Kwan Yin. You could also choose the spirit of an eagle, the sun, or even a lightbulb; maybe it responds to you by flickering on and off. Your guide must be beyond human flaws, unlike figures such as Mother Teresa or Nelson Mandela, who, despite their greatness, were still human and fallible. Your grandmother or your parents won't work here because they're also human, and they've made mistakes.

This step is vital because your body will try to deceive you to maintain safety. Choosing an unimpeachable guide, not subject to human biology, is a little hack that doesn't sound like it would work, but it does. You won't be able to pretend you did the Reset Process; you actually have to feel your way through it to get results.

Some people use the same guide for every reset, while others choose to mix it up. Do whatever works best for you. Whether you believe the guides are real doesn't matter; their role in your subconscious matters. Christianity focuses on forgiveness, Islam on surrender, and Buddhism on compassion. You might choose a guide based on the intention you've set for your work. And if you choose an inanimate object like a lightbulb, you can make up the spiritual meaning on your own. It's about choosing someone or something that resonates with you.

Place your guide in your mental reset environment. I like to place mine above me and to the right. Visualize your guide in this space, where they'll always be watching and paying attention, but not in a creepy way. This external accountability prevents you from tricking yourself into thinking you completed the process when you didn't.

Step Three: Select a Trigger Person and Event

This step can be tricky, so read this part twice. Choose a recent, minor event that upset you for your first reset. Avoid tackling major issues, huge societal problems, or chronic stressors initially; think of this as learning to walk, not climbing Everest. People have used the Reset Process to forgive the greatest wrongs in the world—like the Nazis, heartbreaking wars, their government—so they're no longer triggered. These are obviously huge events. You'll get there eventually, but that's not where you'll start.

Start with something small, like someone cutting you off in traffic or a rude coworker. Focus on *one* specific person and *one* specific incident. For example, instead of forgiving your boss for everything they've ever done to piss you off, forgive your boss for a specific time they criticized you in front of others. Your body remembers distinct moments of feeling unsafe, threatened, or disrespected, often tied to earlier experiences that we see as unrelated, sometimes from childhood.

Choose *one* person and *one* event at a time. Don't try to forgive Mom and Dad simultaneously; forgive Mom for yelling at you for spilling something and Dad separately for not protecting you. This focused approach prevents you from feeling overwhelmed. It also ensures the reset is complete before moving on to the next trigger person and event.

The more you practice, the easier it gets. Like learning to ride a bike, you might not be great initially but will improve with time. Consistent practice, whether in five intensive days at 40 Years of Zen or an hour daily over a month, will help you master the Reset Process. Eventually you can reset quickly, sometimes in just a few seconds or a minute. You can learn how to handle multiple resets simultaneously after you have some practice, but first, let's go deeper into the process.

Step Four: Name the Trigger and the Feeling

In this step, be precise about what triggered you and how it made you feel. Avoid generalizations like "My boss made me mad." Instead, specify the event: "[Boss's name], you criticized me unfairly in a meeting in front of others, and it made me feel angry and embarrassed." Identify the exact feeling you felt. Don't just say, "He was mean." Describe the act: "He criticized me using a condescending tone of voice." Precision is key. Always phrase it like this: "[Person's name], you did X [event], and it made me feel Y [feeling]."

For example: "[Person's name], you stole a million dollars from me [event], causing me to lose my house. It made me feel betrayed, helpless, and unlovable." This level of detail is crucial. And yes, it works. I know because this betrayal happened to me twice—once from a family member. It was awful then, but I could let it go after doing the Reset Process.

If you ask around, you'll find this kind of betrayal has happened to many successful entrepreneurs, but nobody talks about it because of shame. After you complete the Reset Process, you won't feel shame about your triggers anymore.

Step Five: Feel It Fully

After naming the trigger, spend two minutes (or no more than five minutes) fully experiencing all the senses/emotions. Your body can replay any emotion, like a voice memo. But doing that doesn't feel good, so we often avoid it. It's okay to sweat, shiver, or feel intense anger. The more you feel it in the pit of your stomach, around your heart, or through the clenching of your teeth, the more effective this step is.

This is the point in the process where you get to unleash. Say whatever needs to be said. Get the stuck emotions out of your body. Imagine yourself speaking to the person (or thing) that hurt you. If the memory is from childhood, imagine yourself as that child who was in pain. Take yourself back to the moment you felt the feeling, involving all your senses. Yes, this is uncomfortable. And your body will try to distract you with better thoughts and feelings. But commit, remain present in your body, feel what you need to feel, and then release it. The *feelings* are what will set you free. Stay with them.

Listen up: you can get stuck in this step (you don't want that).

That's why you don't want to exceed five minutes—ideally, keep it *under two minutes*. You can set a timer to help and just go as deep as possible in that time. Avoid getting stuck in these emotions, especially when they feel really big. It's easy to lose track of time and overwhelm yourself, which is counterproductive.

We discussed dissociation in a previous chapter, and that's important here, too. Don't visualize yourself from a distance (disassociate); be in your body and experience it. Believe it or not, feeling uncomfortable is a good sign. This brief reexposure helps prevent future reexperiencing. It's a short burst of courage, and you can handle it. Avoiding feelings due to fear of retraumatization (which is a real thing) is common. Your protection is that you will only do this part for two minutes.

The Reset Process puts your brain in Reset Mode and permanently cancels the trigger. This technique won't retraumatize you when you follow the steps. And if it feels like it's too much, congratulations. You can stop feeling it and move on to the next step. There's no need to sit with negative emotions and uncomfortable bodily sensations. Only go as deep as you can safely. The more you feel it, the better it works, but don't push yourself to the point of overwhelm or paralyzing fear.

Important note: If you're dealing with severe trauma, like war or abuse, consider working with an EMDR practitioner or therapist. Listen and honor your body. You know what you need.

Step Six: Find the Spark of Gratitude; One Good Thing That Happened Because of the Trigger

This step is crucial and often overlooked. To truly forgive and let go, you must first experience gratitude. Find one good thing that resulted from the trigger, no matter how small.

Let's return to the example of your boss criticizing you publicly. Well, maybe one of your coworkers took you to lunch to discuss it and remind you of human decency. Or, if someone stole money from you, perhaps you're grateful you still have one hundred dollars left. Maybe your parents moved to a different country to give you a better life because of the war. The war wasn't good, but it led to a positive outcome. The tiniest spark of gratitude can ignite the process of letting go.

Without gratitude, the Reset Process will fail. If you find it extra challenging to find something good, it's okay. Ask a friend for help. Remember, you can always be grateful that you're here, going through this process, working on the things holding you back. Every cloud has a silver lining, even if it's small.

Gratitude can also come from learning. Let's say you were in a narcissistic relationship that crushed your confidence. You might have learned to spot the signs sooner to avoid repeating that mistake. This learning experience itself is something to be grateful for. Finding the spark of gratitude involves turning on curiosity, which extinguishes fear. When you become curious about finding something good, you shift from "this sucks" to "something good came from this." And that's the thing about your body: it's easy to fool. This subtle yet profound shift lightens the heaviness in your heart.

If you get stuck here, evoke a sense of awe; this turns on gratitude. Think of a beautiful sunset, the birth of a child, or a playful puppy. The closer the feeling is to the trigger you're working to release, the better. It won't work if you think about gratitude but don't feel grateful. You have to feel every step. Your body likes to feel gratitude, but sometimes it's hard to access. Changing your body's state from reactivation (fear) to curiosity and gratitude opens the door to freedom, with the Reset Process as the bridge.

Step Seven: Forgive It Fully

The first step in forgiveness is deciding to forgive, inspired by Nelson Mandela's approach. Remember, forgiveness doesn't mean condoning the action or telling the person you forgive them. It simply means shifting your state so you're no longer triggered. This shift can be private and still be profound. If the word *forgiveness* triggers you, you might need to use the Reset Process to let that go. It's for your sake.

To step into forgiveness, look at the trigger person you placed in your reset environment and ask, "What made them this way?" Consider their upbringing, possible traumas, or even a bad day. They may be operating from their unresolved triggers, possibly things similar to what you're consciously choosing to work on right now.

Visualize your trigger person as a child or an innocent baby. Understand that they're flawed, like all humans, acting out of their programming, not their core kindness. It's not an excuse for their poor behavior, but with this understanding, you create compassion. Feel this sense of compassion in your chest. Maybe it has a color, a shape, or feels warm or fuzzy. Breathe into it and let it expand, transforming your perception of them from a threat to just another flawed human who messed up. The power that your nervous system gave them is now gone, and you realize you can feel empathy and compassion toward them, even though you don't like what they did. Sometimes, during this process, people feel like their chest opens up to reveal their heart. This "heart opener" is something you might see in a loving-kindness meditation; your anger turns to softness, and you find it easy to connect to the other person's heart.

If the person triggered you repeatedly, you will run the Reset Process for each incident. Initially you realize that your intense emotions are your body's way of keeping you safe. Now you see them as another deeply flawed person, possibly still dangerous but not deserving of your hate. Hate is too expensive. As you forgive, you may experience profound release and even spiritual sensations, similar to neurofeedback or psychedelics. This process restores your power, removing the other person's control over your heart and nervous system.

You can't overdo this step. You'll know when you're done. Continue until the feelings dissipate. You just see this person as another human and understand that humans are one species. We are one. The freedom from their control is liberating, making you impenetrable to their actions.

Step Eight: Check In with Your Guide

Even if you feel like you've completed the task, your body may resist, making you believe you're done as a way to keep you safe from potential harm (feeling anything more). This is where your guide comes in. Keep your eyes closed, but turn your gaze to wherever you've placed your guide, and either mentally or out loud, ask them, "Am I done for now?" Your guide will give you a sign. If it's not a clear yes, it's a no.

You might think, *I just made up the guide. How would it know?* Your body and mind do many things that are invisible to you. There might not be a logical reason for not getting a clear yes. Take this as a message from your subconscious that you still have work to do. Your guide's response might vary: if you're using a lightbulb, it turns on or doesn't; if a deity, they give a nod, thumbs-up, or high five. If the signal is unclear, it's a no. Take a deep breath. You've removed a layer, but another remains.

If it's unclear or you get a no, return to Step Three: Select a Trigger Person and Event. Then begin the process again. Ensure that your selection is precise. Identify *one* person and *one* specific action, not vague feelings or multiple events. Precision is crucial to effectively completing the Reset Process.

ADVANCED PRACTICE #1: EXPLORE THE ROOT CAUSE

Once you've completed a few resets and understand the process well, you can deepen your practice. When you're in Step Five: Feel It Fully, pause and ask yourself, *When is the first time I ever felt this way?* An image or memory might pop up that seems unrelated at first. Most people dismiss this as an intrusive thought, but it's your subconscious revealing the root of your feelings.

When I felt a sense of injustice from being unfairly attacked by a media celebrity for something I didn't do, a forgotten memory from first grade resurfaced. Why? My body was helping me identify the source of my emotions. I could have run the Reset Process on that incident with Joe, but going from that point back to first grade would be a lot of work. So, I returned to first grade, and the trigger surrounding the experience with Joe dissipated.

Instead of running the Reset Process on each incident over the years, you can use these advanced practices to feel the emotion and think back to when you first remember feeling it. Then you can focus on forgiving the initial event that created the emotional trigger in the first place. This approach saves time and energy. By understanding and forgiving the root cause, you can clear many subsequent triggers simultaneously, making the Reset Process even more powerful and efficient.

ADVANCED PRACTICE #2:
TIME TRAVEL

"Time travel" piggybacks on the root cause practice, taking it even further. When you trace back to the first time you felt a particular way, you might initially jump back a few years. But when you sit down to do the reset, you might notice you jump back even further in time, another ten years. Most people end up remembering childhood stuff that, as an adult, is insignificant. However, these memories are what programmed your initial trigger because, as a child, these events were impactful.

By resetting the earliest occurrence of the emotion, you effectively reset every subsequent instance of that trigger, just as I did with Joe and the memory from first grade. For example, if you reset the first time your heart was broken, often in high school, the pain from all the subsequent breakups might feel less or be gone altogether. This is why the Reset Process doesn't take a lifetime to master. Once you address the root cause, all related memories are affected. You remember them, but they no longer carry the same emotional charge. You can recall these impressionable events without increased heart rate, stress, anxiety, or wavering voice. You're at peace. It can initially be confusing because you might think you are supposed to always feel pain about the horrible thing that happened. Until you realize, *Oh my gosh, I don't have to carry all that old baggage anymore. I can be free!*

This time-travel practice is powerful because science has proven that your body stores memories in your brain with emotions.[3] By changing your emotional response from anger or fear to peace, you retain the memories without reexperiencing the negative feelings. This is what makes the Reset Process so profoundly transformative.

ADVANCED PRACTICE #3: RESET INANIMATE OBJECTS

Another advanced practice involves forgiving *things*. This might seem irrational as an adult, but it can be crucial for resolving childhood triggers. For instance, if you were five and learning to ride a bike and ran into a tree, you might need to forgive both the bike and the tree. To do this, follow the same process but place the object, the bike, in this example, instead of the person in your mental environment. It might feel silly, but five-year-olds are a bit silly. If that's when you formed the trigger, acknowledge your feelings toward the object. You could say, "Tree, you smacked me in the face. It hurt, I was scared, and it left a scar on my forehead." Then find one good thing from the incident, like learning to steer your bike or use the brakes properly.

While this may seem minor, it's essential, especially in situations like car accidents. Forgiving the other car can be as crucial as forgiving the driver. Yes, it seems strange. But your body's responses don't have to make logical sense; this is how they work.

ADVANCED PRACTICE #4: RESET GROUPS, ORGANIZATIONS, AND CONSTRUCTS

For deep feelings of anxiety or betrayal, sometimes you need to forgive a group, organization, or construct. If you're angry about societal issues, such as the financial state or social media's addictive nature, your feelings are justified. However, being triggered makes you easily programmable. When you're aware and no longer triggered, you can address these issues from a place of consciousness rather than reactivity.

Forgiving constructs like financial elites or social media involve visualizing a representation, such as a logo or icon. Nearly everyone I've ever worked with has run a reset against their government for acting unfairly and selfishly. Even if you like your government, chances are it has done at least one dumb thing that has made you angry. So, visualize a representation, whether a figurehead, a dumpster, a whirlwind, or an abstract symbol that resonates with your anger or betrayal. Use this in your mental environment during the Reset Process.

This is not going to take away your power. It's going to enhance it. Anger is terrible long-term fuel. Sure, it can ignite change. But if you fuel yourself with anger, you will become an empty husk of a human, and you'll suffer greatly. If you become peaceful about an injustice, you can break free from it.

These advanced resets take practice; eventually you can enter them at will. Start with simpler resets before tackling faceless constructs.

ADVANCED PRACTICE #5: FORGIVE YOURSELF

The most challenging and valuable practice is forgiving yourself. This is something I've had to work on extensively. You might have taken a job with a terrible boss, suffered silently in a bad relationship, or set up a system that allowed a family member to steal a million dollars. Even if you didn't know it then, you were complicit, which often leads to feelings of shame. If you forgive others and the things that caused the triggers but don't forgive yourself, you miss a crucial part of the healing process. After completing the Reset Process for others, turn it inward.

To do this, place yourself in your reset environment. Visualize yourself at the age or state when the trigger occurred. Run the same Reset Process. It's harder to feel empathy, compassion, and love for yourself. Your body fears that letting go of guilt, shame, and fear might make you less reactive to potential dangers like a tiger chasing you down the streets of New York City. Yes, many things you fear are illogical, but they feel real, so acknowledge them. Don't make yourself wrong for your feelings.

Self-forgiveness is the most challenging but also the most valuable. Just don't start there. Start with the easier resets, move back in time, and forgive things and constructs. Then, when you get to yourself, you'll have the skills and emotional resilience to do the work necessary to set yourself free.

| NOW WHAT? |

When you've completed your Reset Process, whether it was a single issue or a list you made all week and tackled Saturday morning, take a moment to congratulate yourself. Turn on your gratitude muscle and acknowledge your progress. Pat yourself on the back, drink a cup of Danger Coffee, take a walk in the park, pet your dog, or hug a friend or loved one. Notice how much lighter and more energized you feel.

Over the last eleven years of my working with clients and refining the Reset Process, many have reported that things feel easier afterward. And it's true: things are easier because you no longer use your energy to run invisible trigger-sensing programs. What once seemed like a giant mountain now feels manageable. You can ask for a raise or ask someone out without the weight of triggers holding you back. You're no longer wasting energy. You're efficiently allocating it like a pro.

This process has profoundly freed over 1,500 people, including industry leaders, parents, children, and people doing big things. Without the burden of triggers, guilt, shame, fear, and anger, it's easier to tap into your creativity, intuition, and problem-solving abilities.

The greatest gift I can give you for reading this book is to encourage you to do the process. Do it until your guide gives you a thumbs-up, at least twice.

As promised, here's the QR code to download and print the quick reference guide. Put this on your fridge or somewhere you'll see it daily. Let this be a reminder that every trigger stems from somewhere, and you have the power to free yourself from its weight. All it takes is your commitment to go all in on the Reset Process and use forgiveness as a tool for healing.

THE 8-STEP RESET PROCESS:
QUICK REFERENCE GUIDE

Step One: Choose Your Environment

Step Two: Select an Unimpeachable Spiritual Being as a Guide

Step Three: Select a Trigger Person and Event

Step Four: Name the Trigger and the Feeling

Step Five: Feel It Fully

Step Six: Find the Spark of Gratitude; One Good Thing That Happened Because of the Trigger

Step Seven: Forgive It Fully

Step Eight: Check In With Your Guide

| PART III |

WHAT'S STOPPING YOU

EAT MORE, SUFFER LESS

When I say, "Eat more, suffer less," I'm not talking about indulging in junk food or drowning your sorrows in alcohol or other harmful substances. It's all about fueling your spirit and supercharging your life-force energy with the right food and environment. Think of it as powering up your body's Wi-Fi signal. When that signal is strong, you're in sync with reality. You feel more connected to yourself, your community, the earth, and maybe even the entire universe. But when the signal is weak, you feel anxious, tired, and disconnected.

Your life-force energy, or chi, is like the invisible fuel that keeps your body and mind running smoothly. And guess what? The quality of your fuel (food) plays a massive role in how strong your signal is. Eating the right foods can supercharge your mitochondria, making you feel more vibrant and alive. Poor food choices can drag you down, making you suffer more than necessary.

I know believing in something you can't see is challenging. That's why faith is tricky for so many people. But if you tune in to yourself, you can feel this life-force energy pulsing through your veins like electrical currents. You can't see it, but you're alive, which proves that your body is using this invisible energy like a pro. You trust your body to do its job so you can focus on things other than how often your heart pumps or your lungs breathe. It's a miraculous leap of faith to rely on your body to keep you going. Of course, it requires your collaborative effort, like feeding it food, which we'll get to shortly.

Blind faith is part of what makes biohacking so impactful. If you do something and get a reliable outcome, you don't have to know all the steps or reasons it works. You just have to understand that to get X results, you need to do Y. Leave it to mystics, neuroscientists, or both, as I do, to untangle all the reasons and stories about why it works. Then focus on just being grateful that it does. Whether you believe in information field theory, spiritual entities, or hidden dimensions, it doesn't matter to get what I'm saying. There's a solid scientific explanation behind it all: mitochondria.

| THE POWER PLANTS OF YOUR CELLS |

You might remember mitochondria from high school biology. They're like tiny power plants inside your cells, cranking out the energy you need to do anything and everything. When your mitochondria function efficiently, they produce enough energy to power not just your physical activities but also your mental and spiritual well-being.

People have accused me of having a mitochondria fetish. While that makes me laugh, the fascination—or "obsession," some might call it—goes way deeper. When you're dealing with chronic fatigue syndrome, and you're so profoundly exhausted, feeling empty, anxious, and triggered, you know your mitochondria are in trouble. I've been there. I yelled at loved ones because I lacked the energy to regulate my emotions. I also didn't have enough awareness and didn't know the techniques from this book to stop the tidal wave of emotions from pouring out in unhealthy ways. If my energy levels had been better, without hunger, cravings, and nutrient deficiencies, I wouldn't have reacted so poorly. We've all had those moments, right? Well, your mitochondria help with mood regulation. That's not an excuse. It's just a fact.

You've heard of being "hangry," or my favorite, "hypogly-bitchy." You probably laughed when you read that, and for good reason. Because you know it's real whether you've experienced it firsthand or been around someone during a full-blown famine fit. Why does this happen? As you learned earlier in the book, the body doesn't like to waste energy. If there's insufficient energy for any reason, it shuts down nonessential functions, whatever it can skip and not die. Things like kindness, supporting your community, and evolving your personal development and spiritual life all get turned off like a light switch. And if you focus on them anyway, they feel much harder to do.

Most of your cells have a few hundred little environmental sensors with antennas, looking at reality in a way you never will. Using the five F's for survival—fear, food, fertility, friends, forgiveness—your mitochondria vote on what action to take. If they're malnourished, they might choose attack mode. You know, the point where the muscles in your middle finger bulge after someone cuts you off in traffic. They're tired and hungry and in desperate need of nutrients.

Some parts of the body are unusually dense with mitochondria. They have sensors, computing power, and the ability to make heat, electricity, sex hormones, and all the other amazing things they do beyond being your body's power plant. The areas in the brain and most parts of the body that have the most mitochondria are, un-surprisingly, the ones that consume the most energy: the neurons in your brain and the tissues in your heart. These cells have thousands of mitochondria each.[1]

The heart has a smaller neuron count than the brain, but it has its own impressive network. About 40,000 neurons form the "heart-brain" or intrinsic cardiac nervous system.[2] They play a crucial role in heart rate and rhythm. They also communicate with your brain, influencing how you feel and how your body responds to different situations. So, while your brain is the command center with billions of neurons, your heart, with its 40,000 neurons, acts like a sophisticated relay station.

The energy demands on these parts are so great that there are specialized systems to move mitochondria around, bringing extra power where it's needed. It's like there are little buses that mitochondria hop on to get to where the action is. Your body works hard to supply energy to the brain for thinking and your heart for feeling. There are well-established connections between the heart and the brain. In fact, 80 percent of the signals between them are from the heart to the brain. So, when you do the Reset Process, you think about things, then feel them in your heart, signaling your emotions. What actually happens, though, is your heart informs your brain before the thought ever happens. My friend and colleague Dr. Roland McCready, from the HeartMath Institute, has shown that signals go from the heart to the brain much more often than the other way around. You just think they started in your head because that was the first conscious signal you felt unless you're really tapped in and have learned to feel your heart first.

We often think the brain and heart are the most energy-dense parts of the body, but scientists sometimes forget the one part that outdoes them all: the ovaries in women, with a whopping 100,000 mitochondria per cell.[3, 4] So, if you want to talk about life-force energy, it's coming from mitochondria. This energy keeps you young and vibrant and supports your spiritual progression.

Mitochondria make you feel more connected, alive, and attuned to the world. But when the system isn't working correctly, it's like running your car with a clogged fuel injector. You might still be able to drive, but it's a bumpy ride. You burn through fuel fast, and eventually, things break down. If these essential players on your team aren't operating like they should be, you feel it big-time. There are a few key reasons this happens: toxins, nutrient deficiencies, chronic stress, and poor lifestyle choices.

| TRASHY TOXINS |

Your environment is full of toxins that mess with your mito-chondria. Most people know that we're swimming in ultrapro-cessed foods (UPFs): anything with an ingredient list that reads like a chemistry textbook. Things like maltodextrin, sodium benzoate, and carrageenan are red flags. These industrial ingredients serve as preservatives, flavor enhancers, and emulsifiers. The problem? Your body doesn't know what to do with them. Refined sugars and trans fats in UPFs mess with your metabolism and mitochondrial function. These foods lack nutrients and fiber. They're high in cal-ories but low in vitamins, minerals, and antioxidants, which your body needs to thrive. Overly processed, these foods barely resemble their original form. Sad but true. These foods include things like white flour, high-fructose corn syrup, seed oils, and hydrogenated oils.

Artificial colors, flavors, and especially artificial sweeteners or flavor enhancers like MSG harm your brain and slow your progress. These chemicals trick your taste buds into thinking you're eating something delicious, but they're liars and deceiving you. You could write an entire book about what these do to the brain. In fact, I did. So, I won't rehash all of that here because it's already available. How-ever, here's a list of the big offenders: food colorings—especially red, blue, yellow, and orange—along with aspartame and monosodium glutamate (MSG). These are the ones that cause the most harm to the brain.

Studies have linked ultraprocessed foods to many health problems, from obesity and diabetes to heart disease and mental health issues like increased anxiety and depression.[5] They may even shrink your brain![6] They're full of mitochondrial toxins that impair your cells' ability to produce energy efficiently, leaving you feeling crappy and not yourself.

If you want to connect to your higher self and tune in to the world around you, having mitochondria that just got poisoned by your last meal is not a good idea. Maybe you're thinking, *Well,* poisoned *is quite a dramatic word, Dave.* But if your mitochondria ran at 70 percent capacity before the meal and are down to 50 percent after, I'd say they got poisoned. They didn't die, but they got weakened. And you got weakened. Spiritually weakened. So yeah, what you put in your mouth matters.

Heavy metals are another sneaky culprit. Too much lead, mercury, or even thallium (which, surprise, comes from eating lots of kale) will take the shine off your mitochondria. They won't stop them outright, but they'll weaken them. And sadly, when your system is weak, you lose your self-evolution and self-regulation first. It takes way more willpower to make good decisions (like going to the gym instead of eating a whole pizza), and there's less electricity to supply that willpower, perpetuating the cycle of unhappiness and disease.

| NUTRIENT DEFICIENCIES |

You are what you eat—at least, your cells are. The nutrients inside your food create some of the most important molecules in your cells. Scientists are looking at how deficiencies in specific vitamins affect one of these essential molecules: DNA.

Take vitamin B_{12}, for example. This vitamin plays a crucial role in DNA stability. Research shows that being low in B_{12} can lead to indirect DNA damage.[7] How? B_{12} is a cofactor for enzymes like methionine synthase and methylmalonyl-CoA mutase, which are necessary for DNA methylation and nucleotide synthesis. Without enough B_{12}, these processes falter, increasing susceptibility to DNA mutations. Plus, B_{12} has antioxidant properties that help protect your DNA from damage caused by reactive oxygen species (ROS). So, if you're skimping on B_{12}, you're letting free radicals run wild on your genetic blueprint.

Vitamin D is another one—it is so much more than the sunshine vitamin. Vitamin D deficiency increases DNA damage.[8] This vitamin helps regulate the expression of DNA repair genes like RAD50 and RAD51. When there's damage to your DNA, someone has to fix it—think of RAD50 and RAD51 as your construction team, finding and fixing the damaged DNA. These genes are essential for keeping your genetic information accurate and maintaining overall cellular health. When you're low on vitamin D, these repair processes don't work as efficiently. This can set the stage for chronic diseases and even accelerate aging.

The list goes on. That's why knowing how to eat is crucial. Professors will tell you about the Shaman's Diet if you go to shaman school. If you visit traditional Chinese Qigong practitioners, they'll guide you on what to eat and avoid. An Ayurvedic practitioner will do the same because food is fundamental to spirituality. It's also why fasting is such a profound practice in many traditions. They understand that what you put in your body, you get out. Quality food and nutrients create happiness, vitality, energy, and brain power. Crappy foodlike substances lead to weight gain, depression, brain fog, and disease.

Your mitochondria need specific nutrients to do their job well. If you miss out on essential vitamins, minerals, and fats, these little powerhouses can't produce energy. Think of it this way: if you need zinc to make a neurotransmitter, or you're low on amino acids, or missing out on essential vitamins like D, A, K, or E, your body has to work overtime to do the basic tasks to keep you alive. These are simple, low-cost supplements that help your body respond better to everything—exercise, meditation, sleep, you name it. Suppgrade Labs[TM][9] makes a supportive stack that includes DAKE—an all-in-one fat-soluble vitamin—and Minerals 101. Minerals fuel the reactions in your body. DAKE shuttles minerals around the body to where they need to go to work their magic. You can get some of these from food, but for most people, eating a healthy diet still won't give you enough. Being low in nutrients or calories makes it way harder to let go of the triggers running in the background, stealing your energy, joy, and genius.

The same thing happens with a diet devoid of animal fats. (You can get animal fats from a vegetarian diet, but not from a vegan one.) Animal fats are crucial because the hormones in your brain are made from them, not canola oil. Your brain is about 60 percent fat. It thrives on fats from animals, packed with omega-3 and omega-6 fatty acids, which are crucial for cognitive function and building cell membranes. These fats are also building blocks for hormones like testosterone and estrogen, so important for mood and metabolism. They help absorb fat-soluble vitamins D, A, K, and E. Animal fats provide steady, slow-burning energy, unlike carbs, which cause spikes and crashes. They also support cell structure and signaling processes. Plus they make food taste delicious and satisfy you, so you don't get the afternoon munchies and find yourself reaching for junk.

Aim for 75 percent saturated fats, such as grass-fed butter, tallow, lard, coconut oil, and ghee. Even pure dark chocolate,[10] with at least 70 percent cocoa in small amounts, is okay. Gear the other 25 percent toward monosaturated fats (olive oil, avocados, almonds, and macadamia nuts) and omega-3s. Avoid excess amounts of omega-6 fatty acids and polyunsaturated fats.

Then there are proteins, the building blocks of life. They're essential for just about every function in your body, from building muscle and repairing tissues to producing hormones and enzymes. Without enough protein, your body can't perform at its peak. Protein supports the production of enzymes that break down food so your body can absorb all those vital vitamins and minerals. They also help transport nutrients across cell membranes, ensuring your cells get what they need to function efficiently.

Curious if you lack protein? You might notice you're getting sick more often, your nails and hair are brittle and breaking, you have mood swings, or you feel tired all the time. Amino acids are the building blocks of protein. Out of the twentysomething amino acids found in nature, nine are essential to your diet because your body can't make them on its own. That means you have to get them from your food or supplements.

You want the good stuff to fuel your MeatOS. My top picks for quality protein and fats come from grass-fed animals, especially grass-fed beef, beef tallow, and grass-fed butter. And no, it's not because grass-fed is trendy. Grass-fed beef isn't just beef. It's like nature's multivitamin. It has more vitamins and antioxidants than its grain-fed counterpart, things like A and E to support a healthy immune system and vision, and antioxidants like glutathione and superoxide dismutase, which help fight oxidative stress. It also provides up to six times more omega-3 fatty acids than grain-fed beef. Omega-3s help reduce inflammation, support heart health, and enhance your brain's performance. The omega-3 to omega-6 ratio makes grass-fed beef a great choice for heart health. And get this: its beneficial fatty acid profile can keep your blood sugar levels in check. This is huge when it comes to diabetes and obesity prevention.

But it's not just about the nutrients. The taste is superior to grain-free beef. Plus, it's better for the planet and the animals. Grass-fed cattle roam freely and eat grass, not corn or soy. You are what you eat, right? So, eating well-fed beef means you're also eating meat that's healthier for you.

Plants are cool, but not all of them are winners. Some can trigger inflammation and contain antinutrients—compounds that affect nutrient absorption. For example, phytic acid, found in grains (like wheat, rice, and oats), nuts, seeds, beans, lentils, and peas, binds to minerals like iron, zinc, and calcium, reducing their absorption. Lectins and gluten are also culprits, interfering with absorption and causing stomach issues.[11] Spinach, beets, and my leafy nemesis, kale, contain oxalates that can bind to calcium and form kidney stones. Then you've got glucosinolates in cruciferous veggies like broccoli and Brussels sprouts, which can mess with thyroid function if you eat too much. Tannins (grapes, berries, and apples) can affect iron absorption, and saponins (found in potatoes and other tubers) can cause gut issues.[12]

If you're constantly tired, stuck in a victim loop, or just can't let go of something, maybe the answer is a really good breakfast with lots of protein and quality fats. Test it for a week and you might find that your outlook on life has completely transformed. You'll feel less anxious and less depressed, and most importantly, you'll have the energy (in the form of calories) and the raw materials (in the form of healthy fats, minerals, and vitamins) to supercharge your brain.

So, what's the antidote to a healthier brain and body? Eat healthy plants, eat animal protein, and, very specifically, eat animal fats. Then supplement with essential vitamins and minerals because, let's face it, you're probably deficient in something. These are the fuels your brain and body need for peak performance. I dive into these topics extensively in my other books *The Bulletproof Diet* and *Smarter Not Harder*.

| CHRONIC STRESS |

Excess stress hormones, like cortisol, can damage your mito-chondria over time. When they're under attack, your energy levels plummet and your MeatOS takes a serious hit. If you're constantly stressed, inflammation ramps up and becomes chronic. Think of chronic inflammation as having a low-grade fire smoldering inside your body. It won't burn your house down immediately but will cause significant damage over time. Plus it accelerates the aging pro-cess, is linked to a ton of diseases, messes with your mental health, and damages your mitochondria, which is entirely counterproductive for your goals as a biohacker.

If you know you tend to be in a state of chronic stress, there are simple strategies you can implement now to help you long-term. Removing toxins is a big one. These tax your system, eventually overburdening it to exhaustion and burnout. Focus on eating high-quality foods and avoiding ultraprocessed foods as much as possible—practice stress-management routines with things like yoga, breathwork, meditation, and time in nature. Make sure you're well hydrated during the day, getting enough minerals and fat-soluble vitamins, and get enough restful sleep at night. All of these things help you lower chronic stress and inflammation.

| POOR LIFESTYLE CHOICES |

Lack of sleep, sitting around too much, and stuffing your face with sugar and junk food are killing your vibe. Your mitochondria crave good sleep, regular movement, and a diet rich in healthy fats and protein, not processed crap. Give them what they want!

Contrary to popular belief, you don't have to lift and throw heavy things for hours daily to get the benefits. Remember the laziness principle we discussed? Your MeatOS wants you to move your body efficiently, not excessively. I wrote all about this in *Smarter Not Harder.*

I used to be a gym junkie, doing 45 minutes of cardio and 45 minutes of strength training six days a week. I ate a low-carb, limited-calorie diet. I did all of this for eighteen months, and you know what? I was still fat. Sure, I was strong under my soft waistline. But in true biohacker fashion, I wanted to be healthy and lean to live until at least 180. And I wanted my brain to be fit, too. Studies show that regular physical activity can reduce your risk of developing dementia by 28 percent and Alzheimer's disease by 45 percent.[13] That stat alone is worth moving for.

Cardio and strength training are important, but you don't have to kill yourself in the gym to reap the rewards of daily movement. Seriously, if you hate the gym, don't go. Take a walk instead. Find an activity you enjoy and do more of it. Dance, have sex, practice yoga, whatever gets you moving. Even ten minutes a day is better than nothing. Start with something realistic, something you know you can stick with. Exercise improves dopamine levels.[14] Studies show that increases in dopamine in the brain's striatum lead to higher motivation and enhanced task performance.[15] That's because dopamine helps the brain evaluate the potential rewards of completing tasks and pushes you to achieve them. Think of your brain's dopamine system as a coach cheering you on inside your head. Plus, exercise promotes BDNF—that compound we talked about earlier that's like fertilizer for your neurons!

Getting started is the hardest part, but with consistency, you form a habit, and good habits are how you get results. Physical activity also contributes to better sleep, a big problem for many people.

Quality sleep is not just a luxury; it's a necessity. And it's the ultimate biohack for your body and brain. While you're sleeping, your body goes into repair mode. This is when your muscles recover, your tissues heal, your cells regenerate, and your brain works to clear out the toxins from the previous day. Sleep is also essential for cognitive function.[16] Studies show that sleep improves learning and problem-solving skills. It also helps to balance your hunger hormones (ghrelin and leptin), aids in weight management, strengthens your immune system,[17] and supports your mood and emotional well-being.[18]

One study at the University of Chicago found that sleep deprivation impairs glucose metabolism and increases cortisol levels, which can lead to weight gain and diabetes.[19] Another study from Harvard Medical School showed that sleep is critical for memory consolidation and cognitive performance.[20] When it comes to sleep, quality trumps quantity. That's why I recommend tracking your sleep with a good sleep tracker like the Oura ring.[21] For most adults, the sweet spot for quality sleep is generally seven to nine hours per night, but it can vary. The bottom line is if you want a healthy brain, you've got to get good sleep.

SLEEP LIKE A CAVEMAN

This book is about allocating energy so you have enough left for the things that matter most. Without quality sleep, everything feels a lot harder. When you get a good night's sleep, you wake up refreshed, ready to face your day with more peace in your heart. It's one of the cheapest forms of health care, yet for many it's tough to master.

In the United States, between 50 and 70 million adults suffer from some form of sleep disorder. Insomnia, the most common, affects approximately 33 percent to 50 percent of the adult population each year.[22] That's a lot of tossing and turning!

So, let's geek out on something cool: biphasic sleep. This isn't just some fringe theory; it's a natural sleep pattern humans have followed for centuries. People typically slept in two phases before electric lights came along and messed with our natural rhythms. They would go to bed shortly after sunset, sleep for about four hours, wake up for an hour or two, and then go back to sleep until sunrise. This middle-of-the-night wakefulness was known as the "watch" or the "second sleep." During this time, people would pray, meditate, write, make love, or relax. They didn't call it insomnia or a sleep disorder. It was just how the body worked. Now, in our fast-paced world, this sounds crazy.

From a different perspective, the hours between 1 and 4 a.m. are significant. Culturally and spiritually, there's something called the "thinning of the veil." This refers to when the boundary between the physical world and the spiritual or supernatural realm is more permeable. Various traditions cite this concept as a period when spiritual activity and communication are more accessible. In folklore, this period is sometimes called the "witching hour" and is associated with heightened supernatural activity. Funnily enough, most of my books are written during that window because it's when my night-owl brain feels most creative. I do it in a room with dim red lighting, and I don't eat or drink coffee so I don't break my circadian rhythm.

Now, if you're routinely waking between these hours, and this is abnormal for you, this may be something to dig into deeper. According to traditional Chinese medicine (TCM), the hours between 1 and 3 a.m. play a role in liver function and waking between 3 and 5 a.m. might signal poor lung function. Thyroid health is also important in sleep patterns. So, if you find yourself staring at the ceiling at 2 a.m., it might not be because you're a werewolf waiting for a full moon; it could be your liver or thyroid calling for attention. Or you're just a night owl, and your creativity is calling.

Historically, this pattern was typical. People only started sleeping in one long stretch when artificial lighting became widespread, and the Industrial Revolution demanded a more regimented schedule. Recent studies support the idea that our modern, monophasic sleep pattern might not be the healthiest option. For example, a study led by Thomas Wehr at the National Institute of Mental Health found that when you expose people to natural light and darkness patterns similar to preindustrial times, they naturally adopt a biphasic sleep pattern.[23] Participants slept in two sessions of about four hours each, separated by one to three hours of quiet wakefulness. This natural rhythm allowed them to feel more rested and less stressed.

Artificial lighting has disrupted our natural rhythm. Bright lights inhibit alpha brain waves, which are helpful for the transition into sleep, while dim red lights do not. At 40 Years of Zen, people wear TrueDark lenses, designed to block five kinds of light and other variables. They're like noise-canceling headphones for your eyes. As part of the program, we use these glasses to maintain meditation states longer.

| KETONES: PREMIUM BRAIN FUEL |

Your body is a highly sophisticated machine. Like any machine, operating at peak efficiency requires the right fuel. The food you eat isn't just calories; it's information for your cells. Same with the thoughts you think. The nutrients in your food influence your mitochondrial function and, by extension, your overall energy levels and spiritual health.

We know that neurons can eat sugar from your blood, which is the default fuel source. Your body turns most food into sugar, even proteins and complex carbohydrates. But if neurons have a choice, they prefer ketones, which come from either fasting, a ketogenic diet, or ketone supplements like MCT oil.

Ketones are like the premium-grade fuel for your brain. When you fast or follow a ketogenic diet, your liver converts fat into ketones, which your body and brain can use for energy. Feeding neurons ketones instead of sugar gives them incredible power because ketones produce more ATP than glucose. This state is called ketosis. Ketosis is your body's way of switching to a more efficient power source. It's like flipping a switch from regular unleaded to rocket fuel.

But here's the thing: getting into ketosis can take a few days of low-carb eating or fasting. That's where ketone supplements come in handy. They help you increase your ketone levels without having to fast or cut carbs. There are three kinds of ketone supplements you can use today. The first is MCT oil—medium-chain triglycerides, popularized by the biohacking movement, turning it into a billion-dollar industry. It's not an actual ketone, but when you take it, it is quickly converted into ketones in your body. It's extracted from coconuts and creates a high peak of ketones with a low impact on the rest of the body. I use C8 MCT Oil. C8 (caprylic acid, 8 carbons) is the best source for maximum ketone body production. Lauric acid (12 carbons) doesn't work, although it's the most common MCT oil due to its inexpensive production costs and long shelf life. The form you use matters.

The next option is ketone esters. They rapidly raise your blood ketone levels, providing immediate energy to your brain and muscles. When you use them, your body doesn't have to convert fats into ketones, so you get an instant boost of clean fuel. They can be hard on the liver because it must break down the ester bonds and release the ketones into your bloodstream. Moderation is best with these.

Lastly, there are ketone salts, which I don't recommend. Ketone salts combine ketones with mineral salts like sodium, potassium, calcium, or magnesium to raise blood ketone levels. The downside? They often have a high mineral load that can cause stomach issues if taken in high doses. Plus, some experts, like Dr. Richard Veech, have raised concerns about the long-term effects of ketone salts on mitochondrial function. I was honored to interview him on *The Human Upgrade* podcast[24] before he died. He studied ketones for forty-seven years and worked with the guy who discovered the mitochondrial cycle of making energy (the Krebs cycle). After decades of research, he found that ketone salts harm mitochondria. And you know how much I love mitochondria.

By understanding and using ketones to your advantage, you can ensure your brain has the energy it needs to function efficiently. This way, you won't run out of fuel, even during intense activities and fasting periods. Your brain and heart will thank you because they operate way better when these are present.

| FASTING TO INDUCE SPIRITUAL STATES |

You know I'm a fan of fasting, but like most things in life, fasting is best in moderation. Mystics used to fast to reach states like samadhi, the ultimate Zen-like state, where profound insights happen, and you feel a sense of oneness with everything. You may even touch a bit of the Divine. Sages and holy people throughout history have fasted for days because it provides their neurons and hearts with more power. This extra power comes from their bodies going into ketosis, but they didn't have this term in the caveman days. It probably went something like, "Me have lots of energy, me go kill animal now," followed by some dramatic chest-pounding and loincloth-flapping in the wind before raising their spear triumphantly above their head.

Newsflash: they didn't have ketone supplements to help them reach ketosis. Back in the day, the only way to get into ketosis was by fasting. Since people had to hunt for food and never knew when their next meal would come, nature often forced fasting. But now, thanks to biohacking (and grocery stores), you can achieve ketosis without having to fast or starve because of bad weather or scarce resources. While you don't have to fast to reach peak states anymore, in some cases it can help.

So, what happens when you fast? You conserve your body's energy since you don't have to digest food. Then your body can put its resources toward other things, like repairing damaged proteins. It's like giving your entire MeatOS a spa day with time to recharge.

Fasting also activates several bodily pathways that promote metabolic health, heart health, and longevity.[25] If you've never fasted before, and you fast for a day or two, you might feel kind of off— lethargic, have a slight headache, be foggy-headed, and moody. This bodily response is totally normal and temporary. It's your body adapting to using fat as its primary fuel instead of carbohydrates.

Adding MCT oil or other ketone supplements to your fasted state helps your body transition into ketosis. It makes fasting so much easier and, dare I say, enjoyable.

Regular intermittent fasting (IF) or occasionally going a day or two without food can lead to profound spiritual experiences. I usually follow the 16:8 IF practice, which means 16 hours in a fasted state, using the remaining 8 hours for meals. Being in a fasted state opens you up mentally, emotionally, and spiritually. Your body isn't working as hard to absorb and process all that food, so you can do more intense spiritual work quickly. That's a gift.

Important Note: While fasting raises ketones and allows for a certain amount of deep work, I don't recommend it in certain circumstances. During intense Reset Mode work at 40 Years of Zen, people who fast eventually hit a wall and run out of energy. When doing hard work, especially for extended periods, you need enough fuel (food) to turn air into electricity, and MCT oil may not be enough. That's why I eat more than usual during Reset Mode or at one of Joe Dispenza's advanced seven-day breathwork retreats. More output requires more input to replenish yourself. So, fasting can be really beneficial. But sometimes you need more food to keep you going. You can learn all about different ways to fast safely and some cool fasting hacks in my book *Fast This Way*.

ENERGY FOR PERSONAL DEVELOPMENT AND EMOTIONAL REGULATION

Here are a few things to keep in mind.

First, if you want to perform at your best, you're better off getting more energy from fat versus sugar. So, if you're gearing up for an intense day of Reset Mode work or heading to a retreat, have a nourishing breakfast full of high-quality fat and protein. Pack some ketone supplements. When I use C8 MCT oil and sometimes other ketone supplements with clients at 40 Years of Zen, they can do about two and a half times more intense reset work than if they're fasting or just eating regular food. The healthy fats supercharge your brain's battery, giving you the energy you need to do the intense work. So, if you find yourself tapped out after a half hour of resets, have some MCT oil and see what your brain can do. You'll be amazed at the difference.

Next up, calories. If you're on a chronic low-calorie kick—maybe because you thought it would help you lose weight, or you're using something like Ozempic so you eat way fewer calories than you need—you might find it hard to do the Reset Process. You might even feel tired and moody because your brain and body are starving, and your mitochondria lack energy, causing stress. They won't be interested in showing you new spiritual realms of healing and personal development. They just want you to eat the muffin. Eating more when doing intense meditation work is okay, just like eating more on heavy workout days is okay. But remember, don't stuff yourself right before meditating; a full stomach has its challenges. Give yourself a couple of hours to digest before you dive in.

Finally, take quality supplements. At 40 Years of Zen, we give people a handful of optional but recommended supplements daily for a reason. Your mitochondria and other systems in your body are desperate to follow your lead. They want to give you the results you're working toward. But if they don't have the nutrients for growth and expansion, you won't get the full benefits of the Reset Process. Listen to your body.

| QUALITY FAT WON'T MAKE YOU FAT |

If you've been part of this community for a while, you know that not all fats are created equal. Quality fats are certainly not the enemy; they're your body's best friend when you choose the right ones. Healthy fats help keep your blood sugar levels steady, fight off inflammation, and support your heart health. I'm talking about saturated fats like grass-fed butter and MCT oil, monounsaturated fats, and omega-3s from wild-caught seafood.

Twenty years ago, while hiking Mount Kailash, I felt really crappy due to lack of oxygen at 18,000 feet. Then this little Tibetan woman gave me a cup of yak butter tea. I drank it, and within five minutes, my brain woke up. I felt better than I had in a very long time. She wasn't handing out canola oil tea for a reason. Yak butter has a ton of high-quality saturated fats that fuel your brain and body. Canola oil is highly processed and often undergoes refining, bleaching, and deodorizing, stripping away nutrients and introducing harmful chemicals.[26] It's also incredibly high in pro-inflammatory oxidized omega-6 fats. I recommend staying away from all vegetable and seed oils for this reason. In the Sydney Diet Heart Study, a seven-year randomized controlled trial in humans, increased vegetable oil consumption increased the risk of premature death by 62 percent—more than physical inactivity, heavy drinking, moderate smoking, increased sugar, processed meat, or excessive sodium.

The saturated fats in butter are a powerhouse for your brain and body.[27] Saturated fats are the most stable, meaning they're difficult to oxidize. In contrast, omega-6s, like the ones in vegetable and seed oils, are highly unstable and create lots of free radicals and inflammation in your cells. When you eat these damaged fats, your body uses them to make unstable and unhealthy cell membranes. When you eat saturated fat, your brain can produce stable, healthy membranes. Butter also has a unique fat called conjugated linoleic acid (CLA), which supports metabolism and reduces inflammation.[28]

The brain and body energy I experienced in Tibet from yak butter tea inspired me to create my own version with mold-free coffee, grass-fed butter, and MCT oil. The results were so incredible I decided to share this recipe with the rest of the world. Now millions start their mornings with a warm cup of Danger Coffee mixed with grass-fed butter and C8 MCT oil. Blending high-quality fats and antioxidants (like the ones in coffee or tea) gives you boundless sustainable energy and helps your brain stay sharp and focused.

That Tibetan woman knew what she was doing.

SUFFERING SUCKS,
SO STOP DOING IT

Suffering sucks. The good news is you don't have to keep doing it. If you're curious about what's causing you to suffer in the first place, you're about to find out. After diving deep into the teachings of ancient Chinese philosophers, Indian gurus, and some lesser-known spiritual leaders, there's a clear pattern when it comes to self-sabotage. This pattern becomes even more apparent when you look inside the heads of 1,500 people who have undergone advanced brain training at 40 Years of Zen.

In my exploration, the best framework for understanding our suffering comes from Buddhism. Buddhism isn't a monolith; there's no Buddhist pope, and the teachings vary widely depending on the country and lineage. So, if you're a devout Buddhist of one persuasion or another, and what I say doesn't align perfectly with your teachings, trust that it will at least make sense directionally. I'm not a practicing Buddhist, but I find immense wisdom in their teachings and those from other spiritual lineages. I know some Buddhist scholars might say I'm oversimplifying things. And they're right, I am. That's my job. Most people don't want to become Buddhist scholars; they want to use this knowledge to improve their lives.

In Buddhism, there are five main hindrances or obstacles to suffering. I've modified the terms to use straightforward language. The five hindrances are ill will, laziness, pleasure, worry, and doubt. Unsurprisingly, they tie into the five F's for survival: fear, food, fertility, friends, and forgiveness.

In biohacking, these obstacles aren't just abstract concepts. They're part of your operating system. Most of them start in your cells before they spark an emotion, then make their way into your thoughts and feel incredibly important, distracting you from what you want to focus on: peace. These distractions can make you pay more attention to emotionally charged things than you want to. This is what I call the Buddhist version of a trigger.

These are the kinds of things you want to be free from to live an unprogrammed, authentic life. By understanding and addressing these hindrances, you can hack your biology to remove these triggers and improve your mental and emotional well-being. It's all about recognizing these patterns and using the wisdom from various teachings to create a life where you're less triggered, more present, and ultimately happier, making peace your default state.

HINDRANCE #1: ILL WILL (FEAR)

One of the most toxic and easiest to spot of these obstacles is ill will. In Buddhism, ill will, or vyapada, is "the desire to strike out at something." It sounds a lot like being triggered. Every time you feel a negative emotion—malice, anger, resentment, hatred, whether toward others or yourself—that's your mitochondria trying to keep you safe. It's just your body giving you a strong emotion to keep you away from something it thinks could be dangerous. It ties into the first F-word, fear. The first thing to notice is that if you feel hatred, your body, not you, is feeling a fear response toward that person or thing. You might not understand what you're so afraid of or why, but the emotion lurks behind the scenes as protective armor. As soon as these emotions come up, they block your ability to be in charge of yourself. This is when you want to tap into your awareness and consciously decide, *You know what? I'm not going to be triggered right now. I'm going to respond with kindness.*

Things will get worse if someone is pushing your buttons and you yell at them. But if someone's trying to push your buttons and you don't have any buttons to push because you're unprogrammable, they'll probably get frustrated and bug someone else while you go about your day. You cannot move into compassion if you're feeling ill will. Anything that blocks compassion is just sucking away the energy you could be using to have fun, evolve, or do something meaningful.

When you feel ill-willed about anything, the Reset Process is the first thing to do. And by the way, I can still be triggered even though I've practiced this for a long time. It rarely happens, but if it does, I've learned to laugh at my dumb body for its reaction after all this work. If I get triggered and yell at someone or raise my voice, I laugh at myself instead of getting mad, and then I apologize for the behavior and ask how I can make it right. It's very easy. But if this sounds hard, just know that's your ego once again trying to keep you in its safety bubble.

For most people, what blocks you from apologizing and owning up to your mistake is anger or resentment toward yourself or a part of your body that you feel betrayed you. As we discussed, betrayal and injustice are two of the biggest triggers for people and create the most trauma.

Let's say you're overweight, and you've done everything on earth to try to lose those extra pounds. You nourished your body with plenty of healthy food and exercised until you couldn't sit on the toilet without feeling like your legs would break, and your pants still don't fit! It's unjust, and it's not fair. You did the work, but you didn't get the results. That frustration you feel is *toward yourself.* Either you're mad at your body for betraying you, or you're angry at yourself for not trying hard enough. How do I know this? Because I used to weigh over 300 pounds. Being overweight and unhealthy was my biggest challenge for years. It's why I meditated in a cave for four days, started fasting, and became obsessed with biohacking to fix what was broken (or just not working right).

If you're stuck in ill will—those negative emotions toward someone, something, or yourself—and don't want to dive into the Reset Process, there's a simple hack to get you out of that state: curiosity. Instead of thinking, *Why am I feeling this?* shift to something like, *That's weird. I wonder why* my body *is feeling this.* When you ask yourself that question, you engage the problem-solving part of your brain that craves a dopamine hit from figuring things out. It's hard to stay mad or afraid when you're curious. Curiosity disrupts those negative emotions and puts you back in control because curiosity cancels fear.

You might say, "I'm not afraid. I'm pissed-off." Trust me, I've said those exact words. The reality is that your emotions, like anger, have nothing to do with rational thoughts. They're just feelings, and feelings aren't rational.

When my daughter was about six or seven, she had a meltdown while walking through the local farmer's market. It turned into a beautiful parenting moment. "Dad, I don't know what's happening, but I have all these feelings in my body." It wasn't a panic attack, but it was a lot of emotional processing. So I sat her down and asked her to describe it. She looked confused, so I said, "What color is it? Where in your body is it? Can you draw a picture of it?" She's a talented artist, so she thought about it, and when we got home, she drew a beautiful picture of herself with a red ball right in her stomach. By being curious about the feelings, she shifted from emotion to discovery mode and dissolved the emotional charge. Adults can do this, too. It's a powerful hack for dealing with ill will.

So, from now on, every time you're pissed-off or angry, instead of judging yourself, get curious. Say, "Oh my gosh, look, my body's doing something weird. I wonder why." Then, decide you don't want to do that again. Take it a step further and run the Reset Process. Those feelings of resentment? You learned them at a very young age, so you might want to reset those memories, too. This is part of the advanced practice of time travel.

I can share this with you because I have watched clients go through this since 2013. These successful clients feel angry toward their parents, siblings, business partners who stole money, and sometimes even the world. Some people are profoundly angry about getting sick or aging. These are just forms of ill will, and you can let them go with the Reset Process.

Remember, this ill will stems from a distributed consciousness of mitochondria that decides you will feel this way. They sent you a fear signal (the first F of survival) to stop you from evolving because you'll remain safe if you stay in your comfort zone. You know, just in case there's a tiger behind whatever you're mad about. And for the record, that's highly unlikely.

HINDRANCE #2: LAZINESS (FOOD)

The next big one, especially in the West, is one of the seven deadly sins: sloth or laziness. In my book *Smarter Not Harder*, I talk a lot about the laziness principle, which is triggering for some people. But this isn't just about not wanting to get off the couch. It's mental and physical laziness. And it's totally normal. This might sound surprising because we just talked about how to get out of feeling ill-willed, but think about it: How often have you been mad at yourself for not being interested in something you think you're supposed to care about? For being tired when you have so much to do? Or for sitting down to meditate while your brain drifts away into sleep or apathy?

I routinely fell asleep for the first five years of my meditation practice. Or, if not fully asleep, my mind would just check out. Neurofeedback fixed that. Now, even if my mind wanders off, it's somewhere useful. Instead of judging these things, why not consider that your brain and body are simply giving you a signal that they need a break?

This laziness comes from your mitochondria. How does this relate to the F words? If ill will is fear, laziness is the second F: food. Your cells, your mitochondria, are terrified of running out of energy. That's why they make you eat all the ice cream. That's also why they make going to the gym feel like a monumental task, so you resist. It's also why meditation feels like such a challenge; meditation forces the brain to exercise, just like going to the gym forces the body to exercise. Your mitochondria do not want you to use one ounce more energy thinking or doing than is necessary to stay alive. Because you might run out of energy, and then you'll probably die. It can be pretty dramatic.

Being efficient is part of what keeps your body alive, even if your mind is running on autopilot. That's why you see dogs eat more food than they need and nap afterward instead of playing. Why waste energy? Your body gives you the feeling that it doesn't want you to waste energy; this is the laziness principle hard at work. We've made it out to be the bad guy when it's just doing its job. That's why it takes willpower to exercise or meditate. Or maybe a little less will-power if you're using technologies like neurofeedback that let you evolve more quickly than you could on your own.

Your mitochondria are efficiency experts, tiny accountants inside your body making sure you don't run out of energy. They're whispering, "Hey, maybe skip your workout today," or "Why don't we just chill and watch TV?" They're just trying to keep you alive, but sometimes they don't realize you have more gas left in the tank. It's up to you to show them.

I've found that sometimes it's not a matter of laziness; it's a belief you have. You think meditation is a waste of time or that you can't do it. But usually that belief is just your body saying, "Don't you dare do something that takes extra energy. You don't have enough to spare. You're going to run out, and you'll be tired. You could die." It's funny because that same energy conservation system gets you to make decisions without enough information, making you think that was the best decision you could have made. We've discussed how some decisions—the ones you think harder about—take a lot of work. But if you just decide quickly, it feels just as rational. That's why we can be manipulated so easily with advertising and political ads. Your brain says, "Oh, that feels true." Therefore, it must be true. Your brain lets you feel something is true without thinking about it because that's less work.

When you sit down to meditate or exercise, a part of you makes you drowsy or skip out early, even though you've chosen to do it. Many people feel guilt and shame, thinking, *I should want to meditate, I should want to exercise.* No, actually, your body should not want to exercise or meditate. But your body will feel better if you exercise, your mind will feel better if you meditate, and so will your heart. But that doesn't mean you should *want* to do it. It means choosing to do it is worth it.

You will never naturally desire to do these things. Unless, maybe, you get addicted to overexercising with endorphins, but that's a different story. Otherwise the state of not wanting to do things is normal. Doing them puts you in a state that lets you change your life and take control of your mind and biology. Laziness, when used to your advantage, isn't a bad thing. It's just a part of your MeatOS that you can learn to work with instead of letting it control you.

Think about it: Every time you push through the resistance and do what you know is good for you, you teach your body who's boss. It feels great. You're rewiring your brain to understand that this takes energy, but it's energy well spent. The guilt and shame? They're just distractions your body throws at you to conserve energy. Laugh at them, recognize them for what they are, and keep moving forward.

Meditating, exercising, and engaging in activities that enhance your well-being is an act of rebellion against your lazy mitochondria. It's telling them, "I know you're trying to conserve energy, but I've got bigger plans." This is how you gain control over your mind and body. It's not about never feeling lazy or unmotivated; it's about recognizing that those feelings are part of the game and pushing through them anyway.

Suppose you're working on meditation or the Reset Process, which has several steps. You keep forgetting the steps even after reading them in writing ten times. Forgetfulness is your distributed consciousness (your subconscious) trying to make you forget because meditating or running the Reset Process will burn electricity. Even more scary, it might put you in charge of your responsiveness to the world. The last thing your ego wants is for you to be in charge. Your ego's job is to ensure that tigers don't eat you, you don't starve, your heart keeps beating, and you keep breathing. It's like having a well-meaning but overly cautious friend who keeps you from taking risks or trying new things.

But here's the thing: you're the one in control, not your ego. It tries to steal that control with negative emotions, making you forget stuff and making you tired when you go to do something that matters. It will even try to control you by making you forget what you read in this book because this book does not make your ego happy. That's why you might choose to read it twice.

| HINDRANCE #3: PLEASURE (FERTILITY) |

The next obstacle is pleasure. Our bodies are constantly driving us toward pleasure through all our senses—taste, smell, sight, sound, and sensation (including sexual things). This information isn't a call to lead an ascetic life like Gandhi, give up all worldly possessions or indulgences, and live in a cave with just a bowl of water. It's about understanding that if you have constant cravings or think you need something outside of yourself to be happy, it's a story your ego made up to keep you trapped.

One of the most common things I hear from people is, "But I love french fries." Sure, french fries are delicious, but nicotine addicts could argue the same about cigarettes. That doesn't make either good for you. Imagine hearing a response like, "But I love heroin." It's not the same thing, except it is. Because what you "love" about these unhealthy choices is based on cravings and an addiction to pleasure.

Your brain knows to seek pleasure and avoid pain. It's a survival mechanism. But in today's world, where pleasure is available at the push of a button, this mechanism can work against you. It's why you might find yourself finishing a family-sized bag of potato chips or scrolling mindlessly through social media for hours. Your brain gets a dopamine hit from these activities and wants more. But just because something feels good doesn't mean it's good for you.

Understanding this can help you break free from the cycle of unhealthy pleasure-seeking behavior. It's about recognizing when your brain is tricking you into thinking you need something to be happy. When you feel that craving, step back and ask yourself, *Do I need this? Or is this just my ego trying to keep me safe?* The trick is to replace those harmful pleasure-seeking habits with ones that truly nourish you. Instead of reaching for junk food, find a healthy snack you enjoy. Instead of mindlessly scrolling through your phone, engage in an activity that brings you genuine joy and fulfillment, like hanging out with your friends in person.

Let's be clear: there's nothing wrong with enjoying life's pleasures. It's about balance and making conscious choices that align with your long-term goals and health. When you become aware of how your brain seeks pleasure, you can start making choices that serve you better. So, if your body says, "Eat all the cake," that's because cake tastes good. But now that you're aware, you know that just because it tastes good doesn't mean you have to choose it.

Here's the truth: some things that produce dopamine are nourishing, while others are not. The difference between porn, which is a misuse of sensual desire, and a sacred sexual encounter with your lover is profound. Take tantric practices, for example. They're not about dopamine release but about showing your body that you can experience pleasure without a fast dopamine rush. Similarly, slowly savoring a beautiful, nutritious meal is better than gobbling down nutritionally void french fries.

Fast food is the porn of food. It gives you a quick hit but lacks real nourishment. Your body needs genuine nourishment to create and sustain energy for what matters. You crave and feel like you have to have these indulgent things like porn and junk food. In reality, choosing mindfully and in moderation will feel better. Your body will lie to you, making you believe that if you don't have sex right now, the species will end. This response is the third F: fertility, voicing its beliefs.

But when you connect with your higher self, you realize that what you actually want is to connect with your lover. Or to experience a beautiful meal with all the sensory delights around you. These things make you happy because they're artful and meaningful. This awareness changes everything. When you crave something, whether it's food, connection, or a sensory experience, pause and ask yourself if it's truly what you need or if it's just a quick dopamine fix. You don't have to stuff your face to feel temporary pleasure; you can choose to be mindful and have an even more profound experience. They are very different vibes.

You've almost certainly felt shame or guilt about some of these things. Maybe it's when you ate all the cake, went out with the entire soccer team, or lost money gambling. We all have cravings for sensory pleasures and make mistakes. It's your mitochondria, the original sensors for all those sensory pleasures, telling you these things are sexier than they actually are. When you learn to train your operating system not to convince you of certain death if you don't eat french fries, you'll realize the truth: not only will you not die, but you might even feel better without them.

The Reset Process, which might include forgiving yourself for having these cravings or desires, helps you drop the guilt and judgment to a point where you can make a clear decision. Here's some advice: After you've done this forgiveness work and feel free from the ego's grip, go ahead and eat the french fries. Just do it once. See how you feel. Be curious and honest about how pleasurable they are while eating them. Then, see how you feel afterward. When you wake up the following day, check in with your consciousness, body, and mind. You might find that your story and attachment to french fries are gone because you did the work and tapped into your truth instead of an outdated story. Then you can decide whether or not to eat french fries without feeling like a good or bad person; you neutralize your conscious decision. Usually, with this new awareness, you choose not to have them (or whatever your craving is) because you like how you feel when you don't eat them. The pain of attachment and cravings vanishes like a plume of smoke.

Learn to savor sensory pleasures without being addicted or attached to them. I still eat foods that I love. I choose foods I love that make me feel better the following day. But I don't always choose perfectly. I choose mindfully instead of letting my operating system choose the foods for me.

Your intuition won't lie about pleasure. We discussed intuition in Chapter 2, but as a reminder, your intuition is the first thing you feel in your body. Then, almost right on top of that nudge, although slightly delayed, will be your emotions (ego) and your programming (thoughts). Your body knows the truth (intuition) before your emotions and thoughts do their best to either validate you or try to change your mind. So, if eating all the cake or dating the entire soccer team is tempting, tap into your intuition. It will tell you if it's a good idea. The key here is to listen closely and honor what comes up.

It might tell you that eating a piece of cake is a good idea today. Or that the person you've got your eye on is compatible with you. Your intuition will guide you on when pleasure is good for you versus just your mitochondria screaming, "I want all of it now!" Deciphering your emotional response can be tricky until it's not because now you know how to tap into your intuition without all the distractions.

No one, including the best meditating monks on the planet, is perfect. If you come across someone who seems to have it all figured out, they've just strengthened their curiosity muscle so well that they notice if they're angry, lazy, tired, or ruminating and worrying. They notice if they want something delicious more than healthy. They realize, *Aha, that's not me. That's my ego.* And from there, they mindfully choose what to do next.

When you catch yourself in these moments of craving or guilt, it's a chance to learn more about yourself. It's an opportunity to understand how your brain and body work and to reprogram them in a way that serves you better. Use these moments to dive deeper into your biology and psychology and make choices that align with your long-term well-being.

HINDRANCE #4: WORRY (FRIENDS)

The next obstacle is worry. When you're agitated or worried about something, a critical inner voice plays like a broken record. Sometimes that agitation feels like restlessness, and you don't know why. Other times it's remorse, wishing you hadn't said or done something. You can't calm your mind while simultaneously feeling guilty about something. You harbor regrets, a typical response to guilt but also unproductive.

People, especially younger ones, often tell me they can't calm their minds down. They have trouble sleeping because they're so worried about mistakes they've made, upcoming decisions, and even things like the state of the planet. And while the planet is important, if worrying about it stops you from sleeping well, you're stuck in a triggered state. You will not change the environment or any other world aspect if you're triggered. Instead of being angry or worrying about it, the only choice is to figure out how to be peaceful so you can do something to improve it.

It's trendy, especially in Western culture, to see yourself as a victim, to feel helpless, or to focus on injustice, one of the biggest triggers. These can be real feelings, but they take away your power over yourself and your power to solve problems. If you're dealing with regrets, guilt, or worry, you can work on releasing these feelings with the Reset Process. Usually these emotions are about running the Reset Process on yourself.

Worry often isolates you and traps you in your head. When you're stuck worrying about the past or future, you're not fully present with the people around you. This disconnect can harm your relationships. You might find yourself less engaged in conversations, less attentive to your loved ones, and less available for meaningful connections. Your friends (the fourth F-word) want to support you. They make you feel loved, offer a different perspective, and bring you back to reality. If they don't? Get new friends.

Buddhist teachings state that community and connection are vital. Surrounding yourself with supportive friends can be a powerful antidote to worry. They can help you process past regrets and future anxieties so you don't get stuck in the emotions and can return to the present moment, where you can make a difference. This kind of supportive relationship doesn't mean dumping all your baggage on your friends. It means allowing yourself to be vulnerable and showing up as an imperfect human, which we all are.

Worry is like a treadmill; it gives you something to do but it doesn't get you anywhere. Your mind keeps spinning its wheels, leaving you feeling exhausted and powerless. The trick is recognizing when you're stuck in this worry loop and pivoting to break free. When you find yourself in this state, ask yourself if it's something you can control or change. If it is, take action. If it's not, find a way to let it go. Sometimes this is easier said than done, but the Reset Process can be helpful here. By practicing the Reset Process, you can train your mind to release the worries and focus on the present moment and what you can control.

Gratitude is another powerful tool to combat worry, and it's a key part of the Reset Process. But if you're in a time crunch or don't feel like going deep into Reset Mode, pause and consider what you're grateful for. This state shifts your focus from doom and gloom to all the beautiful things in your life. It's a simple and effective way to change your mindset. Worrying is often a habit. And like any habit, you can break it and create better ones with practice and persistence.

It's also important to give yourself permission to make mistakes. We all make them; it's part of being human. Acknowledge your mistakes, learn from them, and learn to let them go without holding on to guilt and shame. It's the grasping tightly that keeps you stuck and stifles your peace. Have you ever felt guilty for not doing enough? Or felt guilty for not being good enough? Or realize you could have done something differently, like buying or selling bitcoin at the right time or leaving an unhealthy relationship sooner? If you said yes to any of those, you're not alone.

Then there's the constant worry about times other than the present moment. You're worrying about something in the past that you can't change, or you're worrying about a future event that's just a story that hasn't happened yet. Both of these worry-loops stop you from being present. Even worse, what you think happened in your past dictates your emotions. You might not remember all the details clearly because that would mean being logical. And emotions aren't logical. If you have ill-willed feelings about anything in the past or future, that's always your ego. And that's something you can change with the Reset Process.

| HINDRANCE #5: DOUBT (FORGIVENESS) |

The final obstacle to overcome is doubt. If I haven't triggered this for you by now, I apologize. I'll have to run the Reset Process on myself. Doubt happens when you're skeptical about anything, whether it's a technology in this book, the Reset Process, or even your ability to succeed. When you harbor doubt, it drastically lowers your chances of success. If you don't believe me, consider the approximately twenty thousand scientific studies of the placebo effect. Doubt and skepticism are active elements in the placebo effect. If something could work but you tell yourself it won't, your operating system is more likely to prove you right. That's just good old confirmation bias.

It turns out that people with an optimistic view of the world have lower risks of cardiovascular disease and die less from all causes compared to pessimists or skeptics. Specifically, being skeptical increases your risk of death and heart attacks. This information comes from the *Journal of the American Medical Association* (the JAMA Network).[1]

Research out of Finland studied whether or not pessimism contributed to poor health outcomes.[2] The Good Ageing in Lahti Region (GOAL) study included 2,267 people ages 52–76. The results? The top 25 percent most pessimistic people had a 2.2 times higher risk of dying from coronary heart disease compared to the lowest 25 percent of pessimists. Interestingly, optimism didn't offer a protective effect. Pessimism alone was a strong predictor of heart disease death, even after adjusting for other risk factors like diabetes, hypertension, and smoking. So, if you're skeptical, everything from meditation to the technologies in this book won't work as well as they might otherwise. Skepticism is another program, like a trigger, that stops you from being effective in the world.

Why do pessimism and skepticism tend to be your default? Because someone tricked you earlier in life, and your body feels like it lost the ability to trust. Now, trust feels dangerous. When trusting feels unsafe, you enter the realm of fear, bringing you back to the first hindrance: ill will. Skepticism doesn't serve you, and neither does naive optimism. The sweet spot is being present, where you're neither skeptical nor unreasonably optimistic but curious. That curiosity puts you in control of your biology and behavior. So, what do you do if you're skeptical and still reading? Doubt may have already made you throw this book against the wall, get up to look at porn, or indulge in some other distraction. Maybe you're eating a cupcake or the whole box of cupcakes as you read this. I get it. This stuff can be confronting. But it's for your own good.

Doubt often stems from a lack of trust, usually because of past disappointments or betrayals. When you doubt, you're holding on to these past experiences and projecting them onto your present and future. This is where forgiveness (the fifth F-word) comes into play. To move past doubt, you have to forgive. This means forgiving other people and, most importantly, forgiving yourself. Forgiveness is a powerful tool that allows you to let go of skepticism and open yourself up to new possibilities. It's about giving yourself permission to trust again, believing that things can work out, and having faith in humanity and your abilities. Forgiveness doesn't mean you forget or condone anything. It means you no longer allow the negative emotions to control you. Instead of being paralyzed by skepticism, shift doubt into curiosity and see what happens.

Run the Reset Process on the first time you remember being disappointed that something wasn't true (this is where your skepticism stems from). This solution might sound pretty out-there, but from working with clients at 40 Years of Zen, it's evident that all humans go through the same experience when we're very young. We believe that our parents are infallible, omniscient beings. Because when you're two years old, they indeed appear that way. When you're two, you don't have much of a prefrontal cortex; this is where your self-control, problem-solving skills, and ability to stay organized come from. You're walking (or stumbling) through the world with rose-colored glasses. Your parents feel like larger-than-life figures. If not for them, you would walk into sharp objects with your eyeballs or jump off balconies without a second thought. They're superheroes, saving you from danger. At least, that's how they appear to your immature brain.

At some point in your life, you realize that your parents aren't perfect and make mistakes. Because you're still operating without an adult mindset, your body says, "My parents lied to me. They told me they were perfect, and they're not!" It's one of the first times you don't feel you can trust the world. Your parents didn't tell you they were perfect. Your body just believed that because the thought made you feel safe; this can be the root of pessimism. Or maybe it was when you were wrong about something and a teacher shamed you. Or when you believed in something and faced betrayal. See how betrayal and injustice keep popping up?

These are the core memories and experiences that create your triggers. This programming tends to happen when you're young, though it can happen later, too. I've been betrayed in my forties by family members and investors; I've had all sorts of things happen. Getting stuck in these triggers is such a waste of energy, though.

If you're someone who always believes the positive or always believes the negative, you probably have some work to do. Always thinking the negative will harm you and always believing the positive, while less likely to harm you, can still be detrimental because you're easier to take advantage of. What you want to do is work on being mindful. The glass isn't half-empty or half-full; it has some stuff inside. You don't know what it is yet, but you're curious to find out.

These hindrances or obstacles are the five things that can take you out of the state you want to be in, and they're not even hard to manage. Your ego just wants you to believe you don't have the energy to manage them. But as you know by now, sometimes your ego is a liar. Anytime you're pissed-off about something and feeling angry (ill will), run the Reset Process. Anytime you can't remember stuff or are exhausted when trying to do something (laziness), run the Reset Process or look at what you ate. If your body's cells feel unsafe, they can trigger these emotions, which is why eating the right foods, getting enough sleep, and taking care of your body make it easier to be present and harder to trigger. If you're feeling distracted by desires (pleasure) you know aren't good for you, and you're mad at yourself for feeling this way, run the Reset Process. Anytime you feel anxious or remorse (worry), run the Reset Process. Skepticism (doubt)? Run the Reset Process.

That's why this practice is so powerful. It's the only thing I've found that works to remove the triggers holding you back. Instead of making you aware of these things and doing what traditional teachers might tell you to do: "Be aware of your thoughts and emotions. Allow them to flow through your body. Be curious. Eventually, they will go away." It's more helpful to be consciously aware of these things, feel them fully, and stop them from recurring without bypassing them. (Bypassing only buries them deeper into the subconscious and causes more problems.) And once you've done that, you can let them go.

In reality, you can turn off the vast majority of these emotions most of the time. But as long as you have a body, you will have an ego. The good news? You can train your body to behave like a service animal instead of acting like an untrained dog that eats poop, humps other dogs, barks all the time, jumps over the fence, and runs into traffic, which is what your ego will do if you let it. You can use your ego to your advantage by training it to alert you to threats you wouldn't otherwise see, to opportunities you wouldn't otherwise notice, to protect you when you're not paying attention, and to inform you of things in the world you're blind to.

These five hindrances—ill will, laziness, pleasure, worry, and doubt—are the primary ways we sabotage ourselves. Ill will, driven by **fear**, can make you lash out and hold grudges. Laziness, tied to **food** and energy, keeps you from doing what you know is good for you. Pleasure, or rather the pursuit of it, distracts you with immediate gratification (**fertility**) over long-term health. Worry traps you in a cycle of anxiety about the past and future, preventing you from being present and connected (**friends**). And doubt, fueled by past disappointments, keeps you from trusting and trying new things (**forgiveness**).

The technologies and techniques in this book will help you manage these hindrances. You don't have to be perfect or even slightly perfect. Just notice one time today when you feel resentment, anger, or malice, then run the Reset Process and see how you feel. You're moving in the right direction whenever you do anything that puts you in a state where you're more aware and in control of your operating system. The practice of consistent discovery and release is ongoing. If you believe in the Buddhist perspective, you will continue doing this until you become fully enlightened. In the meantime, you can suffer a lot less and have more peace and happiness, naturally making you act more kindly toward others and yourself, attracting the same in return. That's why the Reset Process is the best thing you can do for yourself and the world. Gratitude plus forgiveness equals grace. It sounds awesome because it is.

| CAUSE AND EFFECT |

Narcissists and sociopaths commonly trigger feelings of betrayal and injustice in others. Understand that these are both ego manifestations that have gone wrong. Fear consumes these people, especially narcissists. They harbor resentment and ill will. They're so ashamed that they hide this from themselves, completely unaware. If you're stuck in that loop and reading this, maybe it's pushing a button, and you'll do some profound healing. But more likely, you will read it and say, "That's not me." When you're curious, you will not see that you're doing this because your operating system is masterful at ensuring it's always in charge.

If your body feels unlovable when you're wrong, it will go to great lengths to ensure that you're not wrong, including destroying other people who might point out a flaw, even if it's real. People stuck in this fear spread so much injustice and betrayal. It takes a lot of Reset Process work to undo the damage they can spread if you let them into your life. That's why awareness is critical and why having good boundaries is crucial.

BEYOND THE EDGE OF YOUR MIND

So if we want to change some aspect of our reality,
we have to think, feel, and act in new ways; we
have to "be" different in terms of our responses to
experiences. We have to "become" someone else.
We have to create a new state of mind . . . we need
to observe a new outcome with that new mind.
—*Joe Dispenza*

You just experienced a wild journey through the mind and body. The best part is that this is only the beginning. From the intricate dance of brain states to the power of breathwork and sexual energy to the science of neurofeedback, you have upgraded your biohacking tool kit. These are the keys to unlocking a level of high performance and inner peace that most people only dream about.

You uncovered how your MeatOS plays tricks on you with outdated survival mechanisms that sabotage your progress. It's a sneaky little thing, but it's also highly trainable. Now that you understand these patterns, you have the power to rewrite your mental scripts, turning triggers into opportunities for growth. It's more than a mental exercise. Your diet, habits, and willingness to lean into discomfort make your human upgrade possible.

THE ZEN OF KICKING ASS: HOW PERFORMANCE AND PEACE GO TOGETHER

Now you know, without question, how high performance and inner peace are seamlessly connected. It's not just about getting more done or being more productive; it's about syncing your actions with a state of being that fosters success and serenity. It's about being efficient! When I talk about "hacking reality," it's not a gimmick. It's a fundamental shift in how you perceive and interact with the world.

Embrace the principles and practices throughout this book; you've stepped into a new paradigm. You're not just increasing your brain's capacity but cultivating a state of mind that allows for deeper connections, greater creativity, and a more profound sense of fulfillment. These tools will help you navigate your journey with clarity and purpose, from EEG and neurofeedback to the transformative power of forgiveness.

FUTURE-PROOF YOUR BRAIN WITH A HIGH-PERFORMANCE MINDSET

As you look to the future, the world of personal development and performance upgrades is constantly evolving. New technologies and discoveries continually emerge, promising even more profound ways to enhance cognitive and emotional well-being. However, the core principles you've learned here are timeless. Regardless of external advancements, mindfulness, balance, and a deep sense of calm will always be relevant states to strive for and attain.

Remember, this is a journey, not a destination. High performance and inner peace require thoughtful attention and care. Challenges and setbacks are part of the process, but with your knowledge and tools, you're better equipped to face them head-on. Mastery is a life-long endeavor, with each step bringing you closer to your best self.

FIND YOUR TRIBE

Throughout this book, we've touched on the importance of community and connection. Whether it's the supportive environment at 40 Years of Zen, biohackers from around the globe, or the broader networks you build in your personal and professional life, surrounding yourself with like-minded individuals is crucial. People who want to see you win and hold you accountable while also inspiring you to follow your wildest dreams.

In the world of high performance, it's easy to fall into the trap of striving alone. But true growth often comes from collaboration and shared experiences. As you continue your journey, seek communities that challenge and uplift you. Share your knowledge without expecting anything in return, and be open-minded as you learn from others. The collective wisdom of community can amplify your growth in ways you might never achieve on your own.

| YOUR PEACEFUL LEGACY |

Ultimately, the greatest gift you can give yourself and the world is the legacy of inner peace. As you transform your mind and body, you become a beacon of calm and clarity in a chaotic world. Your ability to navigate stress, make thoughtful decisions, and maintain a sense of equilibrium will benefit you and those around you.

Inner peace is contagious. When you embody it, you inspire others to seek it in their own lives. This ripple effect can profoundly change families, communities, and even societies. Committing to your journey of high performance through inner peace contributes to a larger movement toward a more conscious and compassionate world.

| UNLEASH YOUR SUPERHUMAN POTENTIAL |

It's important to acknowledge the transformative potential within each of us. The neuroscience of high performance isn't just about understanding the brain; it's about unlocking the vast, untapped potential within. By integrating the insights and practices from this book, you're embarking on a path that goes beyond conventional limits. This journey invites you to explore the farthest reaches of your mind, challenge your preconceived notions, and embrace the full spectrum of human potential. Becoming more than you ever thought possible means expanding not just in achievement but also in depth, presence, and impact.

Pursuing high performance and inner peace is a noble and worthy endeavor. It's a journey that demands dedication, courage, and a willingness to explore uncharted territories. But clarity, fulfillment, and a profound sense of purpose are immeasurable rewards. Your commitment to unlocking your brain and achieving high performance through inner peace is not just a personal victory; it's a contribution to a brighter, more harmonious future for us all. Keep pushing boundaries, stay curious, and never stop seeking the extraordinary.

| ACKNOWLEDGMENTS |

By now, you've already learned that gratitude is the key that unlocks the fire of forgiveness. And you know that forgiveness unleashes untold energy for everything you do in life. So, this book wouldn't be complete without allowing the opportunity for me to express gratitude to the many honored elders and masters who have helped to shape what you've learned here, or the business leaders who have helped to make biohacking into a $63 billion industry, and to the countless fans and supporters who stop me on the street to share how important this path has been to their lives. So, thank you, thank you, thank you. I humbly receive everything.

Many thanks to my writing team; Sheree Medeiros, my writing partner; Rachel Kambury, my editor; and Celeste Fine, my agent. Words do not express how grateful I am for your time and energy. A very special thanks to Nicole Petersen, RD, for bringing her knowledge and expertise. Super thanks also to Christine, my stellar assistant who manages my time, and to Maja, who manages space for me. Without their wise juggling and coordination, I wouldn't hit my deadlines so I can be a father, CEO, author, and podcaster and still have time to biohack and upgrade myself every single day.

Then there are the 1,500 and counting people who have invested a week of their lives to attend 40 Years of Zen. You didn't just upgrade yourself; you upgraded everyone around you, including me. And to the 40 Years of Zen team, thank you for holding space for radical growth and transformation every single week: both Heather Fs, David, Lisa, Travis, Noah, Ariana, Carlee, Pierre, and Natasha.

An acknowledgment isn't complete without gratitude to my biggest teachers, my family: Lana, the mother of my children; and my teenagers, Anna and Alan. May you benefit from the knowledge in this book when you are called to it.

Special thanks to my leadership team across Danger Coffee and Upgrade Labs, Events, and Media: Miranda, Amy, Ryan, Lily, and Rebecca.

I am grateful to have had the opportunity to talk to many of the world's top leaders who have guided me. Special thanks to Dr. Daniel Amen, who helped me get my brain in order years ago, and to my dear friend Mike Koenigs for his moral support and AI expertise. Thanks also to all the spiritual teachers and masters who have supported me and educated me on the path to creating this book. You know who you are and are at the point in your evolution where that's all you desire. Thank you.

Assuming you are still reading this, I would like to thank you, too, for being curious and investing your time and attention in this book. I sincerely hope it was more than worth the effort you put into it.

Remain curious and continue seeking and evolving!

NOTES

INTRODUCTION: UNLOCKING YOUR ZEN

1. Blake K. Barley, Chenlu Gao, Taylor Luster, Abbye Porro, Mojgan Parizi-Robinson, Dena Quigley, Paul Zinke, and Michael K. Scullin, "Chronotype in College Science Students Is Associated with Behavioral Choices and Can Fluctuate Across a Semester," *Chronobiology International* 40, no. 6 (2023): 710–24, https://www.tandfonline.com/doi/full/10.1080/07420528.2023.2203251.

CHAPTER 1: HURRY, MEDITATE FASTER

1. "Temple Grandin," Wikipedia, last modified July 11, 2024, https://en.wikipedia.org/w/index.php?title=Temple_Grandin&oldid=1225530181.
2. "About," Scott Barry Kaufman, accessed July 17, 2024, https://scottbarrykaufman.com/bio/.
3. Phattaraporn Boonnate, Suttipong Waraasawapati, Wasana Hipkaeo, Supaporn Pethlert, Arun Sharma, Carlo Selmi, et al., "Monosodium Glutamate Dietary Consumption Decreases Pancreatic β-Cell Mass in Adult Wistar Rats," *PLoS ONE* 10, no. 6 (2015): e0131595, https://doi.org/10.1371/journal.pone.0131595.

CHAPTER 2: WHY YOUR BODY WILL PUNCH ITSELF IN THE FACE

1. Upgrade Labs, last modified 2024, https://upgradelabs.com.
2. TrueDark, last modified 2024, https://truedark.com.
3. Kathryn Boere and Olav E. Krigolson, "The Effects of Multi-Colour Light Filtering Glasses on Human Brain Wave Activity," *BMC Neuroscience* 25, no. 21 (2024), https://doi.org/10.1186/s12868-024-00865-0.
4. P. Grandjean and P. J. Landrigan, "Developmental Neurotoxicity of Industrial Chemicals," *Lancet* 368, no. 9553 (2006): 2167–78.
5. Robert D. Oades, Marc R. Dauvermann, Benno G. Schimmelmann, Michael J. Schwarz, and Ashok M. Myint, "Attention-Deficit Hyperactivity Disorder (ADHD) and Glial Integrity: An Exploration of Associations of Cytokines and Kynurenine Metabolites with Symptoms and Attention," *Behavioral and Brain Functions* 6 (2010): 32.
6. Philip R. Nielsen, Michael E. Benros, and Søren Dalsgaard, "Associations Between Autoimmune Diseases and Attention-Deficit/Hyperactivity Disorder: A Nationwide Study," *Journal of the American Academy of Child & Adolescent Psychiatry* 56, no. 3 (2017): 234–40.e1.
7. Lidy M. J. Pelsser, Klaas Frankena, Jan Toorman, Huub F. J. Savelkoul,

Anthony E. J. Dubois, Rosa R. Pereira, and Jan K. Buitelaar, "Effects of a Restricted Elimination Diet on the Behavior of Children with Attention-Deficit Hyperactivity Disorder (INCA Study): A Randomised Controlled Trial," *Lancet* 377, no. 9764 (2011): 494–503.

8. M. F. Bouchard, D. C. Bellinger, R. O. Wright, and M. G. Weisskopf, "Attention-Deficit/Hyperactivity Disorder and Urinary Metabolites of Organophosphate Pesticides," *Pediatrics* 125, no. 6 (2010): e1270–e1277.

9. Martin Holtmann, Stephanie Steiner, Simon Hohmann, Lukas Poustka, Tobias Banaschewski, and Sven Bolte, "Neurofeedback in Autism Spectrum Disorders," *Developmental Medicine & Child Neurology* 53, no. 11 (2011): 986–93.

10. Robert Coben, Michael Linden, and Thomas E. Myers, "Neurofeedback for Autistic Spectrum Disorder: A Review of the Literature," *Applied Psychophysiology and Biofeedback* 35, no. 1 (2010): 83–105.

11. Jaime A. Pineda, Kevin Carrasco, Michael Datko, Stephanie Pillen, and Martin Schalles, "Neurofeedback Training Produces Normalization in Behavioural and Electrophysiological Measures in Children with Autism," *Philosophical Transactions of the Royal Society B: Biological Sciences* 369, no. 1644 (2014): 20130183.

12. James H. O'Keefe, Evan L. O'Keefe, Carl J. Lavie, and Loren Cordain, "Debunking the Vegan Myth: The Case for a Plant-Forward Omnivorous Whole-Foods Diet," *Progress in Cardiovascular Diseases* 74 (2022): 2–8, https://doi.org/10.1016/j.pcad.2022.08.001.

13. Shankar Vedantam, "Do You Suffer from Decision Fatigue?" *Wired*, April 27, 2011, https://www.wired.com/2011/04/judges-mental-fatigue/.

14. C. Loriette, C. Ziane, and S. Ben Hamed, "Neurofeedback for Cognitive Enhancement and Intervention and Brain Plasticity," *Revue Neurologique* 177, no. 9 (2021): 1133–44, https://doi.org/10.1016/j.neurol.2021.08.004.

15. Tanya Lewis, "Scientists Have Finally Pinpointed an Area of the Brain for Intuition," *Live Science*, July 8, 2016. https://www.livescience.com/54825-scientists-measure-intuition.html.

CHAPTER 3: MY EGO IS SMALLER THAN YOURS

1. Brescia University, "The Pratfall Effect: Why 'Being Human' Increases Your Likability," accessed July 17, 2024, https://www.brescia.edu/2017/06/pratfall-effect/.

2. Bessel A. van der Kolk, *The Body Keeps the Score: Brain, Mind, and Body in the Healing of Trauma* (New York: Penguin Books, 2015), https://www.amazon.com/Body-Keeps-Score-Healing-Trauma/dp/B08TX585RN/.

CHAPTER 4: IF YOU CAN BE TRIGGERED, YOU'RE HOLDING A LOADED GUN

1. H. G. Tudor, *Escape: How to Beat the Narcissist*, independently published, 2016, https://www.amazon.com/Escape-H-G-Tudor-2016-07-18/dp/B01N8Q7HPJ/.

2. Michael R. Hamblin, "Mechanisms and Applications of the Anti-Inflammatory Effects of Photobiomodulation," *AIMS Biophysics* 4, no. 3 (2017): 337–61, https://doi.org/10.3934/biophy.2017.3.337.

3. W. H. Li, I. Seo, B. Kim, A. Fassih, M. D. Southall, and R. Parsa, "Low-Level Red Plus Near Infrared Lights Combination Induces Expressions of Collagen and Elastin in Human Skin In Vitro," *International Journal of Cosmetic Science* 43, no. 3 (2021): 311–20, https://doi.org/10.1111/ics.12698.

4. TrueLight, "About Us," last modified 2024, https://shoptruelight.com/about/.

5. Paweł Krol, Magdalena Piecha, Krzysztof Slomka, Grzegorz Sobota, Aleksandra Polak, and Grzegorz Juras, "The Effect of Whole-Body Vibration Frequency and Amplitude on the Myoelectric Activity of Vastus Medialis and Vastus Lateralis," *Journal of Sports Science and Medicine* 10, no. 1 (2011): 169–74, PMID: 24149311; PMCID: PMC3737908.

6. Carlos Cristi-Montero, María J. Cuevas, and Pedro S. Collado, "Whole-Body Vibration Training as Complement to Programs Aimed at Weight Loss," *Nutrición Hospitalaria* 28, no. 5 (2013): 1365–71, https://doi.org/10.3305/nh.2013.28.5.6656.

7. M. de O. Pereira, N. de S. Pinto, M. de O. Monteiro, S. D. Santos-Filho, F. S. Carmo, C. L. Diniz, P. J. Marin, and M. Bernardo-Filho, "Influence of Whole-Body Vibration on Biodistribution of the Radiopharmaceutical [99mTc] Methylene Diphosphonate in Wistar Rats," *International Journal of Radiation Biology* 89, no. 8 (2013): 668–72, https://doi.org/10.3109/09553002.2012.715790.

8. Francine Shapiro, "The Role of Eye Movement Desensitization and Reprocessing (EMDR) Therapy in Medicine: Addressing the Psychological and Physical Symptoms Stemming from Adverse Life Experiences," *Permanente Journal* 18, no. 1 (2014): 71–77, https://doi.org/10.7812/TPP/13-098; PMID: 24626074; PMCID: PMC3951033.

9. Rong Chen, Alexandra Gillespie, Yifan Zhao, Yuchao Xi, Yi Ren, and Leslie McLean, "The Efficacy of Eye Movement Desensitization and Reprocessing in Children and Adults Who Have Experienced Complex Childhood Trauma: A Systematic Review of Randomized Controlled Trials," *Frontiers in Psychology* 9 (2018): 534, https://doi.org/10.3389/fpsyg.2018.00534; PMID: 29695993; PMCID: PMC5904704.

CHAPTER 5: BRAIN STATES 101

1. Koichi Kobayashi, Hironori Okabe, Shigeyuki Kawano, Yasuyuki Hidaka, and Katsuhiko Hara, "Biophoton Emission Induced by Heat Shock," *PLOS ONE* 9, no. 8 (2014): e105700, https://doi.org/10.1371/journal.pone.0105700.

2. Antoine Lutz, Louis L. Greischar, Nancy B. Rawlings, Matthieu Ricard, and Richard J. Davidson, "Long-term Meditators Self-Induce High-Amplitude Gamma Synchrony During Mental Practice," *Proceedings of the National Academy of Sciences of the United States of America* 101, no. 46 (2004): 16369–73, https://doi.org/10.1073/pnas.0407401101; PMID: 15534199; PMCID: PMC526201.

3. Thomas Misgeld and Thomas L. Schwarz, "Mitostasis in Neurons: Maintaining Mitochondria in an Extended Cellular Architecture," *Neuron* 96, no. 3 (2017): 651–66, https://doi.org/10.1016/j.neuron.2017.09.055; PMID: 29096078; PMCID: PMC5687842.

4. Stephen S. Hall, "Could Mitochondria Be the Key to a Healthy Brain?" *Scientific American*, March 2016, https://www.scientificamerican.com/article/could-mitochondria-be-the-key-to-a-healthy-brain/.

CHAPTER 6: UNDER THE COVERS: BREATHWORK AND SEXUAL ENERGY

1. Shawna I. Hopper, Shannon L. Murray, Lisa R. Ferrara, and Joanne K. Singleton, "Effectiveness of Diaphragmatic Breathing for Reducing Physiological and Psychological Stress in Adults: A Quantitative Systematic Review," *JBI Database of Systematic Reviews and Implementation Reports* 17, no. 9 (2019): 1855–76, https://doi.org/10.11124/JBISRIR-2017-003848; PMID: 31436595.

2. Kalyani Singh, Hemant Bhargav, and T. M. Srinivasan, "Effect of Uninostril Yoga Breathing on Brain Hemodynamics: A Functional Near-Infrared Spectroscopy Study," *International Journal of Yoga* 9, no. 1 (2016): 12–19, https://doi.org/10.4103/0973-6131.171711; PMID: 26865766; PMCID: PMC4728953.

3. Ranil Jayawardena, Priyanga Ranasinghe, Hemantha Ranawaka, Niluka Gamage, Deshanie Dissanayake, and Anoop Misra, "Exploring the Therapeutic Benefits of Pranayama (Yogic Breathing): A Systematic Review," *International Journal of Yoga* 13, no. 2 (2020): 99–110, https://doi.org/10.4103/ijoy.IJOY_37_19; PMID: 32669763; PMCID: PMC7336946.

4. Carolina Ferreira-Vorkapic, Cláudia J. Borba-Pinheiro, Márcia Marchioro, and Diego Santana, "The Impact of Yoga Nidra and Seated Meditation on the Mental Health of College Professors," *International Journal of Yoga* 11, no. 3 (2018): 215–23, https://doi.org/10.4103/ijoy.IJOY_57_17; PMID: 30233115; PMCID: PMC6134749.

5. Tracee Stanley, YouTube channel, https://www.youtube.com/@traceestanley108.

6. Karuna Datta, Hruda Nanda Mallick, Manjari Tripathi, Navdeep Ahuja, and K. K. Deepak, "Electrophysiological Evidence of Local Sleep During Yoga Nidra Practice," *Frontiers in Neurology* 13 (2022), https://doi.org/10.3389/fneur.2022.910794.

7. Dave Asprey, "Conscious Rest and Deep Relaxation—Tracee Stanley–#1133," *The Human Upgrade with Dave Asprey* (podcast), January 12, 2023, https://daveasprey.com/tracee-stanley-1133/.

8. Dave Asprey, "Mastering the Mind for Peace & Purpose—Gurudev Sri Sri Ravi Shankar–#1020," *The Human Upgrade with Dave Asprey* (podcast), February 2, 2022, https://daveasprey.com/gurudev-sri-sri-ravi-shankar-1020/.

9. Maria Kozhevnikov, John Elliott, J. Shephard, and Klaus Gramann, "Neurocognitive and Somatic Components of Temperature Increases During G-Tummo Meditation: Legend and Reality," *PLOS ONE* 8, no. 3 (2013):

e58244, https://doi.org/10.1371/journal.pone.0058244, e-pub March 29, 2013; PMID: 23555572; PMCID: PMC3612090.

10. Dave Asprey, "Take Control of Your Body Using the Wim Hof Method—Wim Hof–#750," *The Human Upgrade with Dave Asprey* (podcast), March 18, 2021, https://daveasprey.com/wim-hof-750/.

11. Dave Asprey, "The Birth of LSD with Dr. Stanislav Grof, Father of Transpersonal Psychology–#428," *The Human Upgrade with Dave Asprey* (podcast), June 28, 2017, https://daveasprey.com/stanislav-grof-428/.

12. J. P. Zuniga-Hertz et al., "Meditation-Induced Bloodborne Factors as an Adjuvant Treatment to COVID-19 Disease," *Brain, Behavior, and Immunity Health* 32 (2023): 100675, https://doi.org/10.1016/j.bbih.2023.100675.

13. Joe Dispenza, "Exciting Early Findings from Our QUANTUM Research Study," *Dr. Joe Dispenza* (blog), June 2022, https://drjoedispenza.com/dr-joes-blog/exciting-early-findings-from-our-quantum-research-study.

14. Joseph O. Baker, "The Variety of Religious Experiences," *Review of Religious Research* 51, no. 1 (2009): 39–54, http://www.jstor.org/stable/25593771.

15. Yoshija Walter and Thomas Koenig, "The Induction of Religious Experiences and Temporal Lobe Activation: Neuronal Source Localization Using EEG Inverse Solutions," *Psych* 5, no. 4 (2023): 1191–1206, https://doi.org/10.3390/psych5040079.

16. "Andmore Presents," last modified 2024, https://andmorepresents.com/.

17. "Miss Jaiya," accessed July 17, 2024, https://missjaiya.com/.

18. Dave Asprey, "Miss Jaiya: What Your Sex Type Says About You—with Jaiya," *The Human Upgrade with Dave Asprey* (podcast), July 2023, https://daveasprey.com/miss-jaiya-1112/.

CHAPTER 7: GO SPANK YOURSELF

1. M. Shamsuddin, "A Brief Historical Background of Sati Tradition in India," *Din ve Felsefe Araştırmaları* 3 (2020): 44–63.

2. Leigh Cowart, *Hurts So Good: The Science and Culture of Pain on Purpose* (New York: PublicAffairs, 2021), https://www.amazon.com/Hurts-So-Good-Science-Culture/dp/B09F4NNHT4/.

3. Ilaria Bufalari and Silvio Ionta, "The Social and Personality Neuroscience of Empathy for Pain and Touch," *Frontiers in Human Neuroscience* 7 (2013): 393, https://doi.org/10.3389/fnhum.2013.00393.

4. Joanna Rymaszewska, Andrzej Tulczynski, Zygmunt Zagrobelny, Andrzej Kiejna, and Tomasz Hadrys, "Influence of Whole Body Cryotherapy on Depressive Symptoms—Preliminary Report," *Acta Neuropsychiatrica* 15, no. 3 (2003): 122–28, https://doi.org/10.1034/j.1601-5215.2003.00023.x.

5. Anika Mehren, Marcus Reichert, David Coghill, H. H. O. Müller, Nadine Braun, and Alexandra Philipsen, "Physical Exercise in Attention Deficit Hyperactivity Disorder—Evidence and Implications for the Treatment of Borderline Personality Disorder," *Borderline Personality Disorder and Emotion Dysregulation* 7 (January 6, 2020): 1, https://doi.org/10.1186/s40479-019-0115-2.

CHAPTER 8: TRIP LIKE I DO

1. William J. Scotton, Lara J. Hill, Amanda C. Williams, and Nicholas M. Barnes, "Serotonin Syndrome: Pathophysiology, Clinical Features, Management, and Potential Future Directions," *International Journal of Tryptophan Research* 12 (2019): 1178646919873925, https://doi.org/10.1177/1178646919873925.

2. Dave Asprey, "Psychedelic Healing: Marijuana, MDMA, Psilocybin, and Ayahuasca—Rick Doblin," *The Human Upgrade with Dave Asprey* (podcast), November 2015, https://daveasprey.com/rick-doblin-psychedelic-healing-marijuana-mdma-psilocybin-ayahuasca-200/.

3. Ana S. Correia, Ana Cardoso, and Nuno Vale, "BDNF Unveiled: Exploring Its Role in Major Depression Disorder Serotonergic Imbalance and Associated Stress Conditions," *Pharmaceutics* 15, no. 8 (2023): 2081, https://doi.org/10.3390/pharmaceutics15082081.

4. "Psilocybin Treatment for Major Depression Effective for Up to a Year for Most Patients, Study Shows," news release, Johns Hopkins Medicine, February 2022, https://www.hopkinsmedicine.org/news/newsroom/news-releases/2022/02/psilocybin-treatment-for-major-depression-effective-for-up-to-a-year-for-most-patients-study-shows.

5. N. Gukasyan, A. K. Davis, F. S. Barrett, et al., "Efficacy and Safety of Psilocybin-Assisted Treatment for Major Depressive Disorder: Prospective 12-Month Follow-Up," *Journal of Psychopharmacology* 36, no. 2 (2022): 151–58, https://doi.org/10.1177/02698811211073759.

6. L. Morgan, "MDMA-Assisted Psychotherapy for People Diagnosed with Treatment-Resistant PTSD: What It Is and What It Isn't," *Annals of General Psychiatry* 19 (2020): 33, https://doi.org/10.1186/s12991-020-00283-6.

7. K. Riaz et al., "MDMA-Based Psychotherapy in Treatment-Resistant Post-Traumatic Stress Disorder (PTSD): A Brief Narrative Overview of Current Evidence," *Diseases* 11, no. 4 (2023): 159, https://doi.org/10.3390/diseases11040159.

8. "MDMA May Reawaken Critical Period in Brain to Help Treat PTSD," news release, Johns Hopkins Medicine, April 2019, https://www.hopkinsmedicine.org/news/newsroom/news-releases/2019/04/psychedelic-drug-mdma-may-reawaken-critical-period-in-brain-to-help-treat-ptsd.

9. Dave Asprey, "Ketamine to Neurofeedback: The Brain Hacking Episode—David Feifel," *The Human Upgrade with Dave Asprey* (podcast), August 2018, https://daveasprey.com/ketamine-to-neurofeedback-the-brain-hacking-episode-david-feifel-513/.

10. S. Srirangam and J. Mercer, "Ketamine Bladder Syndrome: An Important Differential Diagnosis When Assessing a Patient with Persistent Lower Urinary Tract Symptoms," *BMJ Case Reports*, September 30, 2012, https://doi.org/10.1136/bcr-2012-006447.

11. S. Xu, X. Yao, B. Li, R. Cui, C. Zhu, Y. Wang, and W. Yang, "Uncovering the Underlying Mechanisms of Ketamine as a Novel Antidepressant," *Frontiers in Pharmacology* 12 (2022): 740996, https://doi.org/10.3389/fphar.2021.740996.

12. H. Wu, N. K. Savalia, and A. C. Kwan, "Ketamine for a Boost of Neural Plasticity: How, but Also When?" *Biological Psychiatry* 89, no. 11 (June 1, 2021): 1030–32, https://doi.org/10.1016/j.biopsych.2021.03.014.

13. Enzo Tagliazucchi et al., "Increased Global Functional Connectivity Correlates with LSD-Induced Ego Dissolution," *Neuropsychopharmacology*, 2016.

14. Juan José Fuentes, Francina Fonseca, Mireia Elices, Magí Farré, and Marta Torrens, "Therapeutic Use of LSD in Psychiatry: A Systematic Review of Randomized-Controlled Clinical Trials," *Frontiers in Psychiatry* 10 (2020): 943, https://doi.org/10.3389/fpsyt.2019.00943.

15. ibid.

16. Leonardo Pasquini et al., "Brain Substates Induced by DMT Relate to Sympathetic Output and Meaningfulness of the Experience," *bioRxiv* (preprint), April 17, 2024, https://doi.org/10.1101/2024.02.14.580356.

17. Alan K. Davis, S. So, R. Lancelotta, J. P. Barsuglia, and Roland R. Griffiths, "5-Methoxy-N,N-Dimethyltryptamine (5-MeO-DMT) Used in a Naturalistic Group Setting Is Associated with Unintended Improvements in Depression and Anxiety," *American Journal of Drug and Alcohol Abuse* 45, no. 2 (2019): 161–69, https://doi.org/10.1080/00952990.2018.1545024.

18. "A study found that 5-MeO-DMT causes structural changes in human brain cells that may inhibit neurodegeneration," UC Berkeley Center for the Science of Psychedelics, accessed July 17, 2024, https://psychedelics.berkeley.edu.

19. Alan K. Davis, J. P. Barsuglia, A. M. Windham-Herman, M. Lynch, and M. Polanco, "Subjective Effectiveness of Ibogaine Treatment for Problematic Opioid Consumption: Short- and Long-Term Outcomes and Current Psychological Functioning," *Journal of Psychedelic Studies* 1, no. 2 (November 2017): 65–73, https://doi.org/10.1556/2054.01.2017.009.

20. G. E. Noller, C. M. Frampton, and B. Yazar-Klosinski, "Ibogaine Treatment Outcomes for Opioid Dependence from a Twelve-Month Follow-Up Observational Study," *American Journal of Drug and Alcohol Abuse* 44, no. 1 (2018): 37–46, https://doi.org/10.1080/00952990.2017.1310218.

21. Thomas K. Brown, "Ibogaine in the Treatment of Substance Dependence," *Current Drug Abuse Reviews* 6 (2013): 3–16, https://doi.org/10.2174/15672 050113109990001.

22. Anette Kjellgren, Anders Eriksson, and Torsten Norlander, "Experiences of Encounters with Ayahuasca—'The Vine of the Soul,'" *Journal of Psychoactive Drugs* 41, no. 4 (2009): 309–15.

23. R. Sheth, E. Parikh, K. Olayeye, K. Pfeifer, and D. Khanna, "The Effects of Ayahuasca on Psychological Disorders: A Systematic Literature Review," *Cureus* 16, no. 3 (2024): e55574, https://doi.org/10.7759/cureus.55574.

CHAPTER 9: BETTER LIVING THROUGH CIRCUITRY

1. Laura Sanders, "How Hans Berger's Quest for Telepathy Spurred Modern Brain Science," *Science News*, July 6, 2021, https://www.sciencenews.org/article/hans-berger-telepathy-neuroscience-brain-eeg.

2. American Institute of Stress, "Workplace Stress," accessed July 17, 2024, https://www.stress.org/workplace-stress/.

3. "Employee Burnout Report: COVID-19's Impact and 3 Strategies to Curb It," Indeed, March 11, 2021, https://www.indeed.com/lead/preventing-employee-burnout-report.

4. "Deloitte Workplace Burnout Survey," Deloitte US, April 2019, https://www2
.deloitte.com/us/en/pages/about-deloitte/articles/burnout-survey.html.
5. "2021 Mental Health at Work Report," Mind Share Partners, October 2021,
https://www.mindsharepartners.org/mentalhealthatworkreport-2021.
6. Habib Yaribeygi, Yunes Panahi, Hedayat Sahraei, Timothy P. Johnston, and
Amirhossein Sahebkar, "The Impact of Stress on Body Function: A Review,"
EXCLI Journal 16 (2017): 1057–72, https://doi.org/10.17179/excli2017-480.
7. Corina Benjet, Evelyn Bromet, Elie G. Karam, Ronald C. Kessler, Katie A.
McLaughlin, A. M. Ruscio, et al., "The Epidemiology of Traumatic Event
Exposure Worldwide: Results from the World Mental Health Survey Con-
sortium," *Psychological Medicine* 46, no. 2 (2016): 327–43, https://doi.org
/10.1017/s0033291715001981.
8. Dave Asprey, "Lt. Col. Dave Grossman: The Science of Killing, Fear Management, and Sleep—Episode 566," *The Human Upgrade with Dave Asprey*
(podcast), April 2020, https://daveasprey.com/lt-col-dave-grossman-566/.

CHAPTER 10: ALL THE TOYS

1. "Introduction to the God Helmet," God Helmet Experiments, accessed July 17,
2024, https://www.god-helmet.com/wp/god-helmet/intro_to_god_helmet.htm.
2. "God Helmet," Wikipedia, last modified June 15, 2023, https://en.wikipedia
.org/wiki/God_helmet.
3. Michael A. Persinger, "The Neuropsychiatry of Paranormal Experiences,"
Journal of Neuropsychiatry and Clinical Neurosciences 13, no. 4 (2001):
515–24, https://doi.org/10.1176/appi.neuropsych.13.4.515.
4. Roxanne Khamsi, "Electrical Brainstorms Busted as Source of Ghosts," *Nature*,
December 9, 2004.
5. S. Bashir et al., "Effects of Transcranial Magnetic Stimulation on Neurobiological Changes in Alzheimer's Disease (Review)," *Molecular Medicine Reports*
25, no. 4 (April 2022): 109, https://doi.org/10.3892/mmr.2022.12625.
6. Joanna Kaszuba-Zwoińska, Jan Gremba, Beata Gałdzińska-Calik, Katarzyna
Wójcik-Piotrowicz, and Piotr J. Thor, "Electromagnetic Field Induced Biological Effects in Humans," *Przegląd Lekarski* 72, no. 11 (2015): 636–41; PMID:
27012122.
7. Martin L. Pall, "Low Intensity Electromagnetic Fields Act via Voltage-Gated
Calcium Channel (VGCC) Activation to Cause Very Early Onset Alzheimer's
Disease: 18 Distinct Types of Evidence," *Current Alzheimer Research* 19,
no. 2 (2022): 119–32, https://doi.org/10.2174/1567205019666220202114510;
PMID: 35114921; PMCID: PMC9189734.
8. O. Erogul, E. Oztas, I. Yildirim, T. Kir, E. Aydur, G. Komesli, et al., "Effects of
Electromagnetic Radiation from a Cellular Phone on Human Sperm Motility:
An in Vitro Study," *Archives of Medical Research*.
9. Ashok Agarwal, Neel R. Desai, Kavindra Makker, Alexander Varghese, Reda
Mouradi, Edmund Sabanegh, et al., "Effects of Radiofrequency Electromag-
netic Waves (RF-EMW) from Cellular Phones on Human Ejaculated Semen:
An in Vitro Pilot Study," *Fertility and Sterility* 92 (2009): 1318–25.

10. Mayo Clinic, "Transcranial Magnetic Stimulation," accessed July 17, 2024, https://www.mayoclinic.org/tests-procedures/transcranial-magnetic-stimulation/about/pac-20384625.

CHAPTER 11: PRESSING THE RESET BUTTON

1. Robert D. Enright and Richard P. Fitzgibbons, *Forgiveness Therapy: An Empirical Guide for Resolving Anger and Restoring Hope* (Washington, DC: American Psychological Association, 2015).
2. Charlotte Van Oyen Witvliet, Thomas E. Ludwig, and Kelly L. Laan, "Granting Forgiveness or Harboring Grudges: Implications for Emotion, Physiology, and Health," *Psychological Science* 12, no. 2 (2001): 117–23.
3. Chai M. Tyng, Hafeez U. Amin, Mohamad N. M. Saad, and Aamir S. Malik, "The Influences of Emotion on Learning and Memory," *Frontiers in Psychology* 8 (2017): 1454, https://doi.org/10.3389/fpsyg.2017.01454.

CHAPTER 12: EAT MORE, SUFFER LESS

1. Xianhua Wang et al., "Mitochondrial Flashes Regulate ATP Homeostasis in the Heart," *eLife* 6 (2017): e23908, https://doi.org/10.7554/eLife.23908.
2. Abdulaziz M. Alshami, "Pain: Is It All in the Brain or the Heart?" *Current Pain and Headache Reports* 23, no. 12 (November 2019): 88, doi:10.1007/s11916-019-0827-4.
3. Dorothy R. Haskett, "Mitochondrial DNA (mtDNA)," *Embryo Project Encyclopedia*, December 19, 2014, ISSN: 1940–5030.
4. Pascal May-Panloup et al., "Low Oocyte Mitochondrial DNA Content in Ovarian Insufficiency," *Human Reproduction* 20 (2005): 593–97.
5. E. E. Martínez Leo and M. R. Segura Campos, "Effect of Ultra-Processed Diet on Gut Microbiota and Thus Its Role in Neurodegenerative Diseases," *Nutrition* 71 (March 2020): 110609, doi:10.1016/j.nut.2019.110609.
6. M. M. Lane et al., "Ultra-processed Food Exposure and Adverse Health Outcomes: Umbrella Review of Epidemiological Meta-Analyses," *BMJ* 384 (2024): e077310, doi:10.1136/bmj-2023–077310.
7. K. Halczuk et al., "Vitamin B12—Multifaceted In Vivo Functions and In Vitro Applications," *Nutrients* 15, no. 12 (2023): 2734.
8. M. I. Lestari et al., "Association of Vitamin D with Deoxyribonucleic Acid (DNA) Damage: A Systematic Review of Animal and Human Studies," *Acta Biochimica Polonica* 70, no. 2 (2023): 379–87, doi:10.18388/abp.2020_6641.
9. "Upgrade Labs Shop," Upgrade Labs, 2024, https://shopsuppgradelabs.com.
10. "Dark Chocolate," The Nutrition Source, Harvard T. H. Chan School of Public Health, accessed July 18, 2024, https://nutritionsource.hsph.harvard.edu/food-features/dark-chocolate/.
11. "Anti-Nutrients," The Nutrition Source, Harvard T. H. Chan School of Public Health, accessed July 18, 2024, https://nutritionsource.hsph.harvard.edu/anti-nutrients/#:~:text=As%20it%20passes%20through%20the,minerals%20at%20the%20same%20meal.

12. David L. Freed, "Do Dietary Lectins Cause Disease?" *BMJ* 318, no. 7190 (1999): 1023–24, doi:10.1136/bmj.318.7190.1023.

13. Qianhong Meng, Meng-Shan Lin, and I-Shiung Tzeng, "Relationship Between Exercise and Alzheimer's Disease: A Narrative Literature Review," *Frontiers in Neuroscience* 14 (2020): 131, doi:10.3389/fnins.2020.00131.

14. Giovanni Bastioli, Jonathan C. Arnold, Martina Mancini, Alex C. Mar, Beatriz Gamallo-Lana, Khashayar Saadipour, Moses V. Chao, and Mark E. Rice, "Voluntary Exercise Boosts Striatal Dopamine Release: Evidence for the Necessary and Sufficient Role of BDNF," *Journal of Neuroscience* 42, no. 23 (2022): 4725–36, doi:10.1523/JNEUROSCI.2273-21.2022.

15. Aria Hamid, Jeffrey Pettibone, Omar Mabrouk, et al., "Mesolimbic Dopamine Signals the Value of Work," *Nature Neuroscience* 19 (2016): 117–26, https://doi.org/10.1038/nn.4173.

16. Silke Diekelmann, "Sleep for Cognitive Enhancement," *Frontiers in Systems Neuroscience* 8 (2014): 46, doi:10.3389/fnsys.2014.00046.

17. Lena Besedovsky, Tanja Lange, and Jan Born, "Sleep and Immune Function," *Pflügers Archiv—European Journal of Physiology* 463, no. 1 (2012): 121–37.

18. Cinzia Baglioni et al., "Insomnia as a Predictor of Depression: A Meta-Analytic Evaluation of Longitudinal Epidemiological Studies," *Journal of Affective Disorders* 135, no. 1–3 (2011): 10–19.

19. Karine Spiegel, Rachel Leproult, and Eve Van Cauter, "Impact of Sleep Debt on Metabolic and Endocrine Function," *Lancet* 354, no. 9188 (1999): 1435–39.

20. Matthew P. Walker and Robert Stickgold, "Sleep, Memory, and Plasticity," *Annual Review of Psychology* 57 (2006): 139–66.

21. Oura, "Oura Ring," 2024, https://ouraring.com/?utm_source=2163&utm_medium=affiliate&cppid=2163&cpclid=24e4745a4788435aad55aa4e4566772 6&utm_campaign=oura&utm_content=&utm_term=The+Dave+Asprey+Group.

22. "The State of SleepHealth in America," SleepHealth.org, 2024, https://www.sleephealth.org/sleep-health/the-state-of-sleephealth-in-america/.

23. Thomas A. Wehr, "In Short Photoperiods, Human Sleep Is Biphasic," *Journal of Sleep Research* 1, no. 2 (June 1992): 103–7, doi:10.1111/j.1365-2869.1992.tb00019.x.

24. Dave Asprey, "Exclusive Interview with Ketone Expert Dr. Richard Veech," *Bulletproof Radio* (podcast), June 18, 2023, https://daveasprey.com/exclusive-interview-with-ketone-expert-dr-richard-veech-299/.

25. Valter D. Longo, Maria Di Tano, Mark P. Mattson, and Nadia Guidi, "Intermittent and Periodic Fasting, Longevity and Disease," *Nature Aging* 1, no. 1 (January 2021): 47–59, doi:10.1038/s43587-020-00013-3.

26. Raphael Adjonu, Zhihua Zhou, Paul D. Prenzler, Jason Ayton, and Chris L. Blanchard, "Different Processing Practices and the Frying Life of Refined Canola Oil," *Foods* 8, no. 11 (2019): 527, doi:10.3390/foods8110527.

27. S. C. Cunnane et al., "Can Ketones Compensate for Deteriorating Brain Glucose Uptake During Aging? Implications for the Risk and Treatment of Alzheimer's Disease," *Annals of the New York Academy of Sciences* 1367, no. 1 (2016): 12–20.

28. Sushma Benjamin and Friedrich Spener, "Conjugated Linoleic Acids as Functional Food: An Insight into Their Health Benefits," *Nutrition & Metabolism* 6, no. 1 (2009): 36.

CHAPTER 13: SUFFERING SUCKS, SO STOP DOING IT

1. Andrew Rozanski, Chirag Bavishi, Laura D. Kubzansky, and Ronald Cohen, "Association of Optimism with Cardiovascular Events and All-Cause Mortality: A Systematic Review and Meta-analysis," *JAMA Network Open* 2, no. 9 (2019): e1912200, doi:10.1001/jamanetworkopen.2019.12200.

2. Matti Pänkäläinen, Tuula Kerola, Olli Kampman, et al., "Pessimism and Risk of Death from Coronary Heart Disease Among Middle-aged and Older Finns: An Eleven-Year Follow-up Study," *BMC Public Health* 16 (2016): 1124, https://doi.org/10.1186/s12889-016-3764-8.

INDEX

Page numbers of illustrations appear in italics.

ABOUT THE AUTHOR

Known as the "Father of Biohacking," Dave Asprey is an award-winning entrepreneur and innovator in the health science space. He's the creator of Bulletproof Coffee and mineralized, mold-free Danger Coffee, the host of the Webby Award-winning number-one rated health podcast, *The Human Upgrade* (formerly *Bulletproof Radio*), and a multi–New York Times bestselling author of *Game Changers*, *Head Strong*, *The Bulletproof Diet*, and *Smarter Not Harder*.

Over the last two decades Dave has worked with world-renowned doctors, researchers, and global mavericks to discover and put into practice the latest, most innovative methods, techniques, and products for enhancing mental and physical performance. Dave has personally spent millions taking control of his own biology—pushing the bounds of what's humanly possible all in the name of scientific evolution and revolution. As the creator of the Bulletproof Diet and Bulletproof Coffee, collagen protein supplements, and many more commercial wellness products, Dave's mission is to empower people not only with information and knowledge, but also the tools and techniques that unlock individual potential for the greater global good. To bring his knowledge to the public, Dave created the Biohacking Conference, the largest, longest-running biohacking conference in the world, celebrating its tenth anniversary in 2024.

Most recently, Dave created 40 Years of Zen, an intensive five-day master program for unlocking and upgrading the brain. This powerful program combines neurofeedback and nutrition with the expertise of top neuroscientists, meditators, and executive trainers in an exclusive retreat setting outside of Seattle, Washington. He is also the creator of Upgrade Labs, the first franchise of biohacking gyms to bring his successful biohacking practices to its members.